CW01496338

Racialization, Islamophobia and Mistaken Identity

Exploring the issue of Islamophobic attacks against Sikhs since 9/11, this book explains the historical, religious and legal foundations and frameworks for understanding race hate crime against the Sikh community in the UK.

Focusing on the backlash that Sikhs in the UK have faced since 9/11, the authors provide a theological and historical backdrop to Sikh identity in the global context, critically analysing the occurrences of Islamophobia since 9/11, 7/7 and most recently post-Brexit, and how British Sikhs and the British government have responded and reacted to these incidents. The experiences of American Sikhs are also explored and the impact of anti-Sikh sentiment upon both these communities is considered. Drawing on media reporting, government policies, the emerging body of inter-disciplinary scholarship and empirical research, this book contributes to the currently limited body of literature on anti-Sikh hate crime and produces ideas for policymakers on how to rectify the situation.

Providing a better understanding of perceptions of anti-Sikh sentiment and its impact, this book will of interest to scholars and upper-level students working on identity and hate crime, and more generally in the fields of Religion and Politics, Cultural Studies, Media Studies and International Studies.

Jagbir Jhutti-Johal is a Senior Lecturer in Sikh Studies in the Department of Theology & Religion at the University of Birmingham.

Hardeep Singh is a freelance journalist, Deputy Director of the Network of Sikh Organisations and Assistant Editor of *The Sikh Messenger*.

Routledge Studies in Religion and Politics
Edited by Jeffrey Haynes
London Metropolitan University, UK

This series aims to publish high quality works on the topic of the resurgence of political forms of religion in both national and international contexts. This trend has been especially noticeable in the post-cold war era (that is, since the late 1980s). It has affected all the 'world religions' (including, Buddhism, Christianity, Hinduism, Islam and Judaism) in various parts of the world (such as, the Americas, Europe, the Middle East and North Africa, South and Southeast Asia and sub-Saharan Africa).

The series welcomes books that use a variety of approaches to the subject, drawing on scholarship from political science, international relations, security studies and contemporary history.

Books in the series explore these religions, regions and topics both within and beyond the conventional domain of 'church-state' relations to include the impact of religion on politics, conflict and development, including the late Samuel Huntington's controversial – yet influential – thesis about 'clashing civilisations'.

In sum, the overall purpose of the book series is to provide a comprehensive survey of what is currently happening in relation to the interaction of religion and politics, both domestically and internationally, in relation to a variety of issues.

Free Speech, Religion and the United Nations
The Struggle to Define International Free Speech Norms
Heini í Skorini

Racialization, Islamophobia and Mistaken Identity
The Sikh Experience
Jagbir Jhutti-Johal and Hardeep Singh

Religion in the Era of Postsecularism
Edited by Uchenna Okeja

For more information about this series, please visit: www.routledge.com/ Routledge-Studies-in-Religion-and-Politics/book-series/RSRP

Racialization, Islamophobia and Mistaken Identity

The Sikh Experience

Jagbir Jhutti-Johal and Hardeep Singh

 Routledge
Taylor & Francis Group

LONDON AND NEW YORK

First published 2020
by Routledge
2 Park Square, Milton Park, Abingdon, Oxon OX14 4RN

and by Routledge
52 Vanderbilt Avenue, New York, NY 10017

Routledge is an imprint of the Taylor & Francis Group, an informa business

© 2020 Jagbir Jhutti-Johal and Hardeep Singh

The right of Jagbir Jhutti-Johal and Hardeep Singh to be identified as authors of this work has been asserted by them in accordance with sections 77 and 78 of the Copyright, Designs and Patents Act 1988.

All rights reserved. No part of this book may be reprinted or reproduced or utilized in any form or by any electronic, mechanical, or other means, now known or hereafter invented, including photocopying and recording, or in any information storage or retrieval system, without permission in writing from the publishers.

Trademark notice: Product or corporate names may be trademarks or registered trademarks, and are used only for identification and explanation without intent to infringe.

British Library Cataloguing-in-Publication Data
A catalogue record for this book is available from the British Library

Library of Congress Cataloging-in-Publication Data
A catalog record has been requested for this book

ISBN: 978-0-815-35262-4 (hbk)
ISBN: 978-1-351-13886-4 (ebk)

Typeset in Times New Roman
by Wearset Ltd, Boldon, Tyne and Wear

Printed and bound in Great Britain by
TJ International Ltd, Padstow, Cornwall

Hardeep Singh – To my wife
Jagbir Jhutti-Johal – For my family

Contents

Illustrations

Figures

Tables

About the authors

Jagbir Jhutti-Johal is a Senior Lecturer in Sikh Studies in the Department of Theology and Religion at the University of Birmingham. Her research over the last 20 years has explored how the British Sikh community is grappling with contemporary societal and ethical issues, including gender inequality and misogyny, mental ill health, identity and community representation. She was a commissioner on the Commission on Religion and Belief in Public Life (2013–15). As a pioneer in the field of Sikh research, Jagbir established the first postgraduate Sikh Studies course in the UK in 2002. She is a much-sought after advisor within the British Sikh community in respect of contentious issues, and she has advised several Government departments and non-governmental organizations on a variety of matters and policy issues relating to the Sikh community. In 2018 she was awarded an OBE for services to higher education, faith communities and the voluntary sector.

Hardeep Singh is a freelance journalist, Deputy-Director for the Network of Sikh Organisations and Assistant Editor of *The Sikh Messenger*. He was a leading member of the Libel Reform Campaign, along with science writer Simon Singh and cardiologist Dr Peter Wilmshurst. He wrote a chapter titled 'Religious Libel: are the courts the right place for faith disputes' for *Legal Cases, New Religious Movements and Minority Faiths*. He has written for the *The Telegraph*, *The Telegraph Magazine*, *The Spectator*, *The Guardian*, *The Independent*, *IBTimes UK*, *Legal Week*, *The Lawyer*, *Media Lawyer*, *Spiked*, *Quillette*, *New Humanist* and *Index on Censorship*.

Foreword

The political and social landscape in the West has changed dramatically following the terrorist outrage of 9/11 and the more recent displacement of refugees fleeing the turmoil in the Middle East. Osama bin Laden, the Muslim mastermind of the 9/11 attack, wore a turban, and one of the first people killed in a 'revenge' attack was a Sikh, Balbir Singh Sodhi, simply because he wore a turban. Other 'mistaken identity' revenge attacks against Sikhs have sadly followed. In 2012 a Sikh *gurdwara* in Wisconsin was targeted by a white supremacist, resulting in the cold-blooded murder of innocent worshippers.

The new environment of suspicion and mistrust has undoubtedly served to polarize communities, and spawned a new wave of anti-immigrant sentiment that is manipulated by those seeking political advantage in the US, here in Britain and Europe more generally. In the US rhetoric such as 'either you are with us, or you are with the terrorists' has been unhelpful and added fuel to the fire. The violent backlash, especially in the US, shows how visible differences were all that were required to fuel hatred, not only against innocent Muslims but also against Sikhs and other minorities, in so-called 'mistaken identity' attacks.

Prejudice and ignorance have also affected British Sikhs, but 17 years on from the Twin Towers attack, the British authorities have tended to ignore hate crimes against Sikhs. The repeated mantra of 'we take all hate crime extremely seriously' is not enough. We urgently need to ensure much greater religious literacy at all levels of society to combat the prejudice and ignorance that give rise to irrational hatred.

This work is important because for the first time the authors Jagbir Jhutti-Johal and Hardeep Singh (from two separate disciplines – academia and journalism) have diligently collated information from a variety of sources – Hansard, police hate crime statistics, media reports and most importantly, first-hand accounts of victims themselves on the extent of hate crime against Sikhs since 9/11 in the UK. The results demonstrate not just the scale of hate crime against Sikhs, but also the laissez-faire approach of the British establishment to such incidents. This is in stark contrast with the historic and continued commitment to Britain's Muslim and Jewish communities. This volume is also the first to highlight this clear disparity of provision through a British Sikh lens, therefore adding value to the available academic literature on this important subject matter.

Hate crime against vulnerable minorities has no place in civilized society and those in authority should always tackle the ignorance and prejudice on which it thrives. In a well-received talk at Lambeth Palace, I observed that in a dense fog, even familiar objects like street lamps and trees can look scary and threatening. In the same way, in a fog of ignorance and prejudice it is all too easy to see those apparently different to us as objects of fear and hate. Remove the fog of ignorance and prejudice and we see people as they really are, ordinary human beings not very different from the rest of us. The tenth Guru of the Sikhs, Guru Gobind Singh, reminded us that people from different cultures and environments, are all members of our one human race.

Whilst I believe that the robust common sense and characteristic sense of fair play of British people make political incitement to violence against minorities as witnessed in history difficult in our country, we cannot afford to be complacent. We must redouble efforts to tackle the root causes of hate crime, and work towards an understanding that different cultures can be affected, and that each one has much to teach us all. I believe that this carefully researched book gives us some valuable direction on a way forward.

Lord (Indarjit) Singh, Director, Network of Sikh Organisations

Acknowledgements

This book has been both a challenging and a rewarding venture in equal measure. Its subject matter has been difficult, sensitive and at times troubling to navigate, but we believe it deserves much wider recognition. First and foremost, we would like to thank all the victims of hate crime who took the trouble to share their stories with us. We would especially like to thank individuals who waived their anonymity, stepping forward to talk of their post-9/11 experiences. A specific thankyou to Suman Kaur, Manpreet Mellhi, Parmjit Singh Dhanda and Amarjit Singh Atwal. Without their assistance, and others who chose anonymity, this project would not have got off the ground.

The same is true for the support of Rob Sorsby, editor, Politics and International Relations at Routledge, who first took interest in the subject back in 2014. Rob's belief in the relevance and importance of this work, along with the support of his colleague Claire Maloney, has been instrumental. Thanks go to Belinda Cunnison for copy editing the manuscript. We would like to thank Parminder Singh Davgun, a PhD student, for his translation of the various *Rehatnamas*. We would also like to thank luminaries in the field such as Professor Simran Jeet Singh, who helped guide us from the start, and Harbakhsh Grewal and Amandeep Madra from the UK Punjab Heritage Association, who helped us to accurately capture the Sikh military contribution during the Great War.

We are grateful to journalists Andrew Norfolk, Kate Mansey and Orlando Crowcroft, who provided us with key insights from a media perspective, as well as Richard Norrie and David Goodhart from think tank Policy Exchange, who advised on findings from our Media Content Analysis.

A final thanks to our families, especially our partners, for their belief in the importance of this book and their tireless assistance in reading manuscripts. Without them this volume would not have been written.

Jagbir Jhutti-Johal and Hardeep Singh

Abbreviations

APPG	All-Party Parliamentary Group
BBC	British Broadcasting Corporation
BF	Britain First
BNP	British National Party
C4	Channel 4
CAA	Campaign against Anti-Semitism
CCHQ	Conservative Campaign Headquarters
CCTV	Closed-circuit television
CPS	Crown Prosecution Service
CRE	Commission for Racial Equality
CS	City Sikhs
CST	Community Security Trust
EDL	English Defence League
EDM	Early Day Motion
EHRC	Equalities and Human Rights Commission
EU	European Union
FBI	Federal Bureau of Investigation
FGM	Female Genital Mutilation
FLA	Football Lads Alliance
FOI	Freedom of Information
GCSE	General Certificate of Secondary Education
GGS	Guru Granth Sahib
HO	Home Office
HMICFRS	Her Majesty's Inspectorate of Constabulary and Fire & Rescue Services
IHRA	International Holocaust Remembrance Alliance
IPSO	Independent Press Standards Organisation
ISIS	Islamic State of Iraq and Syria
MEP	Member of the European Parliament
MET	Metropolitan Police Service
MHCLG	Ministry of Housing, Communities & Local Government
NA	National Action
NDP	New Democratic Party (Canada)

NF	National Front
NPCC	National Police Chiefs' Council
NSC	National Sikh Campaign
NSO	Network of Sikh Organisations
NUS	National Union of Students
QC	Queens Counsel
RE	Religious Education
SALDEF	Sikh American Legal Defense and Education Fund
SAS	Sikh Awareness Society
SC	Sikh Coalition
SCUK	Sikh Council UK
SFUK	Sikh Federation UK
SGPC	Shiromani Gurdwara Parbandhak Committee
SikhPA	Sikh Press Association
SN	The Sikh Network
SYM	Southall Youth Movement
SYUK	Sikh Youth UK
Tell MAMA	Tell Measuring Anti-Muslim Attacks
TfL	Transport for London
UKIP	United Kingdom Independence Party

Introduction

Sikhs are considered a 'model minority' community, due not only to their economic and educational attainments, but also their integration into British society. These successes do not mean that the Sikh community's experiences have always been without problems. For example, one is consciously aware that they have always experienced and been subject to some form of racism. This racist discourse changed after the Salman Rushdie affair in 1989 and the (first) Gulf War, when South Asian communities such as Hindus and Sikhs became targets for attack due to racial similarities to the Muslim community. This was particularly so for Sikhs because the male Sikh identity, especially of turban-wearing males, was and continues to be conflated with Muslim identity. Amritdhari (initiated Sikhs) or non-initiated turban-wearing Sikh men as a result have become particularly vulnerable, because the Sikh *dastaar* (turban) and *kesh* (unshorn hair) have been confused with Osama bin Laden's *kaffiyeh* (headdress) and beard.[1] Attacks on Sikhs intensified in the immediate aftermath of 11 September 2001, when the Sikh turban was transformed from a sacred piece of religious attire to an object of marginalization and a target for discrimination.[2] This anti-Sikh sentiment in the United Kingdom (hereinafter UK) has intensified since 9/11.

Alongside the global attacks, there have been a number of subsequent attacks nationally, like the 7/7 terrorist atrocity (2005), the killing of Drummer Lee Rigby (2013), the attacks in Paris (January 2015, November 2015 and April 2017), Manchester 2017 and Westminster 2017–18. These have resulted in Sikhs being victims of attack due to prejudice against the 'Muslim-looking other'. This prejudice is not always a result of terror attacks, political discourse also plays a part. For example, during and after the European Union (hereinafter EU) Referendum vote and since the election of Donald Trump as US President, Sikhs along with other minorities have experienced what can be defined as an Islamophobic backlash, a phenomenon that has taken the community by surprise.

This backlash has been evident in Britain through the numerous verbal and physical assaults on not only Sikhs, but also attacks on Sikh places of worship. Notably, the first places to be targeted in the UK after 7/7 were a Sikh *gurdwara* in Kent,[3] and another in Bradford.[4] On occasion, Islamophobic slogans have been sprayed on Sikh *gurdwara*s. Northampton *Gurdwara* and its Sikh community have been attacked on numerous occasions since 2009, for example, when the *gurdwara* was targeted with racist graffiti, including far-right extremist logos and a swastika. In April 2015, members of the Sikh community in Glasgow found the message 'Fuck Islam, No Sharia!' next to a Nazi swastika on a wall of the Glasgow Central Gurdwara.[5] At the Shri Guru Nanak Gurdwara and Sikh Community Centre in Thornaby, Middlesborough, vandals sprayed 'White power', 'Death to Allah' and 'die Muslims die' on the outside wall.[6] This graffiti demonstrates a devastating combination of hate and ignorance. Most recently in August 2018, Guru Nanak Gurdwara Sahib, in Leith, Edinburgh was firebombed, and the perpetrator received a four-year jail sentence.[7]

There have been a number of attacks on individuals. On 16 August 2005, a Sikh man had his turban pulled off and was racially abused in Northampton. Another, Arjan Rhode, was attacked in Liverpool in 2008, again having his turban ripped off. During heightened community tensions post-Charlie Hebdo in 2015, a Sikh dentist, Dr Sarandev Singh Bhambra, was almost beheaded by a 'Jihadi John'-inspired neo-Nazi in Wales. On 14 May 2016, the Manchester United versus Bournemouth match at Old Trafford was cancelled due to a bomb scare. There was Twitter fury as an Arsenal supporter, 'Arsenal Craig', blamed Sikh football fans for the evacuation by posting an image of Sikh turban-wearing men, with a caption that read 'Bomb threat at Old Trafford, I know where my investigation would start'. Most recently was a physical attack on Ravneet Singh outside Parliament on 2 February 2018. The latter two incidents highlight how, due to a lack of religious literacy, Sikhs are mistaken for Muslims. As polarized debates about Islamophobia continue, it is clear that Sikhs and other South Asians, who have also suffered from Islamophobia and anti-Muslim sentiment, have gone unnoticed. This backlash against Sikhs in the UK particularly due to 'mistaken identity' has been largely absent from government and media narratives on race hate crime, and therefore Sikhs have become 'silent' and 'invisible victims'.[8]

The rise in hate crimes against Sikhs in the United States (hereinafter US), has been a focus on research since 9/11. A groundbreaking book in the US context, Sidhu and Gohil's book *Civil Rights in Wartime: The Post 9/11 Sikh Experience* (2009),[9] focuses on the American context and the Sikh experience of race hate crimes since 9/11. It highlights how the first person to be murdered in retribution for 9/11 in the US was Sikh gas station owner Balbir Singh Sodhi in Mesa, Arizona, on 15 September 2001. It focuses less on global repercussions (including those in Britain). An article by Ahluwalia and Pellettiere, 'Sikh men post-9/11: Misidentification, discrimination, and coping',[10] focused primarily on the US perspective, citing examples such as the attack on Columbia University Professor Prabhjot Singh, who suffered injuries, including a fractured jaw, when attacked by a group shouting 'get Osama' and 'terrorist',[11] or Inderjit Singh Mukker, who was left unconscious by an attacker who told him, 'Terrorist, go back to your own country, bin Laden'.[12] There have also been a number of journal articles that address the issue of race hate crime in the US, such as Grewal's 'Racial sovereignty and "shooter" violence: Oak Creek massacre, normative citizenship and the state',[13] which addressed how on 5 August 2012 Sikhs were victim of a shooting on a *gurdwara* in Oak Creek, Wisconsin, US, where six worshippers were killed;[14] and Puar '"The turban is not a hat": Queer diaspora and practices of profiling'.[15] Prema Kurien considered Sikh activism in relating to changing identities and census categorization in response to the increasing attacks on them since 9/11,[16] and Verma focuses on 'Trauma, cultural survival and identity politics in a post-9/11 era: Reflections by Sikh youth',[17] to name a few.

Alongside the academic literature there has also been much media reporting of attacks in the US in the national press and via social media. Activists like Professor Simran Jeet Singh and Valarie Kaur a lawyer, activist and filmmaker, amongst others, have facilitated such reporting and coverage. They have made considerable contributions to both the debate and existing literature on the subject matter in the US by raising the issue of attacks on social media and in the mainstream media. They have highlighted the numerous cases of race hate crime against Sikh men such as Sandeep Singh, Inderjit Singh Mukker and Surjit Singh Malhi. Sandeep Singh was run over and dragged 30 feet after being called a 'terrorist' in New York City in August 2014. Inderjit Singh Mukker was attacked and allegedly called a 'terrorist' and 'bin Laden' in Chicago in 2015. Surjit Singh Malhi was assaulted in Central Valley, California, in 2018 and his vehicle daubed with a white nationalist symbol along with the words 'go back to your country'.[18] By making sure such incidents are reported in the media, activists have managed to make raise the issue confronting the Sikh community with the wider American community.

Research from the US highlights such cases, but what is still evident is that most research on the subject of Islamophobia and race hate crime focuses primarily on Muslim communities, and research addressing the Sikh experience in the US is still largely thin on the ground.

There is a large body of sociological, legal and psychology literature on Islamophobia and race hate crime in the UK, such as *Islamophobia* by Chris Allen (2010), *Islamophobia, Victimisation and the Veil* by Irene Zempi and Neil Chakraborti (2014); *The Leicester Hate Crime Project: Findings and Conclusions* by Neil Chakraborti et al.;[19] *Islamophobia: Lived Experiences of Online and Offline Victimisation* by Imran Awan and Irene Zempi;[20] 'The harms of hate: Comparing the neighbouring practices and interactions of hate crime victims, non-hate crime victims and non-victims' by K. Benier,[21] and *What is Islamophobia? – Racism, Social Movements and the State* by David Miller.[22] Although there is much information available on Islamophobia and Muslim communities, little has been written by scholars focusing on the experiences of Sikhs in a post-9/11 environment, and it is fair to say the post-9/11 Sikh experience has been largely ignored or subsumed within the broader debate of an anti-Islam backlash focusing primarily on Muslims.

There have been no books that focus solely on the Sikh experience in the UK. However, recently research is beginning to appear that explores the experience of non-Muslims who are mistaken for Muslims. Examples are N. Hall's *Hate*

Crime;[23] Awan and Zempi's report, 'We are accused of being ISIS terrorists: The experiences of non-Muslim men who suffer Islamophobia because they look Muslim' (2017); and 'Encountering misrecognition: Being mistaken for being Muslim' by Peter Hopkins et al., which focuses on Scotland.[23] In this study, Professor Hopkins and his team conducted 45 focus groups and 224 interviews in Scotland with a total of 382 participants from various ethnic and religious backgrounds. Hopkins et al. discovered that Sikhs, Hindus and black and Caribbean participants were often misidentified as Muslim in encounters in public spaces,[25] and nearly all the Sikh participants (of both sexes) in the study were mistaken for Muslims.[26]

Whilst this literature refers to the Sikh diaspora's experiences in Britain, it is very limited in detail. There has been academic literature on Sikh identity generally in which this issue is addressed. For example, Virendar Kalra has written about the turban and raises the issue of mistaken identity.[26] Katy Sian has addressed the issue in a number of articles she has written, but the issue is normally a subsection in another discussion on losing one's identity, or the tensions between Muslims and Sikhs (2010,[28] 2012,[29] and 2013[30]).

Whilst academic research is lacking, so is policy research and government action because of the community being 'invisible' victims, resulting from the government's focus on what they view to be priorities. For example, since 9/11 the government has invested significant funds into researching extremism and radicalization in the Muslim community, and in turn a plethora of academics have focused their energies on Muslims, feeding into various commissions, government working groups, All-Party Parliamentary Groups (hereinafter APPGs) and other influential bodies. For example, Professor Sophie Gilliat-Ray, from Cardiff's Islam UK Centre, was appointed to the Citizens Commission on Islam, Participation and Public Life chaired by the former Attorney General Dominic Grieve QC, and advised that Islamophobia was a factor contributing to the 'radicalization' of Muslims.[31]

Successive governments in the UK have also supported the Abrahamic faith communities in addressing the issue of race and religious hate crime due to the rise in Islamophobia and anti-Semitism. There have been various commissions and reports on this issue, such as Professor Gordon Conway's seminal report in 1997 *Islamophobia: A Challenge for Us All*,[32] and the Runnymede twentieth-anniversary report *Islamophobia: Still a Challenge for Us All* (2017).[33] In 2018 there was the publication of the National Union of Students (hereinafter NUS) report 'The experience of Muslim students in 2017–18'.[34] There were also initiatives to establish the Independent Advisory Group on Hate Crime, Prejudice and Community Cohesion (Scotland), and the work of APPGs on Anti-Semitism and Islamophobia. All this activity has meant that data and analysis have been available on the Jewish and Muslim communities, who have received significant assistance and protection from government compared to other faith communities because of their visibility. For example, the government has financed Tell Measuring Anti-Muslim Attacks (hereinafter 'Tell MAMA'), a national project that records and measures anti-Muslim incidents in the UK since 2012.[35] This monitoring has also equalled visibility resulting in government action, via the publication of the government's four-year hate crime action plan 'Action against hate' (July 2016)[36] led by Amber Rudd, the former home secretary, which pledged £13.4 million to guard every Jewish school, college and nursery and synagogue in the UK.[37]

However, in all of these initiatives and monitoring, Sikhs were invisible. Whilst the authors recognize that attacks in the Sikh community are not at the level encountered by the Muslim or the Jewish community, there was no equivalent funding in place exclusively for Sikhs for either hate crime monitoring or the protection of *gurdwara*s or Sikh schools. Even though Sikhs have been confused for Muslims, the hate crime action plan 'Action against hate' (2016) completely ignored Sikhs.

To increase visibility and to fill the lacunae in policy reporting on the issue, Sikh community groups, having noted that there was a problem, collected data on the issue to inform government policy and have published a number of reports. For example, City Sikhs (hereinafter CS), through their British Sikh Report,[38] and the Sikh Network (hereinafter SN) through their UK Sikh Survey 2016.[39] The British Sikh Report (2017) reported that since the EU referendum:

> 13% of all respondents said that they had been victims of hate crime, and this was similar in all age groups and for men and women.
>
> When asked if they had ever experienced hate crimes in Britain, over 60% said yes. About half of these experiences had been before the year 2001, 12% between 2001 and 2010, and 9% between 2011 and 2015. In these recent periods, those aged 20 to 34 were more likely to be victims.[40]

Meanwhile, the UK Sikh Survey 2016 reported:

> 18% of Sikhs (nearly 1 in 5) have encountered discrimination in a public place in the last 12 months.
>
> Over 100,000 hate crimes against Sikhs aged 16 and over in the last 12 months.[41]

Research conducted by Sikh organizations to better inform policy and decision making is useful, but one needs to analyse data and conclusions carefully. Questions need to be asked about methodology, sample size and selection, and responder characteristics (age, gender, etc.) so that the data can be understood and interpreted correctly.

Whilst it is important to note some of the caveats with such research, evidence and data collected by community groups, such as CS and SN, have been used in lobbying the British government to incorporate Sikhs and others into the narrative of race hate crime victims. Alongside these surveys, Freedom of Information (hereinafter FOI) request disclosures on 'Islamophobic hate crime' for 2015, 2016 and 2017 were also helpful in this regard. The government did offer to assist the Hindu and Sikh community to report hate crime via True Vision, the police hate crime portal.[42] In January 2017, some Sikh groups came together to set up a website feeding into the True Vision portal called 'Sikh Aware UK'. Such community activism has ensured that this issue is understood, monitored and dealt with by government.

Having recognized the gap in the literature and paucity of data the authors provide a detailed account of the theological and historical backdrop to Sikh identity in the global context, before critically analysing how the Sikh turban became transformed from a sacred piece of religious attire to a visible target for 'anti-Muslim' sentiment in the West, particularly the UK, and how the community has remained invisible. Drawing on media reporting, government policies and the emerging body of inter-disciplinary scholarship and empirical research, the authors highlight the Sikh experiences of race hate crime, and provide an academic analysis of media reporting and political discourse to contribute to the slender body of literature that exists on anti-Sikh hate crime in the UK, and put forward recommendations for the community, media and government to address the issue. The book does not intend to advance theory and will not undertake an in-depth analysis and critique of the concept of Islamophobia or race hate crime; instead, it will focus on the post-9/11 Sikh experience from a British Sikh perspective, whilst reflecting on the experience of our American co-religionists.

Methodology

When addressing the issue of race hate crime the definition as given in the Home Office (hereinafter HO) publication *Hate Crime, England and Wales, 2016/17* will be used:

> Any criminal offence which is perceived, by the victim or any other person, to be motivated by hostility or prejudice towards someone based on a personal characteristic.

There are five centrally monitored strands of hate crime:

1   race or ethnicity
2   religion or beliefs
3   sexual orientation
4   disability
5   transgender identity

For the purposes of this book, the authors focus on race hate crime arising due to race, colour, nationality, and ethnic and national origin.[43]

To address what has happened since to the Sikh community since 9/11 in the UK a combination of methodologies were used:

1   Analysis of media reports
2   FOI disclosures from the Metropolitan Police (hereinafter MET) on the breakdown of 'Islamophobic hate crime' data

3   Empirical data – interviews with British Sikhs who had experienced race hate crime.

Analysis of media reporting

The media content analysis was done via an audit of Nexis.com, a comprehensive news and business information online research tool. The two survey periods were August 2014 to August 2015, and August 2016 to August 2017, and the focus of this audit was to study articles that included reference to the word 'Islamophobia' anywhere in the text, and to see whether Sikh issues were addressed. To refine the search criteria, articles with fewer than 500 words, newswires or group duplicates as well as websites were excluded during both survey timeframes referenced above. Articles that included the key search word 'Islamophobia', were analysed to see whether or not they mentioned Sikhs, and if not, whether there was a (1) general reference to Islamophobia or (2) a specific reference in the context of Muslim communities. For example, an article with reference to Islamophobia specifically affecting Muslim communities, titled 'I'm a Muslim woman, Mr Cameron: here's what your radicalisation speech means to me', was published in *The Guardian* on 24 July 2015 but the article 'Totalitarianism in the age of Trump: lessons from Hannah Arendt', published in *The Guardian* on 1 February 2017, mentions Islamophobia in passing, with no specific reference to Muslims. This analysis was essential to see if observable trends could be established; such as whether the majority of coverage on 'Islamophobia' provided specific reference to Muslims, or examples of anti-Muslim hate crime. Separately, the number of articles that mentioned 'Islamophobia' and also referred to 'anti-Semitism', and whether there was an observable trend in this regard, were also considered.[44]

Freedom of Information requests and police disclosures on the breakdown of 'Islamophobic hate crime' data

To support the media data, a series of FOI requests were submitted to the MET for disclosures on the breakdown of 'Islamophobia hate crime' data, from 2015 to the end of 2017. West Midlands Police and Greater Manchester Police were also asked for the same information, although they capture this information using different hate crime flags.[45] This information was then analysed alongside the MET data.

Interviews

To support the academic and media analysis, empirical research was undertaken to gather information on individual experiences of mistaken identity and Islamophobia amongst the Sikh community, mostly in the UK but also in the US. Views of respondents were garnered using a semi-structured interview-based questionnaire. The final study questions were not too academic or lengthy and the questionnaire was kept reasonably short (11 questions) to avoid respondent fatigue. The interview questions were formulated to enable understanding the experiences of race hate that had been encountered, and to elicit responses that highlighted thoughts, feelings and attitudes towards race hate crime.

Both authors were in a very fortunate position in terms of the research because both authors were Sikh and therefore 'insiders'. As insiders they were in a privileged position because they had access to the community that an 'outsider' could not have. Being insiders served as an important addition to the other methodological strategies employed and provided added value to the academic discussion of 'mistaken identity' and how it is experienced and responded to. By virtue of their embeddedness in daily life in the community, the authors could access and utilize their own networks of family, friends and contacts to locate respondents. For example, contacts in big *gurdwaras* in London and in the Midlands were approached to advertise the research and to encourage members to get involved, particularly those who had experienced race hate crime owing to their Sikh identity. The authors then used a snowball sampling approach to gain more participants via these networks. These methods in the round allowed access to Sikh respondents from diverse backgrounds. There was significant interest; however, many of those who expressed interest did not qualify to participate as they had not suffered directly from incidents of hate themselves, and they were informed of this.

Altogether, there were 76 participants. A sample of 62 Sikhs in the UK were interviewed. In addition to the 62 UK respondents, three respondents who were interviewed waived their anonymity. They were the former MP Parmjit Singh Dhanda, Suman Kaur (artist) and Amarjit Singh Atwal (Northampton *Gurdwara* committee member), who had written or spoken publicly about the issue. For some additional insight into race hate crime, the interview questionnaire was circulated to Sikhs in America via a colleague in the US, and responses were returned to Dr Jhutti-Johal via email; if comments were not clear, the respondents were contacted for clarification. Five responses were received via email, and six interviews were conducted in person whilst Dr Jhutti-Johal was in New York in March 2018. Thus, in total, the authors had 76 responses: 71 respondents were interviewed and five respondents from the US had emailed their responses.

The respondents were all adults between the ages of 20 and 66. They included first-, second-, third- and fourth-generation Sikhs from various social classes, age groups and localities. Whilst all first-generation informants were born and brought up in India, all second-, third- and fourth-generation informants were born in Britain, although some had spent a short time in their parents' country of birth. Nearly all participants had had received formal education when they were young, and most were university educated.

Interviews were conducted either in a *gurdwara* or in another neutral space. The interviews with elders were conducted mostly in Punjabi, but some were conducted in English. Interviews with second-, third- and fourth-generation respondents were conducted mainly in English, but some respondents did regularly lapse into Punjabi. All UK interviews were one-to-one interviews and lasted a minimum of one to two hours. Notes were taken and if the respondents consented, the interviews were recorded and then transcribed.

Throughout the interviews, the authors developed a rapport with the participants, actively listening and responding with appropriate comment(s) and/or follow-up questioning. Although the interviews were based on set questions, flexibility was granted to gain a broadened, deepened understanding of individuals' experiences and understanding of race hate crime. Responses were intensely personal and revealing, and since the respondents were from different age groups, and from a wide cross-section of the society in which they lived, it became clear, when they were discussing their experiences of 'mistaken identity' with surprising frankness, that their perception and experiences of race hate crime varied.

It was also clear that the responses varied according to a number of factors, including age, location, economic status, educational background, and degree of religious observance and practice. For example, the age of the respondents influenced certain responses. The views of some of the elderly Sikhs varied considerably from those of the younger generation. For example, older respondents were more willing to ignore incidences of race hate crime, whilst the younger respondents felt it was their responsibility to address it. It was also apparent that respondents who were university educated and working in white-collar jobs had different responses to those of respondents who had limited education and were working in blue-collar jobs. Different levels of religious commitment also caused respondents to offer different answers and responses on how to address race hate crime. It is also important to note that conversations and interviews sometimes varied depending on attributes such as age, gender, religious observance and social status (of authors as well as respondents), and in the case of Jhutti-Johal her relationship status, i.e. whether she was married and had children (something she was questioned about by several older male and female respondents). It was clear that how some people responded and engaged was sometimes influenced by their social position *vis-à-vis* others.

The interviews gave the authors a detailed insight into how the respondents experienced incidents of race hate crime. Most importantly, they were able to explore the respondents' perceptions of what constitutes a race hate crime. Respondents in their interviews were frank and honest about their experiences. Some of the interviews were painful due to these experience, not least resulting from the apathy that prevented race hate reporting in their community. It was very clear from the young respondents' comments that they recognized the complexities of living in a pluralistic, multicultural and multi-faith society, but were surprised about how the EU referendum and the election of President Trump has reignited a debate centred on immigration.

In the book, when direct quotes have been used the authors have endeavoured to retain them in the spirit in which they were made; the authors are aware of the problems of decontextualization, and the danger of using quotes to support any given argument or to make generalizations, particularly when the sample size is so small. Apart from three respondents, participant names are not used because respondents were informed that the process would ensure confidentiality and anonymity throughout the processes of data collection, data cleaning and dissemination. Instead, pseudonyms were used or markers for individuals participating in the interviews, such as 'an older man'.

The authors are conscious of the shortcomings of the study, for example the small sample size and the fact that respondents' comments may not be representative of those of all Sikhs; but these empirical data are useful in highlighting not only the variety of experiences that Sikhs have encountered and how respondents feel have dealt with their experiences, but also how they feel the government and the community has responded. This valuable information, when cross-referenced with other research studies, echoes a similarity in attacks, slurs and experiences and provides a general understanding of perceptions and the impact of anti-Sikh sentiment.

To enhance understanding of what was happening with regards to US activism, Hardeep Singh spoke to community leaders such as Professor Simran Jeet Singh, Jaideep Singh, co-founder of the Sikh American Legal Defense and Education Fund (hereinafter SALDEF); Amrith Kaur, legal director of civil rights group the Sikh Coalition (hereinafter SC); and other American Sikhs who are engaged in advocacy in order to learn about and understand how and why certain decisions are made. It was clear from discussions that the challenges and environment that American Sikhs continue to face is different from the UK context. For example, American Sikhs have taken a robust approach by prosecuting hate crime, and the SC has led in this regard. There also appear to be mixed views on the 'We Are Sikhs' campaign, and this may be in part related to political affiliations, be they Democrat or Republican.

Structure

The book is divided into four chapters. Chapter 1, 'The evolution of the Sikh *dharam* and identity', provides an overview of the Sikh religion, its history and basic theological tenets, and the religious significance of the turban. To address the significance of the Sikh identity, primary and secondary sources were used. The primary source of reference was the *Guru Granth Sahib*, the holy book of the Sikhs, the Sikh's Eternal Guru and perpetual guide, and the epitome of the spiritual teachings of Sikhism. Other primary sources included the *Dasam Granth* (a book attributed to the tenth Guru of the Sikhs, Guru Gobind Singh), *Janam Sakhis* (a hagiographical life account of Guru Nanak), and other key references (including Bhai Gurdas Ji's writings) and *Rehatnamas*, since they are essential in understanding the role and importance of the turban. The *Rehat Maryada* (1945/1950) is also used in defining the significance of the turban. Having provided a primer on Sikhism, the chapter then considers the global presence of Sikhs, highlights the increasing visibility and accommodation of turban-wearing Sikhs in the UK, and introduces the new challenges faced by turban-wearing Sikhs post-9/11.

Chapter 2, 'Sikhs in Britain post-9/11', focuses on the situation in the UK. British Sikhs in the UK are viewed as an integration success story, but the chapter will focus on the racism that Sikhs encountered when they first migrated. The chapter draws on the Race Relations Act (1976) and its accompanying amendments and then its repeal and replacement, the Macpherson Report and the Equality Act (2010).

The nature of anti-Muslim hate crime in Britain – from the rhetoric of the National Front (hereinafter NF) in the 1970s and the British National Party (hereinafter BNP), and post-9/11 prejudice in which turbaned Sikhs, like Muslim women in headscarves, have faced the brunt of Islamophobia – are discussed.

The chapter provides an overview of how Islamic extremist attacks in the US and Europe are driving Islamophobia in the West, and how despite Sikhs encountering a backlash, their story has been subsumed or dismissed within the wider debate. Prominent cases in the US will be discussed, such as the murder of Sikh gas station owner Balbir Singh Sodhi in Mesa, Arizona, on 15 September 2001, Sikhs killed on 5 August 2012 in a *gurdwara* in Oak Creek, Wisconsin, and an Islamist attack on a *gurdwara* in Essen, Germany, on 16 April 2016.

This analysis is then followed by a discussion of attacks on Sikhs in the UK, such as on Sikh dentist Dr Sarandev Singh Bhambra in Wales by a neo-Nazi influenced by 'Jihadi John'. Alongside this analysis, there is also an analysis of the trolling, memes and harassment that Sikhs have encountered on social media platforms like Twitter/Facebook/Instagram.

Chapter 3, 'UK – do Sikhs count?', follows.[46] In the US since 2015, the Federal Bureau of Investigation (hereinafter FBI) has been separately monitoring hate crime against Sikhs, Hindus, Arabs and Muslims. This was following calls for parity after the 2012 Wisconsin *gurdwara* massacre. American Sikhs have tackled racial profiling at airports, which has been a major priority for them. The SC, for example, designed an app called FlyRights for Sikh passengers. Individuals like Valarie Kaur, filmmaker (*Divided We Fall: Americans in the Aftermath*), a lawyer and founder of Groundswell, has been raising the Sikh issue in the mainstream media along with other luminaires like Professor Simran Jeet Singh, and Vishavjit Singh, a cartoonist who dresses up as Sikh Captain America in order to tackle bigotry head on.

This chapter highlights how in the UK there has not been the same concerted effort by the community, but things are beginning to change with groups like the Network of Sikh Organisations (hereinafter NSO), the Sikh Council UK (hereinafter SCUK) and CS raising the issue with government. For example, the NSO pushed back against the 'Abrahamic-centric' focus of the hate crime action plan resulting in the HO announcing (in February 2017) that Sikhs and Hindus would receive some support in reporting hate crime via the police-sponsored site True Vision. In April 2017, Sikh groups launched Sikh Aware UK – a portal that aimed to feed into True Vision.

The focus of UK governments and influential British think tanks on 'Islamophobia' directed at Muslims and anti-Semitism is discussed alongside an analysis of policy funding and hate crime recording strategies introduced by government, such as the start-up funding (2012) for Tell MAMA, and government reports, such as 'Action against hate' (2016), which made no commitments to support non-Abrahamic victims of hate crime. This discussion is supported by an analysis of Hansard and newspaper articles to see whether attacks on Sikhs have been adequately reported.

This chapter, whilst providing a comparative lens, recognizes that the experiences, situations and even challenges faced by Sikhs in the UK and the US remain markedly different. The authors are not presenting the two as analogous.

Chapter 4 concludes. Having considered the rise in race hate attacks against Sikh men due to their religious appearance, illustrating the consequences of misguided hatred fuelled by a rise in Islamophobia, the final chapter highlights how although some changes have occurred in the UK, this does not mean the community no longer suffers from anti-Muslim sentiment. It is argued that Sikhs remain victims, and that the community and government need to tackle the misguided hatred and Islamophobia, and engage seriously in this debate so that the problem can be tackled from both a community and a government perspective. A series of practical recommendations for both government and the Sikh community itself are made.

Notes

1 Whilst most of the attacks that have been reported have been those that have occurred on men, in the last decade (most recently since the EU referendum of June 2016) initiated Sikh women wearing the turban, but also Sikh women who do not wear the turban, such as Suman Kaur in February 2018, have been victims of abuse. However, the narrative on the gendered dimension to Sikh race hate crime is not as strong as that within the Muslim community, for whom most attacks are perpetrated on women wearing the *hijab* or *burkha*.
2 Other domestic issues, such as 'sexual grooming' gangs, female genital mutilation (hereinafter FGM) and opposition to sharia courts have also placed Sikhs on the frontline of anti-Islam sentiment.
3 Institute of Race Relations (2005). 'The anti-Muslim backlash begins'. [online] Available at: www.irr.org.uk/news/the-anti-muslim-backlash-begins/ [Accessed 13 August 2017].
4 V. Mason (2016). 'Hate crime attack at Sikh temple'. *Bradford Telegraph & Argus*. [online] Available at: www.thetelegraphandargus.co.uk/news/14683946.Hate_crime_attack_at_Sikh_temple/ [Accessed 13 March 2018].
5 BBC News (2015). 'Anti-Islamic graffiti on Sikh temple'. [online] Available at: www.bbc.co.uk/news/uk-scotland-glasgow-west-32284473 [Accessed 12 December 2017].
6 M. Blackburn (2015). 'Yobs spray "die Muslims die" in graffiti attack – on Sikh temple'. *Gazette Live*. [online] Available at: www.gazettelive.co.uk/news/teesside-news/yobs-spray-die-muslims-die-9985403 [Accessed 14 April 2018].
7 BBC News (2018). 'Petrol bomb attack on Sikh temple probed'. [online] Available at: www.bbc.co.uk/news/uk-scotland-edinburgh-east-fife-45330820 [Accessed 28 August 2018].
8 J. A. Abel (2005). 'Americans under attack: The need for federal hate crime legislation in light of post-September 11 attacks on Arab Americans and Muslims'. *Asian Law Journal*, 12, p. 41; K. M. Blee (2005). 'Racial violence in the United States'. *Ethnic and Racial Studies*, 28(4), pp. 599–619; E. Hanes and S. Machin (2014). 'Hate crime in the wake of terror attacks: Evidence from 7/7 and 9/11'. *Journal of Contemporary Criminal Justice*, 30(3), pp. 247–267.

9 D. S. Sidhu and N. S. Gohil (2016). *Civil Rights in Wartime: The Post-9/11 Sikh Experience*. London: Routledge. The authors had written about the issue prior to the publication of their book: N. S. Gohil and D. S. Sidhu (2008). 'The Sikh turban: Post-911 challenges to this article of faith'. *Rutgers Journal of Law & Religion*, 9, pp. 10–72.

10 M. Ahluwalia and L. Pellettiere (2010). 'Sikh men post-9/11: Misidentification, discrimination, and coping'. *Asian American Journal of Psychology*, 1(4), pp. 303–314.

11 J. Cannold (2013). 'Sikh professor beaten in possible hate crime in New York'. CNN. [online] Available at: http://edition.cnn.com/2013/09/23/justice/new-york-sikh-possible-hate-crime/index.html [Accessed 6 January 2018].

12 J. Dean (2015). 'A Sikh man was battered by a racist who called him "bin Laden"'. *The Mirror*. [online] Available at: www.mirror.co.uk/news/world-news/sikh-man-battered-racist-thug-6424786 [Accessed 6 January 2018].

13 I. Grewal (2013). 'Racial sovereignty and "shooter" violence: Oak Creek massacre, normative citizenship and the state'. *Sikh Formations: Religion, Culture, Theory*, 9(2), pp. 187–197.

14 S. Hundal (2012). 'Wisconsin temple shooting: Sikhs have been silent scapegoats since 9/11'. *The Guardian*. [online] Available at: www.theguardian.com/commentisfree/2012/aug/06/wisconsin-temple-shooting-sikh-scapegoats [Accessed 14 July 2017].

15 J. K. Puar (2008). '"The Turban is not a hat": Queer diaspora and practices of profiling'. *Sikh Formations: Religion, Culture, Theory*, 4(1), pp. 47–91.

16 P. Kurien (2018). 'Shifting US racial and ethnic identities and Sikh American activism'. *The Russell Sage Foundation Journal of the Social Sciences*, 4(5), p. 81.

17 R. Verma (2006). 'Trauma, cultural survival and identity politics in a post-9/11 era: Reflections by Sikh youth'. *Sikh Formations: Religion, Culture, Theory*, 2(1), pp. 89–101.

18 C. Fuchs (2018). 'Police investigating alleged assault of California Sikh man as hate crime'. NBC News. [online] Available at: www.nbcnews.com/news/asian-america/police-investigating-alleged-assault-california-sikh-man-hate-crime-n898456 [Accessed 13 September 2018].

19 N. Chakraborti, J. Garland and S. J. Hardy (2014). *The Leicester Hate Crime Project: Findings and Conclusions*. Retrieved from www2.le.ac.uk/departments/criminology/hate/documents/fc-full-report [Accessed 23 December 2018].

20 I. Awan and I. Zempi (2016). *Islamophobia: Lived Experiences of Online and Offline Victimisation*. Bristol: Policy Press.

21 K. Benier (2017). 'The harms of hate: Comparing the neighbouring practices and interactions of hate crime victims, non-hate crime victims and non-victims'. *International Review of Victimology*, 23(2), 179–201. Available at: https://doi.org/10.1177/0269758017693087 [Accessed 22 December 2018].

22 There are also other works that focus on Islamophobia that highlight policy implications and the impact of the media and the far right: N. Chakraborti (2014). 'Re-thinking hate crime: Fresh challenges for policy and practice'. *Journal of interpersonal violence*, 30(10), pp. 1738–1754; N. Chakraborti and J. Garland (2012). 'Reconceptualizing hate crime victimization through the lens of vulnerability and "difference"'. *Theoretical Criminology*, 16(4), pp. 499–514; G. Mason (2005). 'Hate crime and the image of the stranger'. *British Journal of Criminology*, 45(6), pp. 837–859; D. Frost (2008). 'Islamophobia: examining causal links between the media and "race hate" from "below"'. *International Journal of Sociology and Social Policy*, 28(11/12), pp. 564–578, and N. Copsey, J. Dack, M. Littler and M. Feldman (2013). 'Anti-Muslim hate crime and the far right'. Available at: http://tellmamauk.org/wp-content/uploads/2013/07/antimuslim2.pdf [Accessed 4 September 2014].

23 N. Hall (2013). *Hate Crime*. London: Routledge.

24 P. Hopkins, K. Botterill, G. Sanghera and R. Arshad (2017). 'Encountering misrecognition: Being mistaken for being Muslim'. *Annals of the American Association of Geographers*, 107(4), pp. 934–948.

25 Ibid.
26 Ibid.
27 V. S. Kalra (2005). 'Locating the Sikh pagh'. *Sikh Formations: Religion, Culture and Theory*, 1(1), pp. 75–92.
28 K. P. Sian (2010). 'Don't Freak I'm a Sikh'. *Thinking through Islamophobia*, pp. 251–254.
29 K. P. Sian (2012). 'Gurdwaras, guns and grudges in "post-racial" America'. *Sikh Formations: Religion, Culture and Theory*, 8(3), pp. 293–297.
30 K. P. Sian (2013). 'Losing my religion: Sikhs in the UK'. *Sikh Formations: Religion, Culture and Theory*, 9(1), pp. 39–50.
31 A. Wightwick (2015). 'Welsh Muslims must be encouraged into public life to tackle extremism'. *Wales Online* [online]. Available at: www.walesonline.co.uk/news/wales-news/poverty-islamophobia-partly-blame-radicalisation-10165980 [Accessed 7 December 2017].
32 Gordon Conway (1997). *Islamophobia: A Challenge for Us All*. [online] Available at: www.runnymedetrust.org/companies/17/74/Islamophobia-A-Challenge-for-Us-All.html [Accessed 14 December 2017].
33 Elahi Farah and Omar Khan (2017). *Islamophobia: Still a Challenge for Us All*. [online] Available at: www.runnymedetrust.org/uploads/Islamophobia%20Report%202018.pdf [Accessed 30 November 2017].
34 NUS (2018). 'The experience of Muslim students in 2017–18'. [online] Available at: www.nusconnect.org.uk/resources/the-experience-of-muslim-students-in-2017-18.
35 A. Gilligan (2013). 'Muslim hate monitor to lose backing'. *The Telegraph*. [online] Available at: www.telegraph.co.uk/journalists/andrew-gilligan/10108098/Muslim-hate-monitor-to-lose-backing.html [Accessed 26 November 2017].
36 Home Office (2016). 'Action against hate: The UK government's plan for tackling hate crime'. GOV.UK. [online] Available at: www.gov.uk/government/uploads/system/uploads/attachment_data/file/543679/Action_Against_Hate_-_UK_Government_s_Plan_to_Tackle_Hate_Crime_2016.pdf [Accessed 30 December 2017].
37 C. Hope (2016). 'Amber Rudd pledges £13.4million to guard every Jewish school, college, and nursery and synagogue in the UK'. *The Telegraph*. [online] Available at: www.telegraph.co.uk/news/2016/11/30/amber-rudd-pledges-134million-guard-every-jewish-school-college/ [Accessed 18 November 2017].
38 British Sikh Report (2017). British Sikh Report. [online] Available at: www.british-sikhreport.org/wp-content/uploads/2017/03/British-Sikh-Report-2017-Online.pdf [Accessed 20 August 2018].
39 The Sikh Network (2016). 'UK Sikh Survey 2016'. [online] Available at: www.thesikhnetwork.com/wp-content/uploads/2016/11/UK-Sikh-Survey-2016-Findings-FINAL.pdf.
40 British Sikh Report, p. 20.
41 The Sikh Network, 'UK Sikh Survey 2016', p. 5.
42 The Network of Sikh Organisations (2017). 'Support for Sikh and Hindu hate crime victims. Network of Sikh Organisations'. [online] Available at: http://nsouk.co.uk/support-for-sikh-and-hindu-hate-crime-victims/ [Accessed 18 November 2017].
43 A. O'Neill (2017). *Hate Crime, England and Wales, 2016/17*. Home Office. [online] Available at: https://assets.publishing.service.gov.uk/government/uploads/system/uploads/attachment_data/file/652136/hate-crime-1617-hosb1717.pdf [Accessed 29 November 2017].
44 This is a brief summary of the methodology, which is detailed in Chapter 4 along with the results, analysis and conclusion.
45 Requests for disclosure of the breakdown of 'Islamophobic hate crime' data were requested from the MET, the Greater Manchester Police and the West Midlands Police:

4 January 2016 – *'Please could you disclose the number of "Islamophobic offences" recorded between Jan–July 2015, where the victim is non-Muslim?'*
27 June 2016 – *'The number of "Islamophobic offences" recorded between July–Dec 2015, where the victim is non-Muslim.'*
4 July 2016 – *'Please could you disclose the number of "Islamophobic offences" recorded between Jan–June 2016, where the victim is non-Muslim?'*
13 January 2017 – *'Please could you disclose the "Islamophobic hate crime" figures as a breakdown with Muslims and non-Muslims for the year 2016?'*
16 January 2017 – *'Please could you disclose the "Islamophobic hate crime" figures as a breakdown with Muslims and non-Muslims for the year 2016?'*
18 October 2017 – *'Please could you provide a breakdown of non-Muslim victims of Islamophobic hate crime for 2016–17 financial year?'*

(Metropolitan Police)

12 December 2017 – *'Please could you provide a breakdown of Muslim vs non-Muslim victims of Islamophobic hate crime for 2016/17?'*
If the non-Muslim victims could be broken down by religion, that would be helpful.'

(West Midlands Police)

23 October 2017 – *'A breakdown by religion to include non-Muslim victims or those of no recorded faith would be helpful and by financial year 2016/17.'*

(Greater Manchester Police)

46 The heading of Chapter 3 is drawn from an opinion-editorial by Simran Jeet Singh and Prabhjot Singh published 24 August 2012 in *The New York Times*: 'How hate gets counted'. [online] Available at: www.nytimes.com/2012/08/24/opinion/do-american-sikhs-count.html [Accessed 3 January 2019].

1 The evolution of the Sikh *dharam* and identity[1]

The Sikh *dharam*

The Sikh *dharam* (more recently also known by the term, 'Sikhi') is one of the world's youngest religions. It originated on the Indian subcontinent in the fifteenth century. It was founded by Guru Nanak, a charismatic leader considered a messenger of God who was born in 1469 CE.

Historically, Guru Nanak's life (1469–1539) coincided with a period of religious renaissance in Europe – Martin Luther (1483–1546) and John Calvin (1509–64) being amongst his contemporaries.[2] In a similar and no less revolutionary way, Guru Nanak challenged the current theologies and practices of his day (i.e. those of Hinduism and Islam) and propagated the message that the liberation of the soul was open to all, irrespective of race, sex, caste or religion. Guru Nanak's life story itself is a tale of the quest for truth, the performance of miraculous deeds, and the ministry of a charismatic leader and teacher who sought to rescue the path to spiritual truth from the human entanglements of social inequality. He was a householder but lived a life devoted to the Divine Truth, both in his external dealings and his internal spiritual pursuit.

Guru Nanak's egalitarian message becomes particularly clear after he achieved divine revelation, or realization, sometime around the age of 30. After disappearing into a river and meditating in the water for three days, Guru Nanak emerged having had a powerful vision of the nature of reality, divinity and human existence. He recorded that vision in the *Japji Sahib*, the 'Song of the Soul', which highlights a philosophy that recognizes the Divine Light (*jot*) dwelling within all of God's creation – from minute creatures to human beings.

Certain ideas that Guru Nanak had, as well as his choice of vocabulary, suggest that some of his teachings may have drawn inspiration from Sufism, a branch of Islamic mysticism, and the *bhakti* or *sant* devotional movements that had originated around the twelfth century in various parts of India. However, he ultimately fashioned his own philosophy, elevating 'truth' to the highest status and recognizing God as being one with truth.

ਬਾਲ ਵਿਚਿ ਤਿੰਨਿ ਵਸਤੂ ਪਈਓ ਸਤੁ ਸੰਤੋਖੁ ਵੀਚਾਰੋ ॥
ਅੰਮ੍ਰਿਤ ਨਾਮੁ ਠਾਕੁਰ ਕਾ ਪਈਓ ਜਿਸ ਕਾ ਸਭਸੁ ਅਧਾਰੋ ॥

ਜੇ ਕੋ ਖਾਵੈ ਜੇ ਕੋ ਭੁੰਚੈ ਤਿਸ ਕਾ ਹੋਇ ਉਧਾਰੋ ॥
ਏਹ ਵਸਤੁ ਤਜੀ ਨਹ ਜਾਈ ਨਿਤ ਨਿਤ ਰਖੁ ਉਰਿ ਧਾਰੋ ॥

Thaal vich tin vastoo peyeo sat Santokh vicharo.
Amrit naam thakar ka payeo jis ka sabs adharo.
Je ko khave ke ko bhunche tis ka hoey odharo.
Eh vast tujee nahi jae nit nit rakh our dharo.

Upon this Plate, three things have been placed: Truth, Contentment and
Contemplation.
The ambrosial Nectar of the Naam, the Name of our Lord and Master,
has been placed upon it as well.
It is the Support of all.
One who eats it and enjoys it shall be saved.
This thing can never be forsaken;
keep this always and forever in your mind.[3]

In practical terms, Guru Nanak taught that the Creator (*Karta Purakh*) was
immanent and accessible to everyone, encouraged charitable works and selfless
service, and promoted the advancement of the status of women. Many Hindus
revere Guru Nanak as an extraordinary *sant* who sought to restore the *dharma*,
which had been degenerating in his time, by travelling throughout India and
beyond to teach the path of truth, unity and humanity. Many great authorities of
Hinduism and Islam were impressed by his clear message and a teaching style
that was accessible to all people from different castes, religions and genders.

Guru Nanak and the succession of Gurus

Before his death, Guru Nanak appointed a successor, Angad, to continue his
mission, which officially established the Sikh tradition. For the next 250 years
this Sikhi tradition continued, each Guru appointing a successor to carry on the
tradition before leaving his mortal body. In all there was a consecutive series of
ten human Gurus, commonly referred to as the 'Golden Chain', and each Guru is
accorded equal status amongst Sikhs. In fact, for many Sikhs the Gurus are considered the spirit of Guru Nanak assuming ten different forms. Therefore, Guru
Nanak and subsequent Gurus are referred to as Nanak I, Nanak II and so on in
the *Guru Granth Sahib*. Each Guru advanced the tradition by adding various
facets to it. For example, in the sixteenth century, Guru Angad collected Guru
Nanak's hymns into a book and added his own compositions. He also gave Sikhs
a new script, *Gurmukhi* (literally 'from the mouth of the Guru'). This gave the
Sikhs a written language, distinct from that of Hindus and Muslims, that helped
to foster a distinctive Sikh identity.[4]

   As the number of Sikhs began to grow, the third Guru, Amar Das, began to
institutionalize the Sikh faith. He accomplished this by appointing territorial
ministers and creating the system of *langar*, or 'Guru's free kitchen', an integral

part of Sikh religion that continues to be an important feature of the Sikh *dharma*. Guru Amar Das also introduced various social reforms such as the prohibition of *sati* (the widely known, but rarely practised custom of self-immolation by Kshatriya widows on their husband's funeral pyres), and sought to free women from archaic customs. He allowed the remarriage of widows, advocated monogamy, denounced the veiling of women and appointed women leaders.

Guru Ram Das, the fourth Guru, established a village that was eventually to become the city of Amritsar – the spiritual and political capital of the Sikhs in Punjab. The fifth Guru, Guru Arjan, oversaw the construction of the holiest shrine, the *Harmandir Sahib*, popularly known as the Golden Temple. Guru Arjan was a prolific writer and composed more hymns than any of his predecessors. His most important achievement was the compilation of the *Adi Granth*, an authoritative collection of his work and the works of the first four Gurus. It also included the poetry of Hindu and Muslim saints whose views echoed those of the Gurus. In 1604, the *Adi Granth* was installed at the *Harmandir Sahib* in Amritsar, Punjab, India. It became the embodiment of Sikh thought that helped catapult Sikh teachings to the masses.

The growing influence of Guru Arjan Dev consequently brought him into conflict with the Mughal rulers of Punjab as his presence and popularity became a threat to their power. The Mughal Emperor Jahangir had him arrested, and whilst in custody Guru Arjan was put to death. Sikhs see Guru Arjan as their first martyr or *shaheed*, and his death marked a turning point for the Sikh community, which began to feel a real and physical threat to their principles and way of life.

The sixth Guru, Guru Hargobind, in reaction to this, added a militaristic dimension to the Sikh faith. He introduced the concept that the Guru has both spiritual authority (*piri*) as well as a worldly and temporal role (*miri*). *Miri–piri* requires one to be a saint first and a soldier second. This means that a Sikh's saintliness and spirituality should come first, and that spirituality should guide them in their worldly and temporal matters. It was a concept central to the Sikh *dharma* from the very outset of Guru Nanak's time right through to the tenth Guru, Guru Gobind Singh. Guru Nanak was a saint, but he was also a family man. He was both an enlightened being and socially concerned – unlike the *yogis* who renounce society completely – and he actively defied the social and political ills of his times. Furthermore, none of the Gurus endorsed the ascetic lifestyle prevalent in Hinduism and other *dharma* traditions, and instead promoted the sanctity of the householder lifestyle.

However, Guru Hargobind took the concept of worldly concern to a different level. This concept is further symbolized through his creation of the *Akal Takht* ('Throne of the Timeless') at *Harmandir Sahib*, as the Sikh *dharam*'s seat of temporal affairs. It is one of the five seats of authority in the Sikh *dharam*.[5] The *Akal Takht* is the highest seat of authority, created to address issues of justice and order in the *Panth*. The Sikhs are asked to embody heroism that is grounded in the Guru's Word:

ਗੁਰ ਕਾ ਸਬਦੁ ਮਨੇ ਸੋ ਸੂਰਾ ॥
ਸਾਚੀ ਦਰਗਹ ਸਾਚੁ ਨਿਵਾਸਾ ਮਾਨੈ ਹੁਕਮੁ ਰਜਾਈ ਹੇ ॥

Gur ka Shabad mane so soora.
Sachee dhargeh sach nivasa mania Hukam rajaye hai

He alone is a spiritual hero, who believes in the Word of the Guru's Shabad (Naam). He alone obtains a true seat in the True Court of the Lord, who surrenders to the Command of the Commander.[6]

Thus, in terms of action, Sikhs must first be attached to the love of God, and they must also have the qualities of a saint in order to be a soldier ready to confront worldly battles against injustices. Through this unique model of Saint-Solider, Guru Hargobind sanctified actions for the protection of the faith and human dignity. By prioritizing saintly qualities and affairs, politics become purified and spiritualized, rather than spirituality becoming politicized.

The period of Guruship between the seventh (Guru Har Rai) and eighth (Guru Har Krishan) Gurus was generally one of peace and the continual spread of Sikh teachings. This peace was shattered during the tenure of the ninth Guru, Guru Tegh Bahadur, who died defending *dharma* and the rights of other religious traditions to practice their faiths. Like the fifth Guru, Guru Tegh Bahadur was executed by the order of the Mughal Emperor, Aurangzeb. Guru Tegh Bahadur also composed many hymns that were later added to the *Adi Granth* by the tenth Guru, Gobind Singh, who also renamed the *Adi Granth* as the *Guru Granth Sahib*. Guru Gobind Singh gave the Sikh community a unique external identity and passed the Guruship to the Holy Scripture, the *Guru Granth Sahib*, which is the Eternal Living Guru for Sikhs today.[7]

External identity: the formation of the Khalsa

In 1699, the tenth Guru, Guru Gobind Singh, was instrumental in creating the Khalsa (the community of the 'pure'), which established the Sikh *dharma* as a distinct religious movement with a unique and separate Sikh identity and code of conduct. This was achieved through both the institution of an initiation ceremony called the *Amrit Sanskar/Amrit Pahul*, which is performed in the presence of the *Guru Granth Sahib*, and the adoption of the five articles of faith, which are commonly known as the Five Ks. The principles of the faith and other key instructions on how a baptized Sikh must live were imparted to the initiates: principles such as devotion to God, service to humanity, fighting against injustice and defence of the weak. The ceremonious receiving of *Amrit* involves sacraments:

On acceptance of these instructions, *Amrit* (nectar of immortality) is prepared by pouring water and sugar in a steel bowl and stirring the mixture with a double-edged dagger while selected verses from the *Guru Granth*

Sahib and *Dasam Granth* (works of the tenth Guru) are read out aloud. Five handfuls of *Amrit* are drunk by the initiate and five handfuls are sprinkled over their hair and eyes. Further prayers are then offered followed by a random reading of a verse from the GGS.[8]

Once initiated into the Khalsa, membership of this sacred order requires the Khalsa Sikh to adopt the *Panj Kakar* (Five Ks). These are five articles of faith whose name in Punjabi begins with a 'K': *kesh* (ਕੇਸ – unshorn hair),[9] *kangha* (ਕੰਘਾ – a wooden comb), *kara* (ਕੜਾ – a simple iron bracelet), *kachera* (ਕਛੈਰਾ – special cotton underwear) and *kirpan* (ਕਿਰਪਾਨ or ਕ੍ਰਿਪਾਨ – a short sword). These articles of faith are symbols of commitment to both spirituality and the defence of justice. Furthermore, to emphasize equality, Khalsa Sikhs were required to use a caste-neutral last name: Singh (Lion) for men and Kaur (Princess) for women. These spiritual last names signify the dignity of both male and female genders and unite Sikhs within the family of the Sikh tradition. Finally, it also requires the adoption of a code of conduct, which prohibits Sikhs from consuming alcohol, tobacco, drugs, and *kuttha* meat (meat of an animal slaughtered slowly, as imposed by the Muslim Halal method). Through the institution of *Amrit* and the tenth Guru's role in creating a distinct Sikh identity, one can see how the sixth Guru's ideology of *Miri–piri* began to take concrete form. The adoption of the Five Ks symbolizes both the embrace of a spiritual shared identity and the restoration of human dignity.

Whilst it is clear from the *Guru Granth Sahib* that the core spiritual or religious ideology of Guru Nanak did not change, it is evident that with each Guru the emphasis of the Sikh movement shifted, in part as a natural evolution of the religious movement but also as a response to changing political and cultural circumstances.

Identity: the turban

It is the order of Soldier-Saints, as instituted by Guru Gobind Singh, that has become the model of the devout Sikh. When one thinks of Sikhs and their unshorn hair and turban, one normally associates this identity with Guru Gobind Singh and the formation of the Khalsa. The requirement to keep long hair was made part of the key requirement to be Amritdhari Sikh only. The turban – *dastaar* (ਦਸਤਾਰ), also referred to as pagri (ਪਗੜੀ), or *pagg/pagh* (ਪੱਗ), has become a mandatory head covering for Sikh men who keep their hair long, irrespective of whether they are initiated or not. Academics such as McLeod[10] have questioned what the exact theological status of the turban is and whether it is a requirement for a Sikh to wear one. Whilst McLeod argues that references to the turban are sparse in the *Guru Granth Sahib* if one reads the *Guru Granth Sahib*,[11] various *Rehatnamas* and the 1945/1950 *Rehat Maryada* one can trace the observance of long hair and the turban for Sikhs back to the time of Guru Nanak.[12]

The socio-religious and symbolic significance of keeping uncut hair (*kesh*) was that it demonstrated that one has accepted *Hukam* (ਹੁਕਮ) – the Will of God.

Guru Nanak taught that the appearance of the Sikh should essentially be that which God Almighty has given according to His Will. Having accepted the *Hukam*'s expectation of maintaining long hair, Sikhs were encouraged to keep the *kesh* intact and tidy and to maintain its sanctity, and hence the turban became a necessity, and acquired a social and political status of its own. The turban, which at the time of Guru Nanak had been reserved for the higher castes, became an article of faith that all Sikhs could wear, thus becoming a symbol of unity, equality, dignity and humility.[13]

Guru Granth Sahib, Dasam Granth and Rehatnamas[14]

The primary sources such as the *Adi Granth, Guru Granth Sahib, Dasam Granth, Vaaran Bhai Gurdas Ji* and a number of *Rehatnamas*, such as *Rehatanama Bhai Chaupa Singh Chibbar, Rehatnama Bhai Nand Lal, Rehatnama Bhai Daya Singh, Rehatnama Bhai Desa Singh* and *Sri Gur Prachin Panth Prakash*, which, as Kalra highlights, provide information 'about the nature of the turban that should be tied, when it should be worn and in what manner it should be tied'.[15] Together they provide information about the presence of the turban from the beginning of the Sikh *dharam*. Within the *Guru Granth Sahib* there a number of quotes that highlight the existence and importance of the turban:

ਮੈ ਗੁਰ ਮਿਲਿ ਉਚ ਦੁਮਾਲੜਾ ॥

Mai gur mil uch dumalṛa.[16]

I, upon meeting the Guru, have tied a tall turban.

ਬੰਕੇ ਬਾਲ ਪਾਗ ਸਿਰਿ ਡੇਰੀ

Banke bal pag sir deri.[17]

You make your hair beautiful, and wear a stylish turban on your head.

ਖੂਬੁ ਤੇਰੀ ਪਗਰੀ ਮੀਠੇ ਤੇਰੇ ਬੋਲ ॥

Khūb terī pagrī mīṭhe tere bol.[18]

How handsome is your turban! And how sweet is your speech.

ਨਾਪਾਕ ਪਾਕੁ ਕਰਿ ਹਦੂਰਿ ਹਦੀਸਾ ਸਾਬਤ ਸੂਰਤਿ ਦਸਤਾਰ ਸਿਰਾ

Nāpāk pāk kar haḍūr haḍīsā sābat sūrat ḍastār sirā.[19]

Purify what is impure, and let the Lord's Presence be your religious tradition. Let your total awareness be the turban on your head.

These and other passages in the *Guru Granth Sahib* indicate that covering the head was a mark of spirituality, but they also emphasize that this is just one of the garment's meanings. The turban also, as mentioned earlier, signifies equality, justice and bravery. There are also some direct statements about covering the head in other texts such as the *Dasam Granth*[20] and the various *Rehatnama*s, and McLeod notes that 'a turban or turbans of some description would certainly be worn by those male Sikhs who accepted initiation into the Khalsa'.[21]

Dasam Granth

ਗੰਜ ਗਾਹ ਬਾਧੇ ॥ ਧਨੁਰ ਬਾਣ ਸਾਧੇ

Ganj gah badhe. Thnur ban sadhe.[22]

Wearing metal ornaments on the turban, stretching the bow the arrow fled the hand.

Vaaran Bhai Gurdas Ji

ਸਿਰੁ ਉਚਾ ਅਹੰਕਾਰ ਕਰਿ ਵਲ ਦੇ ਪਗ ਵਲਾਏ ਡੇਰੀ।

Sir ucha ahankaar kr val de pag valaay deree.[23]

The head is proud of its high place (status) so upon it a turban is tied.

In another verse the significance is highlighted:

ਠੰਢੇ ਖੂਹਹੁੰ ਨ੍ਹਾਇ ਕੈ ਪਗ ਵਿਸਾਰਿ ਆਇਆ ਸਿਰਿ ਨੰਗੈ
ਘਰ ਵਿਚਿ ਰੰਨਾ ਕਮਲੀਆਂ ਧੁਸੀ ਲੀਤੀ ਦੇਖਿ ਕੁਢੰਗੈ।

Thnde khuhu nhae kai pag visar aaea sir nungai
Ghar vich runa kumleeaa this lete dekh kudngai.[24]

After taking a bath on the well, an individual forgot to tie the turban on his head and returned home without his turban on.

Rehatname

The various *Rehatname* also refer to the turban. *Rehatname* are argued to be written at the time of the tenth Guru. Although academics such as McLeod and Padam state that the *rehatname* date to the mid-late 1700s, tradition amongst Sikh *gyanis*, *kathavachicks* (religious speakers) and saints states that these codes of conduct were written during the period of the tenth Guru.

Tankhanama (*Manual of Penances*), Bhai Nand Lal

ਕੰਘਾ ਦੋਨਉ ਵਕਤ ਕਰ ਪਾਗ ਚੁਨਹਿ ਕਰ ਬਾਂਧਇ

Kanga donau vakt kar, pag cunhe kar bandaee.[25]

Comb, with a Kanga, your hair twice a day and tie your turban fresh each time.

ਨਗਨ ਹੋਇ ਬਾਹਰ ਫਿਰਹਿ ਨਗਨ ਸੀਸ ਜੋ ਖਾਇ
ਨਗਨ ਪ੍ਰਸਾਦ ਜੋ ਬਾਂਟਇ ਤਨਖਾਹੀ ਬਡੋ ਕਹਾਇ

Nagn hoe bahr firhe, nagn sees jo khae
Nagn Parsaad jo batae, Tankhahi budou khae.[26]

One who wanders naked or eats without covering their head [with a Turban].
Or one who distributes Parshad naked [no Turban or dress] is a serious offender of the Rehat.

Sakhi Rehat Ki (*Story of the Rehat*), attributed to Bhai Nand Lal

ਗਾਇਤ੍ਰੀ ਤਰਪਣੁ ਪੂਜਾ ਅਰਚਾਂ ਧੋਤੀ ਬੰਨ ਕੇ ਸਿਰੀ ਨੰਗਾ ਖਾਵਣਾ ਨਾਹੀ

Gayatri, tarpn pooja, archa, toti ban ke, sir nanga khavna nahi.[27]

Renounce, reading Gayatri [other] mantra, ancestor worship rituals, archana wearing a *toti* [Hindu garb] and eating without covering the head [with a Turban].

ਅਤੇ ਜਨੇਊ ਪਾਵਣ ਦਾ ਅਰਥ ਇਹੁ ਹੈ ਜੋ ਹਿੰਦੂ ਸਿਆਣੀਐ । ਸੋ ਖਾਲਸੇ ਨੂੰ ਏਹੁ ਨਿਸਾਨੀ ਲਗੀ ਹੈ । ਜੋ ਲੱਖ ਹਿੰਦੂ ਅਤੇ ਲੱਖ ਮੁਸਲਮਾਨ ਹੋਵਨਿ ਤਾਂ ਭੀ ਸਿਖੁ ਵਿਚ ਛਪਦਾਂ ਨਹੀ । ਕਿਉਂਜੋ ਹੱਛਾ ਦਾੜਾ, ਸਿਰ ਤੇ ਕੇਸ ਸੋ, ਕਿਥੋ ਛੁਪੈ॥

Ate jeneoo pavn da arth eh jo hindu sianeai. So khale nu ehu nisanee lugi hai. Jo lakh hindu lakh musalman ta bhi sikh vich chapda nahi. Kioujo jucha dhara sir te kes, so kitho chupai.[28]

The wearing of the sacred Hindu thread is a practice for the Hindus. Not for the Khalsa. The Khalsa has such an identity marker, that it makes them stand out amongst thousands of Hindus and Muslims. How can the Khalsa hide when they have the turban, uncut beard and uncut *kesh*?

ਅਤੇ ਪੂਜਾ, ਅਰਚਾ, ਕਰਮ ਕਿਰਿਆ, ਧੋਤੀ ਬੰਨਣਾ, ਸਿਰਿ ਨੰਗੇ ਖਾਵਣਾ ਸੋ ਉਨਾਂ ਜੁਗਾਂ ਕਾ ਧਰਮੁ ਹੈ । ਅਤੇ ਕਲਿਜੁਗ ਵਿਚ ਗੁਰਮੁਰੀਦੀ ਪਰਵਾਨ ਹੈ ।

Ate pooja, archa, karm kiria, toti bnana, sir nanga khavna so ona jug aka dharam hai. Ate Kaljug vich gurmuridi Parvaan hai.[29]

Idol worship, archana, Brahmin rituals, wearing the *toti* and eating without covering your head [with a Turban] were actions permissible in the previous ages. In this age of Kalyug, it is required that one follows the Guru.

Rehatnama Bhai Prahilad Singh

ਹੋਇ ਸਿਖ ਸਿਰ ਟੋਪੀ ਧਰੈ । ਸਾਤ ਜਨਮ ਕੁਸ਼ਟੀ ਹੁਇ ਮਰੈ

Hoe sikh sir topi turai. Sat Janam kushtee huei mrai.[30]

Being a Sikh, if he wears a hat [a Turban not tied fresh each time or a literal 'hat']. He will suffer seven lives as a leper.

ਪਾਗ ਉਤਾਰਿ ਪ੍ਰਸਾਦਿ ਜੋ ਖਾਵੈ । ਸੋ ਸਿਖ ਕੁੰਭੀ ਨਰਕ ਸਿਧਾਵੈ

Pag othaar parsad jo khavai. So sikh kumbhi nark sidhavai.[31]

Removing the turban and eating, such a Sikh will go to the pits of hell.

Rehatnama Bhai Daya Singh[32]

Bhai Daya Singh's *Rehatnama* highlights the importance of wearing the turban like Bhai Chaupa Singh:

ਜੂੜਾ ਸੀਸ ਕੇ ਮੱਧ ਭਾਗ ਮੈ ਰਾਖੇ ਔਰ ਪਾਗ ਬੜੀ ਬਾਂਧੇ ਕੇਸ ਢਾਂਪ ਰਖੇ ਕੰਘਾ ਦੋਵੇ ਕਾਲ ਕਰੇ ਪਾਗ ਚੁਨਕੇ ਬਾਂਧੇ

Joora sees ke madh bhag mai rakhai, aur pag burhee Bandai, kes dhanp rakhai, kanga dovo kal kure, pag chunke bandhai.[33]

Tie the *Kesh* in a topknot on the head and cover it with a turban. Do not leave it uncovered. Comb the hair twice a day and tie the turban a fresh each time.

ਲੋਹ ਕੀ ਕਰਦ ਸੀਸ ਮੈ ਰਖੇ

Loh ki kard sees mai rukhai.[34]

Carry a small weapon [*Kard*] on your head [in the turban].

ਉਚਾ ਬੁੰਗਾ ਜੋ ਸਜੈ ਨਾਮ ਨਿਹੰਗ ਸੁਜਾਨ

Ocha bunga jo sujai nam Nihang sujan.[35]

One who wears the high turban, know him as a Nihang.

Rehatnama Bhai Chaupa Singh Chibbar

According to the Rehatnama Bhai Chaupa Singh Chibbar, a contemporary of Guru Gobind Singh Ji, the five *Kakar* of Sikhism were the steel bracelet, sword, comb and small turban:

ਜੋ ਸਿਖ ਸਿਖ ਦੀ ਪੱਗ ਤੇ ਹੱਥ ਪਾਏ ਸੋ ਭੀ ਤਨਖਾਹੀਆ

Jo Sikh, Sikh de pag te hath paee, so bhe tankhaia.[36]

If a Sikh puts his hand on another Sikhs turban he is to be penalised.

ਜੋ ਸਿਖ ਦੀ ਅਪੇ ਪੱਗ ਉਤਾਰੇ ਸੋ ਭੀ ਤਨਖਾਹੀਆ

Jo Sikh de ape pag othare, so bhe tankhaia.[37]

If a Sikh removes another Sikhs turban he is to be penalised.

ਜੋ ਪੱਗ ਨੂੰ ਬਾਸੀ ਰਖੇ ਸੋ ਤਨਖਾਹੀਆ

Jo pag nu basi rakhai, so tankhaia.[38]

He [the Sikh] is to be penalised if he keeps his turban in a tied state when it is off (taking the turban off as if it were a hat).

ਪੱਗ ਰਾਤੀ ਲਾਹਿ ਕੇ ਸੋਵੇ ਸੋ ਭੀ ਤਨਖਾਹੀਆ

Pag rathe lahe ke sovey so bhe tankhaia.[39]

Taking the turban off at night and sleeping bareheaded is a violation of the Rehat.

ਨੰਗੇ ਕੇਸੀ ਭੋਜਨ ਕਰੇ ਸੋ ਤਨਖਾਹੀਆ

Nange kesi bhojan kure so tankhaia.[40]

Eating bare headed [without the turban] is a violation of the Rehat.

Rehatnamas written in the late 1700s and early 1800s also make reference to the turban.

Rehatnama Bhai Desa Singh[41]

ਕੰਘਾ ਕਰਦ ਦਸਤਾਰਹਿ ਬਾਂਧੇ

Kanga kard dastareh bandhe.[42]

The Dastaar is to be tied afresh with the Kanga and Kard [inside the turban].

Mukatnama (Liberation Manual), Bhai Sahib Singh

ਗੁਰ ਕੀ ਛਾਪ ਸਿਰ ਕੇਸਕੀ

Gur ke chaap sir keski.[43]

The signature/stamp of the Guru is the Keski ((small) turban) on the head.

As McLeod notes, 'obviously the compilers of *rahit-namas* are interested in the wearing of the turbans, and equally obvious is the close connection which they draw between the turban and the *kes*'.[44]

Sri Gur Panth Parkash, Rattan Singh Bangu

The Sikh historian Rattan Singh Bhangu, who wrote the *Sri Gur Panth Parkash*[45] almost two centuries ago, writes:

ਦੋਇ ਵੇਲੇ ਉਠ ਬੰਧਯੋ ਦਸਤਾਰੇ । ਪਹਰ ਆਠ ਰਖੱਯੋ ਸ਼ਸਤਰ ਸੰਭਾਰੇ

Doi vele uthe bandeyo dastare. Pehr aath rakheyo Shastar sanbare.[46]

Tie the turban afresh twice a day. And wear Shastar 24 hours a day with care.

ਕੇਸਨ ਕੀ ਕੀਜੋ ਪ੍ਰਤਿਪਾਲ । ਨਹਿ ਉਸਤ੍ਰਨ ਕਟਯੋ ਬਾਲ

Kesn ki kejo pritpal. Neh ustarn katyo bal.[47]

Take care of your hair. Do not cut it your hair with a blade.

Rehat Maryada

In recent times the Sikh *Rehat Maryada: The Code of Conduct and Conventions* notes:

> For a Sikh, there is no restriction or requirement as to dress except that he [or she] must wear Kachhehra [a drawer type of garment] and turban. A Sikh woman may or may not tie a turban.[48]

Whilst the various sources mention the importance of a turban, and how one should treat it, there are also primary sources that describe the role of the turban in succession. McLeod notes:

> Guru Angad personally dressed him in fresh garments, placing a saffron turban on his head and the symbol of spiritual authority on his forehead. Before him he laid five copper coins and a coconut, thus appointing him his successor as Guru.[49]

Art

Alongside the religious texts and *Rehatnamas* there are also a number of pieces of art that corroborate this development; for example Sikh art nearly always shows the Gurus wearing a head covering,[50] and academics such as W. H. McLeod highlight that:

> the turban is a neat and tidy means of covering the hair which must be left uncut. There is no other satisfactory form of covering for the hair. One need only imagine uncovered hair to realize how superior the turban is as a means of containing and controlling the hair which has to be tied on the head in a topknot.[51]

Thus, it is an incontrovertible fact that the custom of covering the head with a turban dates from the outset of the Sikh faith, more than 500 years ago and the turban has become a fundamental religious symbol in the Sikh *dharam*.

Sikhs in the global diaspora

The Sikh *dharam* is more than either an Indian or a UK-based phenomenon. Sikhs have migrated in large numbers across the world. Sikhs can be found in the US, Canada, Australia, Singapore, Malaysia and countries in Africa, such as Kenya. Recently, we have begun to see a sizeable presence of Sikhs in other European nations such as France, Denmark, Italy and Germany.

The global presence of Sikhs is evidenced by the increasing visibility of turban-wearing Sikhs in media portrayals internationally. From images of Sikh soldiers who fought in the First and Second World Wars[52] to the Sikh warriors of Peter Dickinson's 1970s BBC trilogy *The Changes*, Kip, the 'sapper' (soldier) for the British, working in demining and bomb diffusion in *The English Patient* (1996). In *Bend it Like Beckham* (2002), which focuses on a young Sikh girl, Jess Bhamra, who wants to play football, the Sikh identity is highlighted by Jess's father (played by Anupam Kher) wearing the identifiable marker of Sikhism, the turban, with his airline uniform. Actor Kabir Bedi played a Sikh character alongside Sir Roger Moore in the James Bond movie *Octopussy* (1983). Actor Sir Ben Kingsley played the role of a turban-wearing Sikh driving instructor named Darwan in New York in the film *Learning to Drive* (2015).

Snoop Dog wore a turban for his song 'Singh is Kinng' for the synonymous Bollywood movie. The turban has also recently appeared in marketing ads for fashion retailers such as GAP,[53] H&M,[54] River Island,[55] has featured as a fashion accessory by designers such as Prada, Chanel and Gucci,[56] and has been worn by celebrities, particularly women such as Elizabeth Taylor and the Queen.

There is also the growing visibility of turban-wearing Sikhs globally in the public arena. For example, Waris Ahluwalia, a turban-wearing actor, has appeared in films such as *Life Aquatic with Steve Zissou, The Grand Budapest Hotel, Ocean's 8, Beeba Boys* and *The Darjeeling Limited*. UK Sikh turban-wearing comedian, TV and radio presenter, Hardeep Singh Kohli has been on Channel 4's *Meet the Magoons*. Other turban-wearing Sikhs have appeared as extras in films or TV programmes.[57]

The election of four Sikhs to the Canadian Cabinet in 2015, including two turban wearers, Navdeep Singh Bains and Harjit Singh Sajjan, has added to this visibility on the global stage, resulting in President Trudeau telling an audience at the American University, 'I have more Sikh ministers than Modi'.[58] In the US, there was the election of Satyendra Huja as Mayor of Charlottesville, Virginia in 2012,[59] through to the recent election of Ravi Bhalla as Mayor of New Jersey (2018),[60] and the Attorney General, Gurbir Grewal of New Jersey who was referred to as 'turban man' on radio.[61]

Sikhs in the UK

The Sikh diaspora, wherever they have settled, have integrated and adapted to the host community. However, this does not mean that they have not faced numerous challenges regarding their religious identity, particularly around two of their articles of faith – the *kirpan* and the *kesh*, and the *kesh's* accompanying turban. The community has had to resort to the law to have their articles of faith recognised, particularly the kesh and the turban. This was not expected since Sikhs who had fought for the British, in battles such as Saragarhi in 1897, and had played a significant role in supporting the allied war effort in both world wars[62] had won the right to keep their hair long and wear the turban. During these wars Sikhs refused to wear the required steel helmet instead of the turban, and exemptions were made.[63] In *Civil Rights in Wartime The post-9/11 Sikh Experience*, Sidhu and Gohil explore Sikh military contribution to Britain whilst adhering to the requirement to maintain the Sikh turban, observing:

> In the British-Afghanistan War, Sikhs fighting for the British were asked to don tin helmets in place of their turbans in battle. The Sikhs refused on the grounds of their religious beliefs, and fearing widespread mutiny, the British withdrew the requirement after having each soldier sign off on the equivalent of a current-day liability waiver. After that, throughout the Sikh involvement in the colonial armed forces, they were never required to remove their turbans.[64]

After the Second World War, Sikhs were part of the large-scale immigration to Britain in the late 1940s to assist in the reconstruction and post-war economic expansion, but also a response to the 1947 Partition of India. For these immigrants, the 1948 legislation enabled them, subjects of the British Empire, to be citizens of the Commonwealth, granting them rights to take up British residency. The 1948 legislation was subsequently amended with new Acts: 1962 Commonwealth Immigrants Bill, the 1968 Commonwealth Act and the 1971 Immigration Act. However, the UK posed challenges to Sikh identity which the Sikh community had to address.

Accommodation of the turban

Whilst the British Home Secretary Roy Jenkins (1966) highlighted how the UK was a multicultural country, questions regarding the turban arose between the late 1950s and 1970s in response to the British feeling threatened by all the changes that migrant communities were introducing into the host community, which many felt where going to damage the fabric of British identity and society. British Sikhs had to fight for exemptions, and as a result of Sikh activism British governments over the decades have made significant accommodation for the Sikh turban to be protected under law (along with other articles of faith like the *kirpan*[65] *and kara*), rights that are not afforded in other European nations like neighbouring France.[66] There are several key cases on the turban: Manchester bus garage worker G. S. S. Sagar; the Wolverhampton bus driver Tarsem Singh Sandhu (1967–9, discussed below) and Sant Singh Shattar, post office worker. Sant Singh Shattar moved to Birmingham from Jalandhar in 1955. His application to work in the Post Office was rejected on uniform grounds, as he could not meet the then requirements to wear a Post Office uniform cap. He challenged the decision in 1961 and in doing so set a precedent by becoming the first postman in the UK postal department to be granted the right to wear his turban on duty.[67] Other cases include The Motor-Cycle Crash-Helmets (Religious Exemption) Act; and *Mandla v. Dowell-Lee* (see below).[68] All of these cases in their own way highlighted the importance of the turban for the Sikh community.[69]

Manchester City Council v. Sagar, bus driver

In 1959, G. S. S. Sagar applied for the post of conductor with Manchester City Council's transport department. His application was turned down because his turban violated the company's uniform rules. Sagar's offer to wear a blue turban with a badge was considered by the transport committee, which, after 'considerable research and discussion', refused to countenance an exception to the rules (*Manchester Evening News*, 22 June 1959). Sagar's case lasted seven years and on 5 October 1966, it was finally decided that turbans should be allowed (*The Daily Telegraph*, 6 October 1966).[70]

Wolverhampton Council v. Tarsem Singh Sandhu, bus driver

A year after Sagar's ruling there was a similar case in Wolverhampton. Tarsem Singh Sandhu, when he joined Wolverhampton Council as a bus driver, was clean-shaven but returned to work wearing a turban, which broke the uniform code, after taking time off due to sickness. His employers, Wolverhampton Transport Committee, dismissed him in 1967 for violating the company dress code.[71] Sandhu, like Sagar, fought to be allowed to wear the turban instead of the peaked cap that was required by his employers. He 'launched a campaign which soon became embroiled in local, national and transnational politics that were vertically divided between supporters of Enoch Powell and Labour on the one hand, and the Indian Workers' Associations (IWA) and the emerging Shiromani Akali Dal (SAD) on the other'. The council was very reluctant to change its position due to the wider community's feelings on the issue of immigrants: 'it is time they [the Sikhs] realised this is England, not India' (*The Express and Star*, 29 November 1967). After two further protest marches, Sohan Singh Jolly, a 65-year-old local leader, declared he would immolate himself on 13 April 1969, if the transport committee failed to change its policy. This threat further inflamed an already volatile situation and led to the involvement of the Indian High Commissioner, who met the transport committee and appealed to the Department of Transport in Whitehall, warning of the serious consequences of a possible suicide with wider ramifications in India. In the event, despite the Mayor of Wolverhampton's description of the Sikh threat as 'blackmail', the council changed its rules on 9 April 1969 because it was 'forced to have regard to wider implications'.[72]

Turbans v. motorcycle helmets

According to Section 32 of the Road Traffic Act (1972), which came into force on 1 June 1973, it was compulsory for motorcyclists to wear a helmet. This posed problems for turban-wearing Sikhs, who did lobby for an exemption but were refused. In the February 1974 general election, MPs with a significant proportion of Sikh constituents were lobbied to support a general exemption for turban-wearing Sikh motorcyclists. Baldev Singh Chahal, a leading activist in the campaign, even stood as a candidate for Ealing, Southall on this single issue. Earlier, following a conviction, Chahal had appealed to the High Court against the new regulation on three grounds:

> that the Ministry of Transport had failed to adequately consult with Sikh groups; that the minister had been remiss in not taking into account the public policy implications of the Race Relations Acts of 1965 and 1968; and that the new act was in contravention of 'the guarantee of freedom of religion enshrined in the European Conventions on Human Rights'.[73]

Lord Widgery dismissed the appeal because:

No one is bound to ride a motorcycle. All that the law prescribes is that if you do ride a motorcycle you must wear a crash helmet. The effects of the Regulations no doubt bear on the Sikh community in this respect because it means that they will be often prevented from riding a motorcycle, not because of the English law but the requirements of their religion.[74]

A subsequent ruling of the European Commission on Human Rights further supported Lord Widgery's argument:

The Commission considers that the compulsory wearing of crash helmets is a necessary safety measure for motorcyclists. The commission is of the opinion therefore that any interference there may have been with the applicant's freedom of religion was justified for the protection of health in accordance with article 9(2).[75]

The exemption was eventually conceded when the Labour government decided to support a Private Members' Bill introduced by Sidney Bidwell, the MP for Southall. The Motor-Cycle Crash-Helmets (Religious Exemption) Act (1976) modified Section 32 of the Road Traffic Act (1972) by declaring that it 'shall not apply to followers of the Sikh religion while he is [sic] wearing a turban', and this was reconfirmed in the Road Traffic Act (1988).[76] In giving support to this measure, the government was quite clear that it was moved by considerations of religious tolerance. As Kenneth Marks, Under-Secretary of State for the Environment, observed during the debate on the Bill:

The Bill is based on religious tolerance and that, too, is an important and vital part of our society … There is no possibility of a compromise on this difficult issue … if Parliament concludes that in this case religious tolerance outweighs road safety and equality, the Government will accept the decision.[77]

In the case of the motorcycle exemption for turban-wearing Sikhs, during a debate on the 'religious exemption' amendment of the Road Traffic Act (1972), Conservative MP Winston Churchill (the grandson of wartime Prime Minister Winston Churchill) said:

There can be no doubt that, as a people, we owe a deep debt of gratitude to the Sikh community over many years. For me it is sufficient that in our time of need twice this century, when we needed the Sikhs to stand by us they did so and, in the case of too many, died beside us in two world wars to enable us to live in the freedom which we today enjoy. We did not then require them to wear a steel helmet in the front line of battle. If it was sufficient to do that when we needed them in a desperate situation, the least we owe them, now that that sort of crisis is past, is to continue respecting these traditions.[78]

Although the Sikh community had government backing for the measure, the host community's response to the new legislation brought forth some amusing episodes. Two persons felt enraged enough to put on a turban before riding a motorcycle. One subsequently apologized, saying he respected the Sikh community and appreciated its religious traditions (*Des Pardes*, 22 July 1983). Another, Brian Nicholas, was given two years' conditional discharge after he attempted to ride a motorcycle wearing a turban. Nicholas maintained that helmet law discriminated against non-Sikhs and he even wore his turban in the court, claiming that a Sikh had actually wound it for him (*Motor Cycle Weekly*, 16 April 1983).[79]

Turbans v. safety helmets

In 1979, the Health and Safety Commission put forward the idea of safety helmets for workers in the construction industry, recommending that the requirement should have statutory force. Sikhs in the construction industry lobbied the Commission to secure an exemption along the lines of the motorcycle legislation. As the threat of legislation loomed, the issue assumed a particular urgency because it was claimed that 40,000 Sikhs worked in the construction industry, with an especially strong representation by the Ramgharias, who specialized in trades associated with carpentry, bricklaying and blacksmithing. To further the case of these workers, the British Sikh Federation conducted an extensive campaign within *gurdwaras* and the Punjabi print media. The government conceded to the pressure from the Sikh lobby by inserting an amendment to the Employment Bill during the Committee stage in the House of Lords. Section 11 of the Employment Act (1989) recognized the Sikh exemption by noting that:

> Any attempt to wear a safety helmet … would, by virtue of any statutory provision or rule of law, be imposed on a Sikh who is on a construction site shall not apply to him any time when he is wearing a turban.[80]

Lord Strathclyde conceded that the measure was necessary because 'the wider issues of religious freedom and relations with the Sikh community must take precedence'.[81]

The value of this legislation appeared to have been compromised almost immediately when the Council of European Communities issued a new directive in June 1989 on measures to improve the health and safety of workers, including the requirement to wear safety helmets. This directive came into force at the end of 1992 in the guise of the Personal Protective Equipment at Work Regulations, and allowed for no exemptions. The implementation of the directive created an anomaly because Sikhs were exempt from wearing safety helmets in the construction industry, but no such general exclusion could be maintained in other sectors. The existence of this anomaly was raised by Jim Marshall MP in a question to the Secretary of State for Employment, with a call to amend the legislation. In his reply, the Minister noted that no such 'universal exemption' had been sought because of the 'risk of challenge'.[82]

Deregulation Act (2015)

The most recent amendment to the exemption of wearing safety helmets on building sites came as recently as 1 October 2015 when Sections 11 and 12 of the Employment Act 1989 was amended by Section 6 of the Deregulation Act (2015), which extended the existing exemption to wear safety helmets in the Employment Act to all workplaces, including factories and warehouses.[83] This extended the right for Sikhs to wear their turbans on construction sites and in safe environments, closing a loophole in the legislation. The new legislation exempts Sikhs from wearing the safety helmet and prohibits disciplinary action against Sikhs who choose to do so with the Deregulation Act (2015).[84]

Mandla v. Dowell-Lee (1983)

The case of *Mandla v. Dowell-Lee* is often cited in discussions about the definition of Sikh identity. It set a precedent for the recognition of Sikhs in a legal setting in the diaspora of the UK. Singh and Tatla argue that it 'marked a major landmark in the development of the community and anti-discrimination legislation in Britain'.[85]

The case centred on a Sikh student, who in 1978 sought admission to Park Grove School in Edgbaston, Birmingham. A. G. Dowell-Lee, the school's headmaster, denied the student's admission because he felt the turban was in violation of the institution's uniform policy. His father lodged a complaint with the Commission for Racial Equality (hereinafter CRE), claiming that his son had been racially discriminated against.

The case went through the county court, the Court of Appeal, and finally the House of Lords where the previous decisions were overturned and the young boy was allowed to wear the turban because of the protected 'ethnic group' test:

> For a group to constitute an ethnic group in the sense of the Act of 1976, it must, in my opinion, regard itself, and be regarded by others, as a distinct community by virtue of certain characteristics. Some of these characteristics are essential; others are not essential but one or more of them will commonly be found and will help to distinguish the group from the surrounding community. The conditions which appear to me to be essential are these, (1) a long shared history, of which the group is conscious as distinguishing it from other groups, and the memory of which it keeps alive; (2) a cultural tradition of its own, including family and social customs and manners, often but not necessarily associated with religious observance. In addition to these two essential characteristics the following characteristics are, in my opinion, relevant, (3) either a common geographical origin, or descent from a number

of common ancestors; (4) a common language, not necessarily peculiar to the group; (5) a common literature peculiar to the group; (6) a common religion different from that of neighbouring groups or from the general community surrounding it; (7) being a minority or being an oppressed or dominant group within a larger community, for example (say, the inhabitants of England shortly after the Norman conquest and their conquerors might both be ethnic groups.) A group defined by reference to enough of these characteristics would be capable of including converts, for example, persons who marry into the group, and of excluding apostates. Provided a person who joins the group feels himself or herself to be a member of it, and is accepted by other members, then he is, for the purposes of the Act, a member. … In my opinion, it is possible for a person to fall into a particular racial group either by birth or adherence, and it makes no difference, so far as the Act of 1976 is concerned, by which route he finds his way into the group.[86]

Thus, British Sikhs had to fight for exemptions from wearing helmets/hard hats whilst riding a motorcycle or a horse or working on construction sites. These battles were in response to the British feeling threatened by all the changes that migrant communities were introducing into the host community, which many felt were going to damage the fabric of British identity and society, something that Enoch Powell stressed in his 'Rivers of Blood' speech. Whilst these legal exemptions and recognition of the importance of the turban have meant that Britain is now arguably one of the most attractive places in the world for Sikhs to enjoy religious freedoms that allow them to wear their religious articles, in the past, it was racist and discriminatory towards the Sikh religious identity.

As a result of the migration process the Sikh diaspora has faced numerous challenges regarding their religious identity, particularly the turban, and the community has had to resort to the law to have the Sikh turban recognized as a fundamental religious article of faith for initiated Sikhs, something that was acknowledged in Parliament by Sydney Bidwell MP for Ealing and Southall on 28 January 1975:

There must be no doubt that the long coiled hair and the turban go together as one of the five K's; as they are called – the articles of the religion dating back over 500 years. Definitions have been clearly made by the Gurus from time to time.[87]

It was also acknowledged by Lord Avery during the Second Reading of the Motor-cycle Crash-Helmets (Religious exemption) Bill on 5 October 1976:

There is absolutely no doubt that the wearing of the turban is an essential part of the Sikh religion. The ten gurus, the founders of the religion and the architects of it, all wore turban themselves.

Having successfully achieved this accommodation Sikhs have become a funda-mental part of pluralist British society, and today there are over 432,429 Sikhs in the UK;[88] as a community, they are well represented in both the professional and public spheres by turban-wearing Sikhs. From figures such as Fauja Singh, the centenarian marathon runner, to Ravi Singh from Khalsa Aid, to Rajinder Tony Singh Kusbia, a Scottish celebrity chef and restauranteur, and comedian Hardeep Singh Kohli, to turban-wearing judges like Sir Rabinder Singh QC and the late Mota Singh QC, but also others like Sir Harpal Singh Kumar, former chief exec-utive officer of Cancer Research UK, and notably the first turbaned Sikh, Lord Singh of Wimbledon, was elevated to the House of Lords in 2011, and then joined by Lord Suri in 2014, and the first Sikh turbaned MP, Tanmanjeet Singh Dhesi, was elected Member of Parliament for Slough in 2017.

British Sikh photographers Amit and Naroop write:

> today in the UK, Sikhs no longer feel they need to mute their turbans to conform. With flamboyant fabrics and accessories, young Sikhs use them as a way to reflect their personality, as well as a symbol of their faith.[89]

As a symbol of the faith, despite the turban being recognized as a sign of a number of principles, such as sovereignty, dedication, courage, faithfulness, peace, equality, tolerance and social activism, the turban for Sikhs has also become an article of faith that has negative connotations due to 9/11. A lack of religious literacy about the way Sikhs look has resulted in 'mistaken identity' and Sikhs being attacked because of the turban, which is not just something that is confined to the Sikh community but is also worn by Muslims and Arabs, and this association has brought Sikhs into a negative spotlight. Eli Sanders in an article 'Understanding Turbans'[90] outlined the differences very clearly, but what is clear from the current context is that although attempts have been made to improve awareness of the difference between Sikhs and Muslims there is still a lack of understanding, which is leading to hostility and 'mistaken identity' attacks.

Against this theological background to the Sikh turban identity, and its pres-ence in the global diaspora, the next chapter considers the racism encountered by Sikhs in the early stages of migration. It will then consider how attacks on Sikhs after 9/11 took a different turn from the racism that they experienced prior to 9/11 and how subsequent terrorist incidents created an environment in which turban-wearing Sikhs were mistaken for Muslims and attacks on the Sikh com-munity in the UK began to rise. Although it is evident that attacks are increasing, the authors have highlighted how the reporting and recording do not reflect this. For example, the latest figures show that the number of hate crimes between April 2017 and March 2018 reached 94,098 – a rise of 17 per cent. Seventy-six per cent were classified as 'race hate'.[91] Where the perceived religion of the victim was recorded, 2 per cent of religious hate crime offences were targeted against Sikhs (117 offences). Whilst this is still a small percentage compared to the attacks on the Jewish and Muslim community, these figures, alongside increasing stories of attacks in the media and data collected by the community[92] suggest that hate crime against Sikhs is on the rise and needs to be addressed by the community and government.[93]

Notes

1 Some parts of this chapter have appeared in J. Jhutti-Johal (2011). *Sikhism Today*. London: Continuum. Some parts of this chapter have appeared in A. Gatrad, A. Sheikh and E. Brown (2007). *Palliative Care for South Asians*. London: Quay Books; and J. Jhutti-Johal (2017). 'Sikh Dharma', in V. R. Howard and R. D. Sherma (eds), *Dharma: The Hindu, Buddhist, Jain and Sikh Traditions of India*. London: I. B. Tauris. Use of this content is with the permission of Quay Books and Continuum.
2 P. Singh (1999). *The Sikhs*. London: John Murray Publishers, p. 28.
3 *Guru Granth Sahib*, Ang 1429.
4 K. Singh (1977). *A History of the Sikhs*, Vol. 1. New Delhi: Oxford University Press, p. 52.
5 The complete list is Akal Takht, Amritsar; Takht Keshghar Sahib, Anandpur Sahib; Takht Patna Sahib; Takht Damdama Sahib, Batinda; and Takht Sachkhand, Hazur Sahib.
6 Guru Nanak Dev Ji, *Guru Granth Sahib*, Ang 1023.
7 Jhutti-Johal, 'Sikh Dharma'.
8 R. Gatrad et al. (2005). 'Sikh birth customs'. *Archives of Disease in Childhood*, 90(6), pp. 560–563.
9 W. H. McLeod (1999). 'Discord in the Sikh Panth'. *Journal of the American Oriental Society*, 119(3), p. 381. Also: Shiromani Gurdwara Parbandhak Committee (1945/1950). *The Code of Conduct and Conventions: English Version of the Sikh Rehat Maryada*. Chapter X. [online] Available at: http://sgpc.net/sikh-rehat-maryada-in-english/ [Accessed 30 April 2019]. *Kesh* is also, in the case of men, normally accompanied by the wearing of a turban or, if the hair is not particularly long (such as for young boys), a topknot. The turban is considered of vital importance to men for a variety of reasons (e.g. hygiene) but mostly because of the importance placed upon tying the *kesh* in a topknot and keeping it neat and tidy; the turban is the best practical method of achieving this. Women are not expected to wear the turban; but some particularly devout Sikh women have chosen to wear it.
10 W. H. McLeod (2001). 'The turban: Symbol of Sikh identity', in P. Singh and N. G. Barrier (eds), *Sikh identity: Continuity and Change*. New Delhi: Manohar. pp. 57–68.
11 The translations of the *Guru Granth Sahib* are voluminous and difficult to locate. Therefore, since the page numbers of the hard copy correspond with a digitized version, the authors have chosen to use all citations from the following digital talk produced by Srigranth.org (2018). *Sri Granth*. [online] Available at: www.srigranth.org/servlet/gurbani.gurbani [Accessed 7 May 2019].
12 For more detail see Sidhu and Gohil, *Civil Rights in Wartime: The Post 9/11 Sikh Experience*, pp. 47–61, and Kalra, 'Locating the Sikh pagh'.
13 There have been debates about whether Guru Nanak wore a turban or a hat. For example, Sarna, using the *Janam Sakhis*, writes:

> Nanak was accompanied by Mardana on his travels, who carried his rabab. He dressed in strange clothes that could not be identified with any sect and symbolized the universality of his message. He wore the long, loose shirt of a Muslim dervish but in the brownish red colour of the Hindu sanyasi. Around his waist he wore a white kafni or cloth belt like a faqir. A flat, short turban partly covered a Qalandar's cap on his head in the manner of Sufi wanderers. On his

feet, he wore wooden sandals, each of a different design and colour. Sometimes, it is said, he wore a necklace of bones around his neck.
(53–54)

N. Sarna (2010). *The Book of Nanak*. New Delhi: Penguin Books India.

14 References for the turban are from *Guru Granth Sahib* [online] Available at www. searchgurbani.com/guru-granth-sahib/ang-by-ang; and from *Dasam Granth* [online] Available at www.searchgurbani.com/dasam-granth/index/chapter/en [Accessed 1 May 2019]. Also see Sri Granth. [online] Available at: www.srigranth.org/servlet/gurbani.gurbani [Accessed 1 May 2018]. Rehatnama translations are by Parminder Singh Davgun; passages from the book are taken from Piara Singh Padam (1989) *Rehatname*. Amritsar: Singh Brothers.

15 Kalra, 'Locating the Sikh pagh'.

16 *Guru Granth Sahib*, Ang 74.

17 Bhagat Ravidas (*Guru Granth Sahib*, Ang 659).

18 Bhagat Namdev (*Guru Granth Sahib*, Ang 727).

19 Guru Arjan Dev (*Guru Granth Sahib*, Ang 1084).

20 A text containing religious writings attributed to Guru Gobind Singh, the tenth Guru of the Sikhs. There is much controversy around this text and whether it was composed by Guru Gobind Singh.

21 McLeod, 'The turban: Symbol of Sikh identity', p. 58.

22 *Dasam Granth*, Ang 120.

23 Searchgurbani.com (2018). Vaaran Bhai Gurdas: Vaar 23, Pauri 12. [online] Available at: www.searchgurbani.com/bhai-gurdas-vaaran/vaar/32/pauri/19/line/1 [Accessed 24 April 2018].

24 Searchgurbani.com (2018). Vaaran Bhai Gurdas. Vaar 32, Pauri 19. [online] Available at: www.searchgurbani.com/bhai-gurdas-vaaran/vaar/32/pauri/19/line/1 [Accessed 24 April 2018].

25 Padam, *Rehatname*, p. 58.

26 Padam, *Rehatname*, p. 59.

27 Padam, *Rehatname*, p. 61.

28 Ibid.

29 Padam, *Rehatname*, p. 62.

30 Padam, *Rehatname*, p. 65.

31 Ibid.

32 Bhai Daya Singh was the first of the *Panj Pyare* to offer his head when Guru Gobind Singh gave a call for the highest sacrifice. He was amongst those five who received the Amrit initiation. The *Rehatnama* was written after the death of Guru Gobind Singh. It outlines the basic ideals of the Khalsa: Padam, *Rehatname*, pp. 57, 61, 62.

33 Padam, *Rehatname*, p. 70.

34 Ibid.

35 Padam, Rehatname, p. 75.

36 Padam, *Rehatname*, p. 97.

37 Padam, *Rehatname*, p. 98.

38 Ibid.

39 Padam, *Rehatname*, p. 103.

40 Padam, *Rehatname*, p.105.

41 Padam, *Rehatname*, p. 105.

42 "According to the Bhatt Vahis, Bhai Desa Singh was the youngest of Bhai Mani Singh's ten sons." W.H. McLeod (2003). *Sikhs of the Khalsa: A History of the Khalsa Rahit*. New Dehli: Oxford University Press, p.114.

43 Padam, *Rehatname*, p. 144.

44 McLeod, 'The turban: Symbol of Sikh identity', p. 60.

45 S. Rattan Bhangu. *Sri Guru Panth Parkash*. Volumes I and II. English translation by Kulwant Singh. Chandigarh: Institute of Sikh Studies.

46 Rattan Singh Bhangu, *Sri Guru Panth Parkash*, Volume I, p. 87.

47 Ibid.

48 Shiromani Gurdwara Parbandhak Committee (1945/1950). *The Code of Conduct and Conventions: English Version of the Sikh Rehat Maryada*, Article XVI (t), Chapter X. [online] Available at: http://sgpc.net/sikh-rehat-maryada-in-english/ [Accessed 29 January 2018].

49 W. H. McLeod (1984). *Textual Sources for the Study of Sikhism*. Manchester: Manchester University Press, pp. 27–28. Also see McLeod (2003). *Sikhs of the Khalsa: A History of the Khalsa Rahit*. New Delhi: Oxford University Press; McLeod (1980). *Early Sikh Tradition: A Study of the Janam-sākhīs*. Oxford: Clarendon Press.

50 There are images showing Guru Nanak wearing a turban. For example, *Guru Nanak with Mardana* [left], *Bala and Twelve Yogis*, Amritsar or Lahore, about 1875 (http://collections.vam.ac.uk/item/O70861/guru-nanak-with-mardana-bala-woodcut-unknown/); *Woodcut*, depicting Guru Nanak with Mardana (left) and Bala, coloured woodcut, Amritsar or Lahore, about 1875 (http://collections.vam.ac.uk/item/O70860/woodcut-unknown/); and 'Painting of Guru Nanak with his parents, c. 1733' (the image appears courtesy of @SikhProf: https://americanturban.com/2012/11/28/celebrating-the-birth-anniversary-of-guru-nanak/). There is also an image of Bhai Lehna (later Guru Angad) and his companions visiting Baba Nanak (Gurmukhi Manuscript Panj. B40, ca. 1733, India Office Library, www.sikhmuseum.com/nishan/khalsa/index.html) [Accessed 19 March 2017]. For more information and images about types and styles of turbans see 'A Visual History of the Sikh Turban' by Jodh Singh (6 March 2019), available at: https://medium.com/@jodhsingh/a-visual- history-of-the-sikh-turban-ca294b58953b [Accessed 7 March 2019]; and 'The old Sikh turban style: A tradition lost to the ages' by @Kharagket (6 March 2019) https://twitter.com/i/moments/1103380915257032708 [Accessed 7 March 2019].

51 McLeod, 'The turban: Symbol of Sikh identity', p. 57.

52 See G. Singh (2014). *The Testimonies of Indian Soldiers and the Two World Wars: Between Self and Sepoy*. London: A&C Black.

53 Y. Hafiz (2013). 'The inspiring way Gap responded to racist graffiti'. *Huffington Post UK*. [online] Available at: www.huffingtonpost.co.uk/entry/gap-ad-sikh-waris-ahluwalia_n_4343586 [Accessed 19 August 2018].

54 J. Dizon (2015). 'New H&M ads feature hijab and turban wearing models'. *Tech Times*. [online] Available at: www.techtimes.com/articles/89799/20151001/new-h-m-ads-feature-hijab-and-turban-wearing-models.html [Accessed 19 August 2018].

55 Twitter (2018). Punjab2000.com on Twitter. [online] Available at: https://twitter.com/punjab2000music/status/1012865902549794816 [Accessed 19 August 2018]; Twitter (2017). LookASingh on Twitter. [online] Available at: https://twitter.com/LookASingh/status/923267900974288896/video/1 [Accessed 4 September 2017]. [Accessed 4 September 2018].

56 In March 2018, the debate around Sikh turbans in Britain took an interesting turn, with the news that Gucci, the high-end Italian fashion house, used turbans as a fashion accessory as part of a catwalk fashion show during Milan Fashion Week. In the ensuing furore, many took to social media accusing Gucci of 'cultural appropriation', whilst others went further suggesting that Gucci had insulted the Sikh religion itself. Aljazeera (2018). 'Gucci accused of culturally appropriating Sikh turban'. [online] Available at: www.aljazeera.com/news/2018/02/gucci-accused-culturally-appropriating-sikh-turban-180223200944130.html [Accessed 4 March 2018].

57 For example, the turban-wearing Sikh postman, and the Sikh couple at Alfie and Kat's wedding in *EastEnders* (www.lookasingh.com/2013/10/eastenders-singh-via-iamdaguy.html). Also see Supakino at www.supakino.com/ for more discussion of turbans appearing in films.

58 I. Tharoor (2015). 'Canada now has the world's most Sikh cabinet'. *The Washington Post*. [online] Available at: www.washingtonpost.com/news/worldviews/wp/2015/11/05/canada-just-appointed-the-worlds-most-sikh-cabinet/?utm_term=.fe231ca3acba [Accessed 27 June 2018].

59 R. Singh (2012). 'Satyendra Singh Huja, Mayor of Charlottesville, VA, in his own words'. American Turban. [online] Available at: https://americanturban.com/2012/01/10/satyendra-singh-huja-mayor-of-charlottesville-va-in-his-own-words/ [Accessed 16 August 2018].

60 Ravinder Bhalla (2018). Ravi Bhalla, Hoboken Mayor. [online] Available at: www.ravinderbhalla.com/ [Accessed 4 September 2018].

61 Nj.gov (2018). State of New Jersey. [online] Available at: https://nj.gov/oag/oag/ag_bio.htm [Accessed 5 November 2018].

62 To illustrate their inordinate contribution, at the outbreak of hostilities in the Great War 20 per cent of soldiers in the British Indian Army were turban wearing Sikhs, despite comprising less that two per cent of British India's population. For their gallantry in the various wars, Sikh soldiers have been awarded 5 Victoria Crosses, the first of which given to Ishar Singh in 1921. *Empire, Faith & War: The Sikhs and World War One* (2016). About. [online] Available at: www.empirefaithwar.com/about#about/intro [Accessed 8 October 2017]. Also see Heike Liebau (2017) 'Martial races: Theory of'. *International Encyclopedia of the First World War*. [online] Available at: https://encyclopedia.1914-1918-online.net/ article/martial_races_theory_of [Accessed 8 October 2017]. And Sikhs in the Army (2016). 'Victoria Cross winners'. [online] Available at: www. sikhsinthearmy.co.uk/vc-winners/4545958279 [Accessed 8 October 2017].

63 M. Rahi (2005). 'Turban and the French law: A question of freedom of conscience'. Globalsikhstudies.net. [online] Available at: www.globalsikhstudies.net/pdf/Turban%20and%20the%20French%20Law-M.S.%20Rahi%20.pdf [Accessed 15 November 2018].

64 Sidhu and Gohil (2016). *Civil Rights in Wartime: The Post*.

65 A *kirpan* is a Sikh ceremonial dagger/sword, and is one of the five articles of faith worn by an initiated Sikh.

66 S. Juss (2012). 'Kirpans, law, and religious symbols in schools'. *Journal of Church and State*, 55(4), pp. 758–795; R. Banakar (2016). *Rights in Context*. London: Routledge.

67 D. Goyal (2019). 'Remembering a Sikh postman whose battle benefits the community in UK even today. *The Indian Express*. [online] Available at: https://indianexpress.com/article/express-sunday-eye/head-heart-5719275/ [Accessed 12 May 2019].

68 For information see G. Singh and D. S. Tatla (2006). *Sikhs in Britain: The Making of a Community*. London: Zed Books; G. Singh (2005). 'British multiculturalism and Sikhs'. *Sikh Formations: Religion, Culture Theory*, *1*(2), pp. 157–173; and D. S. Tatla (2003). 'Sikhs in multicultural societies'. *International Journal on Multicultural Societies*, *5*(2), pp. 177–192. More information can also be found in S. Juss (1995). 'The constitution and Sikhs in Britain'. *Bingham Young University Law Review*. Issue 2, Article 6, pp. 481–533; S. Poulter (1998). *Ethnicity, Law and Human Rights: The English Experience*. Oxford: Clarendon Press.

69 The authors have quoted from Singh and Tatla, *Sikhs in Britain*, pp. 127–135; G. Singh, 'British multiculturalism and Sikhs', pp. 157–173; Tatla, 'Sikhs in multicultural societies', pp. 177–192, because they have covered the case law and material significantly.

70 The authors have quoted from Singh and Tatler, *Sikhs in Britain*, pp. 127–128.

71 D. Beetham (1970). *Transport and Turbans: A Comparative Study in Local Politics*. Published for the Institute of Race Relations, London: Oxford University Press.

72 All material in this paragraph taken from G. Singh, 'British multiculturalism and Sikhs', including the Beetham reference at the top of the paragraph and the final quoted words, which are also taken from Beetham, *Transport and Turbans*, p. 63.

73 S. Poulter (1998), *Ethnicity, Law and Human Rights: The English Experience.* Oxford: Clarendon Press, p. 293.

74 Ibid.

75 Poulter, *Ethnicity, Law and Human Rights*, p. 324.

76 Poulter, *Ethnicity, Law and Human Rights*, p 297.

77 Poulter, *Ethnicity, Law and Human Rights*, pp. 295–296.

78 Sikh Missionary Society (2003). *The Turban Victory – The House of Commons.* [online] Available at: www.gurmat.info/sms/smspublications/theturbanvictory/chapter1.html [Accessed 28 January 2018].

79 Singh and Tatla, *Sikhs in Britain*, pp. 127–135; G. Singh, 'British multiculturalism and Sikhs' (the source of external references used in this paragraph).

80 Poulter, *Ethnicity, Law and Human Rights*, p. 320.

81 Hansard. HL Deb (16 October 1989) Employment Bill, series 5, vol. 511 col. 738. [online] Available at: https://api.parliament.uk/historic-hansard/lords/1989/oct/16/employment-bill [Accessed 26 May 2019].

82 Hansard. HC Deb, (11 May 1995) Business of the House vol. 259 cols 901–902. [online] Available at: https://api.parliament.uk/historic-hansard/commons/1995/may/11/business-of-the-house [Accessed 26 May 2019]. 'Today the matter stands between statutory exemption in the United Kingdom and the Unchanged EU directive on public health and safety for the construction industry' (Singh and Tatla, *Sikhs in Britain*, p. 242).

83 Department for Work and Pensions (2015). 'Government overturns turban workplace rule'. GOV.UK. [online] Available at: www.gov.uk/government/news/government-overturns-turban-workplace-rule [Accessed 8 October 2017].

84 National Archives (2015). Deregulation Act 2015 – *Explanatory Notes.* [online] Available at: www.legislation.gov.uk/ukpga/2015/20/notes/division/5/6 [Accessed 15 September 2018].

85 Singh and Tatla, *Sikhs in Britain*; *Mandla v. Dowell-Lee* [1982] UKHL 7 (24 March 1982); [1983] 2 AC 548.

86 *Mandla v. Dowell-Lee.*

87 S. Bidwell (1987). *The Turban Victory*. Kent, UK: Sikh Missionary Society.

88 According to the 2011 Census, there were 432,429 Sikhs throughout the United Kingdom, the vast majority of them in England alone. The number of Sikhs in the nations forming the United Kingdom were:

   England: 420,196
   Wales: 2,962
   Scotland: 9,055
   NI: 216

89 A. Amin and N. Jhooti (2019). 'The 4,000-year history of the Sikh turban'. [online] *CNN Style*. Available at: https://edition.cnn.com/style/article/turbans-tales-history/index.html [Accessed 15 February 2019].

90 E. Sanders (2001). 'Understanding turbans: Don't link them to terrorism'. *The Seattle Times*. Community.seattletimes.nwsource.com. [online] Available at: http://community.seattletimes.nwsource.com/archive/?date=20010927&slug=turban270 [Accessed 8 January 2018]. Also reproduced in Sidhu and Gohil, *Civil Rights in Wartime*.

91 Home Office (2018). *Hate Crime, England and Wales, 2017 to 2018.* Assets.publishing.service.gov.uk (2018). [online] Available at: https://assets.publishing.service.gov.uk/government/uploads/system/uploads/attachment_data/file/748598/hate-crime-1718-hosb2018.pdf [Accessed 28 October 2018].

92 Whilst the authors recognize the importance of research conducted by community groups, such as CS and SN, they are cautious about results due to sample size and extrapolations being made.

93 In November 2018, the APPG Group on British Muslims launched the Islamophobia Defined report announcing a working definition following two years of consultation: 'Islamophobia is rooted in racism and is a type of racism that targets expressions of Muslimness or perceived Muslimness.' The report acknowledged Sikh victims of Islamophobia, further to written and oral evidence from the Network of Sikh Organisations, who subsequently gave evidence to the Home Affairs Committee expressing concern that the definition could censor free and open debate about aspects of Islam and history.

2   Sikhs in Britain post-9/11

Introduction

Despite a wide recognition of Sikh military contribution, the *dastaar* (turban), like the *hijab* worn by Muslim women, has been an article of faith subjected to significant hostility and resentment. Following the US administration's decision to attack the Taliban (whom they accused of harbouring bin Laden) in the aftermath of 9/11, derogatory references to turbaned Sikhs in Britain began to include the slur 'Taliban' and 'bin Laden',[1] adding to the repository of hate-filled language. The precursor, of course, being 'Paki'. Sikhs have become increasingly misidentified as Muslim in encounters such as those highlighted in recent research owing to the lack of religious illiteracy about who is a Sikh.

A Glaswegian Sikh respondent named Kudoo from Hopkins et al.'s 2017 study[2] highlighted the ignorance and prejudice he had faced:

> Umm, when I was about 17, it was New Year's Eve … and one of the guys said, 'Oh is that a bomb in your bag?' Typical, and that is one incident that does stick out, and me being me I was, if someone said something to me I would go, Yes, and I am going to put it under your chair!' And the guy crapped it ha ha, he was drunk anyway so I don't think he knew what was happening. The guy crapped it and just left the restaurant and the manager came and said sorry to me and x, y, z, but I got a free meal ha ha. Got a free meal for the inconvenience, but again that incident does stick out … it was New Year's Eve, he was fairly drunk, he was about seventy, so I don't think he knew what who was who.[3]

Dr Imran Awan and Dr Irene Zempi presented their findings[4] from a smaller study to MPs in 2017, as part of hate crime awareness week and they highlighted a Sikh example:

> When Taranjeet, 36, had his shop windows smashed, he felt both helpless and scared. He also found it extremely difficult to explain to his wife and children, why they had been targeted with a horrific Islamophobic attack, when they themselves are not Muslim. 'Both my wife and kids have had it really bad. When the shop windows were smashed, they were inside and I

was out. My wife is always scared now. Actually, she did not want to go back to the shop for a whole month. My kids at home always say "Daddy why are they hurting us? Is it because they don't like us? But we haven't done anything wrong to them." What should I say to them? That they are hitting us because they think we are Muslim?"[5]

Those on the frontline dealing with the post-9/11 backlash in Britain recall the challenges on the ground at the time. Retired Metropolitan Police Detective Sergeant Gurpal Virdi (who is of Sikh heritage himself) described the frightening level of ignorance about Sikh identity:

> I dealt with a lot of complaints – we had attacks on individuals, even on women. When it [9/11] happened, I was going around police stations to tell the officers the differences between the Taliban and a Sikh because they didn't know either. And this is London, a multicultural area. It doesn't help when they kept showing images of [Osama bin Laden] and in the UK, it's the Sikhs who wear a turban.[6]

Analysing the Sikh experience through a British lens

With the growing evidence of race hate crime against Sikhs an analysis of the post-9/11 Sikh experience from a UK perspective cannot be complete without first reflecting on the history of racism and its evolution in modern Britain.

Post-war migration

After the Second World War, immigrants from the former British Empire, many of whom had some role in supporting the allied war effort, started moving to Britain en masse. Britain needed to rebuild after the war, with fears she would be unable to turn around her crippled post-war economy or alter a declining birth rate without immigrants, who were in the large part of Irish or European descent. However, many came from the British Empire in India.

The bloody partition of India in 1947 had triggered a significant wave of migration from the Indian subcontinent. Punjab, the birthplace of Sikhism, like Bengal, was split between the newly formed nations of India and Pakistan. In 1948, the British government set up a working group considering the employment of colonial labour. There was little restriction put on immigrants from the Commonwealth nations, and this passed through law as the British Nationality Act (1948). For the first time, significant numbers of immigrants from the Caribbean, India and Pakistan came to work and settle in Britain. It was in the 1950s and 1960s that the majority of immigrants from the Indian subcontinent arrived: seeking better economic opportunities and joining family members, they established themselves in the manufacturing and textiles sectors. They included Sikhs from east Punjab, Hindus from Gujarat and Muslims from Pakistan and modern-day Bangladesh.

Rather than seeking economic fruits, some came to Britain to escape religious or political persecution in India, but they also went elsewhere in the world. In August 1972 the then President of Uganda, Idi Amin, gave Asians 90 days to leave the country.[7] Tens of thousands escaping Amin's rabid 'Indophobia' (which included Muslims, Sikhs and Hindus) emigrated to the sanctity of Britain's safe shores. A further wave of Sikhs came to the UK in the aftermath of 1984, following the Indian army's military assault on the Golden Temple in Amritsar (codenamed Operation Bluestar) and the subsequent Delhi anti-Sikh pogroms following the assassination of Indira Gandhi by her Sikh bodyguards to avenge Bluestar.[8] In the 1990s, Afghan Sikhs rushed to escape persecution at the hands of Islamic extremists in Afghanistan and Pakistan's tribal regions, seeking refuge in countries like Britain.[9]

Since the early 1960s, many of the new arrivals were not always welcome and a section of the 'host' community opposed Britain's open immigration policy. This hostility came from some unexpected quarters. For example, an advert taken out by Leicester City council in the Uganda Argus in 1972 actively discouraged Indians preparing to flee Uganda from settling in the city.[10] Despite this, 44,000 ethnic Indians had settled in Leicester by 1981. They were largely middle-class Hindus and Sikhs who had fled Amin's regime, and they not only added value to the local economy but also integrated well into the host society.[11]

Despite successful integration, it is clear that the migration process created tensions due to identity, multiculturalism and assimilation, and it appears that the Sikhs' historical contribution during the two world wars and the concession given to Sikh soldiers allowing them to wear their turbans[12] were not matters to which politicians like Enoch Powell had given much consideration.

Echoes of Enoch Powell's notorious 'Rivers of Blood' speech at the Conservative Association meeting in Birmingham on 20 April 1968 are still being felt in Britain today. The speech came at a time of significant tensions on the issue of immigration, something that we have more recently become familiar with in the context of the debate around the EU referendum and forthcoming Brexit.

Enoch Powell, in 1968, then MP for Wolverhampton South West, declared that mass immigration would produce social breakdown – that 'like the Roman, I seem to see the River Tiber foaming with much blood'.[13] He feared that the consequences of mass migration of immigrants and their descendants settling in Britain would be 'like watching a nation busily engaged in heaping up its own funeral pyre'.[14] These words may have marginalized him at the time and ended his political career, but his views are enjoying somewhat of a posthumous revival. So much so that in 2015, columnist and author Simon Heffer wrote an article in response to the November Paris terror attack headlined, 'Paris is tragic proof that Enoch Powell was right about threats to our country'.[15]

Decades on, the speech remains the subject of significant debate and discussion, with a recent *The Telegraph* article suggesting that Powell, amongst other things, was right on the European project being 'a great deception'.[16] It also raises a difficult debate around the failures of multiculturalism. The view that British multiculturalism has failed was legitimatized after the 7/7 London bombings, with the realization that despite being born, bred and educated in Britain, 'home-grown' extremists despised everything that Britain stood for. The bombers' allegiance lay with Islam and their sympathies with the *ummah* (the global Muslim brotherhood), not Britain or British values. Whilst the failures of multiculturalism resurrect the spectre of Powell's incendiary intervention, the writings of Huntingdon, in his 'clash of civilizations' hypothesis, also stressed religious and cultural identity, in particular Islam, would be a driver for post-Cold War conflicts globally.

Issues of immigration and Europe were at the heart of the 2016 EU referendum vote for Brexit. The steady rise in Islamic extremist attacks have involved 'home-grown' terrorists, but also immigrants, as in the case of Ahmed Hassan, the Parsons Green tube bomber, Mohamed Lahouaiej Bouhlel, the Nice Bastille Day jihadi, and Anis Amri, the Berlin Christmas market terrorist. This new wave of extremism in the West continues to raise serious questions about Europe's approach to immigration, especially Chancellor Angela Merkel's open-door policy during the Syrian refugee crisis. It is therefore unsurprising that much of what Powell said in the 1960s resonates with groups like Britain First (hereinafter BF), the English Defence League (hereinafter EDL), or proscribed groups like National Action (hereinafter NA) today. The former two organizations campaign primarily on an anti-Islam platform. Powell's comments would of course strike a cord around the current debate on the *hijab*, the *niqab*, the *jilab* and in particular the *burkha*.

Whilst when people think of Enoch Powell's speech in today's context they are likely to focus on Islam, what is less widely acknowledged is that Powell's specific focus at the time was British Sikhs and how their demand to wear a turban would destroy the British way of life. Referring to a campaign for the right to wear the turban, he said, 'The Sikh communities' campaign to maintain customs inappropriate in Britain is much to be regretted. Working in Britain, particularly in the public services, they should be prepared to accept the terms and conditions of their employment.'[17] He continued, claiming that asking for special rights leads to 'a dangerous fragmentation within society'. In fact, in 1969, after a long-running campaign, Sikh bus drivers in Powell's constituency of Wolverhampton won the right to wear their turbans whilst on duty.[18] Many consider this moment in history as an important milestone in the battle for religious equality in the workplace. However, Powell, like Labour Minister John Stonehouse said, 'This communalism is a canker; whether practised by one colour or another it is to be strongly condemned'. In other words, fighting for civil liberties was destructive and comparable to a fungal disease, and Sikhs in doing so, were 'dangerous and divisive elements'.

This was not the first or the last time that the Sikh turban became the subject of prejudice, marginalization and discrimination in the UK. Sikhs have had to fight for the turban to be recognized as outlined by Tatla,[19] and Singh and Tatla,[20] (discussed in Chapter 1). Indeed, British Sikhs have been an integral part of the British civil rights movement since the 1960s by virtue of standing out from the crowd, but also because standing up for human rights is a central tenet of Sikh teachings. From defending the right to wear articles of faith, like the landmark 'turban case' (*Mandla v. Dowell-Lee*),[21] or the '*kara* case' (*R (Watkins-Singh) v. Governing Body of Aberdare Girls' High School & Anor*),[22] to lobbying for changes in equality law, through to opposition to fascist groups – it is no exaggeration to suggest that Sikhs, in many ways, have almost always been on the front line. Nevertheless, today the British Sikh community is considered an integration success story. Sikh teachings of tolerance, equality and justice for all fit hand in glove with Western democracy.

Racism since the late 1970s

Before Islamic extremism became a serious issue for British authorities, it is worth reflecting on events in the late 1970s and early 1980s that were to shape history for those fighting against the fascist ideologues of the then NF. During this period Muslims, Hindus and Sikhs faced hostilities together, collectively labelled with the derogatory term 'Pakis'. The racist murder of turbaned Sikh pupil Gurdip Singh Chaggar in 1976[23] was an event that served as a catalyst for the fledgling Southall Youth Movement (hereinafter SYM). Southall, a suburb of West London, was a place where many Sikh migrants had settled by the 1970s and it became fondly known as 'Little Punjab'. With growing racial tensions, the SYM became instrumental in pushing back against the NF's often-unprovoked physical assaults on those from the Indian subcontinent, described as 'paki bashing'. Ongoing tensions culminated in the Southall race riots in 1979, and once more in 1981.[24]

In the 2014 documentary 'Young Rebels – The Story of the Southall Youth Movement',[25] members of the SYM speak openly about violent assaults, racism and prejudice in schools, where a racist policy of 'bussing' was implemented in 1965, by the then government.[26] Immigrant children from the Indian subcontinent and Afro-Caribbean's were sent to schools outside of Southall, throughout the London Borough of Ealing, due to complaints from white parents campaigning against the increasing number of immigrant children in the local primary schools.[27]

An accompanying report to the documentary by the Asian Health Agency in partnership with Digital Works (funded by the Heritage Lottery Fund)[28] states:

> This first generation to attend schools in England experienced racial abuse, racist attacks and discrimination as a daily feature of life both in the playground and on the way to and from school as well as on the streets while their parents struggled and worked to provide for their families, Asian children and young people were learning to live with and cope in a different environment without any family or community support against this overt racism. Their personal experiences shattered the myths and beliefs, instilled in them by their parents, that the English were tolerant, fair and just and that the police, educational and other public institutions and professionals be afforded almost unchallengeable respect.[29]

As a result of growing racism, a movement for equality began with significant changes in legislation designed to protect minority rights. Following previously unsuccessful bills, it was towards the end of 1965 (coinciding with the time of 'bussing') that the first Race Relations Act achieved Royal Assent, outlawing discrimination on the 'grounds of colour, race, or ethnic or national origins' in public places.[30] At the time of the Act being passed there were approximately one million immigrants in the UK, largely from Commonwealth countries.[31] It was subsequently strengthened by the Race Relations Act (1968), which extended the laws remit to housing and employment, later to be repealed by the Race Relations Act (1976),[32] which saw the establishment of the CRE. Later, the Equalities and Human Rights Commission (hereinafter EHRC), a non-departmental public body, was established by the Equalities Act (2006) and became Britain's national equality body. The Equalities Act (2010) brought together 116 pieces of legislation together, including the Race Relations Act (1976), into a single Act of Parliament.[33]

Despite some positive steps along the way, Britain in 1976 remained a nation divided on racial lines, with suspicion of ethnic minorities and significant social inequalities. The first of the two Southall riots on 23 April 1979 was a turning point, when the SYM and allied anti-fascist protestors of the anti-Nazi league demonstrated against a provocative NF meeting being held in the Town Hall. It was during these events that anti-racism activist Blair Peach was tragically murdered. His death became a rallying point for the burgeoning anti-fascist movement, and his funeral a poignant moment in the battle for equality. Thirty years later, it was revealed an elite riot squad officer of the MET most likely killed him.[34]

Anti-immigrant sentiment and the rise in anti-Islam politics

Anti-immigrant sentiment, which was to later diversify specifically into an anti-Islam, anti-sharia or a 'counter-jihad' narrative, continued to be a rallying point for nationalist groups in Britain in the 1970s. A decade or so after the speech that ended Powell's political career, Nick Griffin, the former leader of the BNP and former Member of the European Parliament (hereinafter MEP), could not have been clearer when it came to policy ideas regarding British Sikhs. He once proposed the voluntary repatriation of Sikhs to India, so that 'West London wouldn't be so crowded at rush hour time'.[35] As recently as 2010 the BNP continued to promote their controversial immigration policy for those defined as 'non-white' British, with voluntary resettlement grants of £50,000 for 180,000 individuals per year,[36] but by then, they had become almost irrelevant. In 2010, they ended up with just two council seats, down from 338, and lost both European seats.[37] Around the time of this political decline, a 78-year-old Sikh, Rajinder Singh, who had lost his father at the hands of Muslim extremists during India's partition, became the BNP's first non-white member.[38] The BNP had been forced to change their constitution to allow non-whites to join, fearing legal action from the EHRC.

Other groups later developed, focused primarily on opposition to the actions of British Muslim extremists. The United People of Luton was the precursor to what became known as the EDL. It was born in Luton in 2009, in response to Islamist protests as the Royal Anglian Regiment paraded through the Bedfordshire town returning from a tour of Afghanistan.[39] Meanwhile demographic changes were afoot. Whilst Christianity continued to see a dramatic decline in adherents, falling from 37 million in 2001 to 33 million in 2011,[40] the increase in Britain's Muslim population from 1.5 million in 2001 to 2.7 million in 2011 (a 72 per cent rise),[41] fuelled fears with stories suggesting that Muslim communities were somehow overtaking white 'Brits'. Headlines such as 'The changing face of Britain: A child in Birmingham is now more likely to be a Muslim than Christian',[42] and 'Muslim population of the UK could triple to 13m following "record" influx',[43] would provide the necessary oxygen for groups like the EDL to feed their concerns about a 'Muslim takeover'.

Unlike the BNP, or NF before it, the EDL focused primarily on an anti-sharia and anti-Islam politics, and many of the street protests by the group over the years have turned ugly. Clashes have occurred with Muslim counter-protestors like the Muslim Defence League, and groups like Unite Against Fascism (hereinafter UAF).[44] Notably Azad Ali, the vice-chairman of UAF, is an Islamist.[45] The EDL's founder Tommy Robinson, who left the group in 2013 admitting that neo-Nazis had infiltrated his street movement,[46] is now an author and former journalist for right-wing Rebel Media.[47] He amassed a significant social media presence, but received a Twitter suspension in 2018,[48] and most recently, he has had his Facebook page deleted. He remains a vocal critic of Islam, and has received a number of death threats as a result.[49] However, unlike older right-wing groups that focused largely on race, the EDL's focus on Islam resonated with disgruntled members of the white working class concerned about mainstream 'political correctness' around Islamic extremism, and Britain's sexual 'grooming gang' problem. It therefore attracted many followers from ordinary backgrounds.

The EDL started using the slogan 'black and white unite' conveniently taken from anti-racism protestors of the 1970s. From the outset, its membership included those from ethnic minorities, so in interviews Tommy Robinson often pushed back against the suggestion the EDL was a racist organization. Moreover, one of the EDL's main spokespersons in its early days, Guramit Singh, was Sikh-born.[50] It promoted Jewish, LGBT (lesbian, gay, bisexual and transgender) and Sikh divisions,[51] and Tommy Robinson, whilst criticizing Islam, continues to promote a pro-Sikh view.[52] During a 27 May 2013 EDL demo in Whitehall, Sikhs campaigning for the release of a Sikh on death row in India were sandwiched between rival EDL and UAF supporters. Tommy Robinson took the opportunity to highlight the Sikh contribution to the great wars. In appreciation, EDL supporters are seen in the same footage chanting 'Sikh, Sikh, Sikh'.[53] This 'Sikhophilic' approach has attracted a small Sikh group in the Midlands, Sikh Youth UK (hereinafter SYUK), who have common ground with Tommy Robinson, particularly on the issue of sexual grooming gangs. Some commentators, especially from within the Sikh community, have viewed this as promoting Islamophobia in itself.[54]

In a video after the Manchester arena terror attack, Robinson visited a *gurd-wara* in Birmingham (where he was greeted by a prominent member of SYUK) and said: 'So many times the Sikh community are wrongly identified as problematic by uneducated people. I've spent the last 6–7 years forming relationships with Sikhs across the country, we couldn't ask, and no one could ask for a better minority, more loyal, more patriotic and more hardworking people.'[55] This 'outreach', along with regular pro-Sikh social media posts, sets Robinson apart from the likes of Griffin, and the leadership of groups like BF, who also continue to primarily campaign on an anti-Islam agenda. On 22 November 2017, Robinson tweeted images of historic Sikh martyrs, Bhai Mati Das, Sati Das and Bhai Dayala, being executed by India's Muslim rulers for 'refusing to get forcefully converted into Islam'.[56] Although the tweet is historically accurate, these kinds of posts play into the hands, amongst others, of India's anti-Islam Hindu nationalists, many of whom follow the former EDL leader on social media.

The newcomer, BF is described as a British ultranationalist party, and was set up in 2011 by former BNP members. BF have promoted petitions on Facebook, like one that requested the HO 'Deports All Islamists!',[57] and its leaders, Paul Golding and Jayda Fransen, were sent to prison in 2018 for religiously aggravated harassment.[58] We have also seen the emergence of the Football Lads Alliance (hereinafter FLA), who conduct 'anti-extremism' marches in their thousands.[59] It was the brainchild of grassroots football fans following the Westminster; Manchester and Finsbury Park terror attacks.

On 24 June 2017, the FLA organized the 'United Against Extremism' street march in London. Mohan Singh from the Sikh Awareness Society (hereinafter SAS), a group that raises awareness about the dangers of sexual grooming gangs, was surprisingly one of the event's speakers.[60] He told the authors that he was worried about retributory attacks on *gurdwara*s following the atrocities, so, when approached, he agreed to make a speech with the aim of helping to educate football fans about Sikhism, and the Sikh stance against all forms of extremism. However, he made it clear he would leave the stage if there were any racist or Islamophobic chants. The FLA later splintered, and some of its activists set up what became known as the Democratic Football Lads Alliance.

However, it was the UK Independence Party (hereinafter UKIP) that brought concerns about Islamic extremism into mainstream political discourse. In 2015 its former leader Nigel Farage MEP, talking about immigration, said some Muslims in Britain want to form 'a fifth column and kill us'.[61] In 2017, a failed UKIP leadership candidate, Anne Marie Waters, set up For Britain, a party purporting to be '[t]he only party speaking up for the forgotten people of Britain',[62] one of its priorities being speaking out against Islamic extremism. In 2018, the party was accused of shifting to the 'populist hard right' when its leader, Gerard Batten MEP, proposed Muslim-only prisons in the party's 'interim manifesto'.[63] Batten also linked Britain's sexual grooming gang problem with Islam.[64]

The increasingly anti-Islam focus across right-leaning (and far-right) politics has become problematic for all Britain's diverse communities, not just Muslims. Moreover, it has not been restricted to hateful speech, social media campaigns, petitions against halal meat, angry street protests or the promotion of divisive politics; it has involved real and direct violence. In fact when the Royal Anglian Regiment staged their homecoming parade in Luton back in 2009, and men from an extremist group called Islam4UK demonstrated, shouting 'Anglian soldiers go to hell', an angry reaction was provoked against 'Asians' per se, and Luton's turbaned Sikh Mayor Lakhbir Singh was kicked to the ground.[65] As this discourse grew, the conflation between race and religion became a more common occurrence in both Britain and the US – a phenomenon that the authors describe as the *racialization of Islamophobia*.

The post-9/11 anti-Sikh backlash

The attacks on the twin towers in America heralded the beginning of a new phase of religious/ethnic hatred and violence – the post-9/11 backlash. Both 'mistaken identity' and the *racialization of Islamophobia* contributed to this phenomenon. It is true that 9/11 heralded a period in history when hate crimes would be driven by major world events, starting with Al Qaeda's declaration of war against 'Jews and Crusaders', and its unswerving commitment to sanctioning the murder of Westerners in the name of Allah. It is also true that rolling images of the Al Qaeda leadership had a more or less similar affect in Britain, which regurgitated the same imagery and narrative as mainstream US television networks, such as Fox News. Bin Laden's *kaffiyeh* (traditional Middle Eastern headdress) and his turban and beard were confused with the Sikh *dastaar* and beard in so-called 'mistaken identity' attacks. Whilst the public vilification of the turban became prevalent after 9/11, this had in fact already begun decades prior to 9/11 because of the Iranian revolution in 1979 and later the *Satanic Verses* affair in 1989.

Images of a black-robed and turbaned Ayatollah Khomeini broadcast across the Western media at the time, according to Chris Allen in *Islamophobia*, 'became the epitome of evil: personifying a rampant and uncontrollable anti-Americanism, the antipathy of Western values, morals and beliefs'.[66] Allen talks about a 'climate of fear', writing:

> it is for this reason that in the immediate aftermath of 9/11, Muslim (and Sikh) men that resembled Usama [sic] bin Laden however insignificantly, possibly only having a beard or wearing a turban – were attacked thousands of miles away from where he himself was alleged to have been.[67]

Allen does not note however, that the majority of turban wearers in Britain are in fact Sikhs, or that this religious minority was becoming increasingly targeted due to 'mistaken identity'.

Verbal/physical attacks

Although British Sikhs routinely faced minor incidents – largely insults and racial slurs like 'Paki' due to racism – it was evident that things were starting to change after 9/11 when they began to face physical attacks alongside the verbal attacks. These attacks were mainly aimed at bearded men who wore the Sikh turban. The *kesh* and the turban, although symbols of religious significance representing justice, tolerance and equality, became symbols of marginalization, hatred and vilification. The racialization of religious identity began to have real and serious consequences.

A British Broadcasting Corporation (hereinafter BBC) report in September 2001 highlighted how British Sikhs in the Midlands felt 'intimidated' in the aftermath of the twin towers attack. One told the BBC, 'a lorry started passing by me and the driver opened the window and said to me "hello bin Laden" '.[68]

An important case highlighting how these images and associations (especially bin Laden) affected British Sikhs is that of Jagdeesh Singh. On 26 September 2004, Singh was subjected to a violent physical assault due to his appearance. At the time, British engineer Kenneth Bigley had been kidnapped by Muslim extremists in Iraq. Despite pleas to the then Prime Minister Tony Blair, the British government refused to meet the demands of his captors, an Al Qaeda affiliate called Tawhid and Jihad, led by the Jordanian Abu Musab Al-Zaqawi. Bigley, who appeared on his knees in videos in an orange jumpsuit before armed masked militants, was subsequently beheaded.[69] Prior to Bigley's murder, Singh was walking home one evening in Coventry with his ten-year-old nephew and was accosted by white males who told him, 'Pakis were causing a great deal of problems in Iraq'. He was repeatedly called 'Paki' and 'bin Laden' during a violent assault in which he was punched 30 times.

Later that year Singh, a well-known activist in the community, gave oral evidence to a Home Affairs Committee outlining his experience as a Sikh in a post-9/11 Britain.[70] Although he had been subjected to racism before, he said this ostensibly Islamophobic attack was 'the worst thing that's happened to me in my life'.[71] Clearly emotional during the committee session, Singh posed some pertinent questions to the committee chairman. He said:

> That particular incident [the assault on Jagdeesh Singh] epitomises the kind of verbal brutality and physical brutality, the verbal aggression and the physical aggression, that members of the Sikh community are suffering. The point is: are we to treat this as part of life? Are we to treat this as part of an ongoing situation? As a community we feel very much exposed, very vulnerable but even more so we feel that the British government has done next to nothing in terms of putting into place any form of measure by way of public statements of support.

Following the 7/7 London bombings, Hardip Singh, a young Sikh studying in Dublin, was blamed for the attacks, called 'bin Laden', set upon and stabbed.[72]

The latter two cases show how Sikhs, like Muslims, were equally vulnerable to extreme violence against the perceived 'enemy' after 9/11.

In the case of initiated Sikhs like Jagdeesh Singh and Hardip Singh, it is clear (due to comments made by their assailants) that the turban and beard, which form an integral part of Sikh identity, had been conflated with the attire of Islamic extremists, like Osama bin Laden and his deputy Ayman al-Zawahiri, who wore turbans and had beards. In *Civil Rights in Wartime: The Post-9/11 Sikh Experience*, Sidhu and Gohil note:

> Bin Laden's image, complete with his white turban and flowing beard, had been seared into the American consciousness, which was still reeling with grief and anger. The visual connection between a turbaned bin Laden and a dark-skinned, turbaned male had been forged.[73]

In 2015, four decades on from the murder of a Gurdip Singh Chaggar in West London, an attack with a claw hammer and machete on Dr Sarandev Singh Bhambra, a trainee dentist from Mold (North Wales), sent shockwaves through Britain's Sikh community. Like Chaggar he was targeted because of his colour, but the motivation behind the attack was more specific still. According to the perpetrator Zack Davies, it was a 'revenge' attack for the murder of Fusilier Lee Rigby by Muslim extremists in Woolwich in 2013. In fact, Davies shouted, 'white power' and 'I did it for Lee Rigby'[74] during the frenzied attack that left Bhambra with life changing injuries.[75]

In September 2015, Davies was sentenced to life imprisonment for racially aggravated attempted murder.[76] It was the brave intervention of an ex-soldier, Peter Fuller, that in fact saved Bhambra's life.[77] After the sentencing, Sarandev's brother Dr Tarlochan Singh Bhambra read a statement outside Mold Crown Court:

> Sarandev was singled out because of the colour of his skin. We are in no doubt that had the racial disposition of this case been reversed this would be reported as an act of terror with a wider media coverage. We as a family have listened intently to the evidence … and are in no doubt given the racial and political motivation that this should be rightly defined as an act of terrorism … Ethnic minorities have and continue to contribute positively to the multicultural Britain of 2015. Sikhs have sacrificed their lives in both world wars to facilitate the freedom that Britain enjoys today.[78]

Remarkably, in this particular incident it was not always entirely clear that the victim had been a Sikh. In January 2015 on a flagship BBC Radio 2 programme, a Muslim guest discussing Islamophobia after the Charlie Hebdo killings with host Jeremy Vine inaccurately implied that Bhambra was a Muslim, which resulted in a complaint to the BBC.[79] Notably, the BBC discussion involved talking to Jewish and Muslim representatives who feared a backlash following the murder of Drummer Lee Rigby, but no one from the non-Abrahamic faith traditions, including Sikhs. BBC *Newsnight* subsequently referred to the incident as 'Islamophobic', again with no reference to the victim's Sikh heritage. In fact, the media, police and British government's primary focus then, and even in today's current context, has been almost entirely on highlighting, tackling and pursuing (Muslim) victims of Islamophobia and anti-Semitism. This has been to the detriment of others, who have largely suffered in silence, and Sikhs in particular, who have been described as the 'invisible victims' of hate crime.[80]

Both the Rigby and the Bhambra attacks were attempted beheadings, and Davies, Bhambra's attacker (known as 'Zak Ali' on Facebook), was not influenced only by neo-Nazi groups, but also by Islamic extremists like the Westminster University-educated Mohammed Emwazi or 'Jihadi John', the infamous British Islamic State (hereinafter ISIS) executioner. Some have gone as far as suggesting Davies was indeed a Muslim convert;[81] in fact 'Zak Ali's' Facebook page quotes violent verses from the Koran.[82] Nevertheless, the British media decided to focus on the connection with the far right, in particular, a group proscribed under the Terrorism Act 2000, NA.[83] This unprecedented attack, along with other incidents, demonstrate how grievances against 'Blacks' or 'Pakis' per se evolved from what can be described as primarily colour-motivated prejudice through to a bigotry motivated by revenge for *jihadist* attacks on Muslims, or those who could be described as the 'Muslim-looking other'. Regrettably, there were no official statements of solidarity from the government to give reassurances to a British Sikh community shaken by Bhambra's case.

The vulnerability of Sikhs to post-9/11 prejudices has been a consistent affair. In the same year as Zack Davies' conviction (2015), a Sikh professional working in central London described how he had been effectively barred from a London nightclub because the door staff said people inside had seen him on closed-circuit television (CCTV) informing him, 'you look intimidating due to the colour of your skin and your beard and you look like a Muslim'.[84] Although prohibition from public places has not been a significant theme in Britain, in the same year Navjot Sawhney, a British aerospace engineer, had a similar experience at the door of a Polish nightclub in Krakow, except that a bouncer called him a 'terrorist' and punched him, knocking off his turban.[85] Polish police are reported to have told Sawhney, 'what do you expect after the Paris attacks'. Although the present focus is Britain, Sawhney's case gives indication of how this is a global problem for Sikhs and is part of the wider European malady.[86]

In April 2017, when ArsenalFanTV interviewed two Sikhs, they informed the host that fellow supporters had tried to take their turbans off, called them 'turbanator' and 'Osama squared'.[87] These kinds of experiences are far from unusual. The irony is that none of the 9/11 terrorists wore turbans, and the majority of them, such as Egyptian national Mohamed Atta, were in fact clean-shaven. The trigger for these hate crimes is in no way different to those motivating violent attacks on American Sikhs.

Racism per se, combined with the stark realities of a post-9/11 era, has been a bitter pill for Sikhs to swallow. In 2009, Dean Nelson, then *The Telegraph*'s Asian editor, wrote an article titled 'Our shameful treatment of Britain's Sikh

Figure 2.1 'Best of Britain'.

Source: Copyright Vishavjit Singh @sikhtoons (2009).

saviours', referring to the awful incident when a group of Sikhs from Luton escaped their burning bus on the motorway hard shoulder, having come back from a seaside trip. Rather than provide assistance, passing motorists instead hurled racist abuse, 'gave them the finger', and told them to get back into the burning inferno.[88]

In 2013, a video of an unprovoked attack on a Sikh pensioner in Coventry by a white teenager went viral;[89] his attacker was subsequently jailed for two years.[90] The following year a Sikh cabbie had his turban ripped off and burnt in Bristol, for which a woman was convicted for a race hate offence.[91] The cases in themselves are not meant to provide an exhaustive list of incidents, but the latter two, at least, illustrate cases in which perpetrators have been convicted.

Attacks on social media

Whilst physical attacks and abuse are rising, another arena in which one sees an escalation of hate crime is in the echo chambers of social media, which serve to further propagate a dangerous narrative (particularly evident in the US) where some ignorantly equated Sikhs with 'terrorists' to a much wider global audience.

In 2014 on Instagram, American Hip Hop artist Joe Budden posted an image of an elderly initiated Sikh going through airport security along with the caption, 'Not on my watch, Homeboy!' He later retracted the anti-Sikh comment and apologized.[92] In June 2017, an American flight passenger sitting in proximity to a turbaned Sikh published a series of images on Snapchat wrongly believing that a turbaned Sikh man was a terrorist. In one image he wrote in an accompanying caption, 'Update I'm still alive', along with an emoji, to indicate his sense of relief. Social media users in the UK have also propagated this dangerous narrative.

On 14 May 2016, when a Manchester United versus Bournemouth match at Old Trafford was cancelled due to a bomb scare, there was fury on Twitter: an Arsenal supporter blamed Sikh football fans for the evacuation by posting an image of turban-wearing Sikh men with a caption that read: 'Bomb threat at Old Trafford, I know where my investigation would start.' What was clear from this was that he had no idea that the image he was using was of Sikh men and not Muslims.[93]

A similar level of ignorance about Sikh identity was on display after the Manchester stadium terror attack in May 2017, when *Cosmopolitan* magazine published an image on Twitter identifying a turbaned Sikh taxi driver (who had helped victims free of charge) as a Muslim. It read, 'Muslim Taxi Drivers Took Kids Trying to Escape the Manchester Ariana Grande Concert Home for Free'.[94] The tweet was taken down following a number of complaints about the error in reporting the man's faith.

Nevertheless, aside from misidentification of those with visible articles of faith (on social media or otherwise), other Sikhs who did not wear turbans or outwardly express adherence to their religious tradition equally faced prejudice in the public space. One of the recent cases that reinforce this wider problem is the curious case of Manpreet Mellhi, which she herself described as 'bizarre'. Mellhi, a Sikh heritage reporter at BBC Gloucestershire, was out shopping in her local Sainsbury's supermarket on 12 November 2016 when she discovered someone had mischievously placed packets of pork scratchings in her shopping basket. On discovering them Mellhi was understandably shocked, tweeting: 'to person who dropped two bags of pork scratchings into my basket in Sainsbury's: your pitiful Saturday activity backfired. I'm not Muslim.'[95] She does not wear a turban, nor wear any visible symbols of Sikhism (discussed in Chapter 1) including the *kara* (steel/iron bracelet).

Manpreet described how she had faced racism before, but this was, 'the first thing to upset me in the last ten years'. The individual(s) had acted with the explicit understanding that pork is forbidden or *haram* to practising Muslims, and thus would be offensive to Mellhi, ignorantly assuming that she was of the Islamic faith. Understanding pork's prohibition in Islam has motivated more serious incidents against other unorthodox Sikhs. Just after the 2010 election, former government minister Parmjit Singh Dhanda had a pig's head thrown in his drive. After nine years' service, his book *My Political Race* notes, 'people didn't even realise [he] was actually a Sikh and not a Muslim'.[96] Under a chapter titled 'The Pig's Head', Dhanda writes:

> It was almost comical that they thought the best way to offend me was by leaving a pig's head on my drive because they assumed I was a Muslim. The subtlety of these people to know the difference between a Sikh and a Muslim would have been a bit much to expect, I guess.[97]

Apart from highlighting the wider ramifications for all Sikhs, both the Mellhi and Dhanda incidents demonstrate that their detractors did in fact have some basic religious literacy when it came to Islam. Furthermore, it illustrates how race and ethnicity have been conflated in some cases with religiosity, presenting a group of hate crime victims who have been largely subsumed within the broader debate. Certainly, from a policy perspective the focus has been on Islamophobia directed at Muslims rather than on non-Muslims or on those of no faith. This 'Abrahamic-centric' approach is discussed in the next chapter.

Attacks on religious places of worship

Moreover, it is not just individuals who faced a problem; religious institutions like mosques and temples have also been targeted. In 2018, two *gurdwara*s were attacked: one in Leeds,[98] and one in Edinburgh.[99] Back in 2015 anti-Muslim graffiti 'die Muslims die', was sprayed outside a *gurdwara* in Thornaby, north-east England.[100] It also included the phrase 'white power', signalling a racially motivated element. In the same year, a *gurdwara* in Glasgow was vandalized with the words 'Fuck Islam! No SHARIAH', along with a Nazi swastika scrawled alongside.[101] This was by no means a recent trend; in fact one of the first places to be attacked in retribution for the 7/7 London bombings was a *gurdwara* in Belvedere, Kent, which was firebombed.[102] Two others were also targeted in Merton and Leeds.[103] Again, it should be noted that the various examples discussed here are by no means an exhaustive list of hate crimes against British Sikhs, but more a representative sample of the kind of hostile environment Sikhs find themselves facing in post-9/11 Britain.[104]

The American Sikh experience

Despite this, many would agree that British Sikhs have fared much better than their American co-religionists, who have continued to suffer horrendous hate crimes since 9/11. As previously highlighted, the first murder in retribution for 9/11 was a turbaned Sikh gas station owner from Arizona, Balbir Singh Sodhi.[105] Gurdwara Gobind Sadan, near Syracuse (New York), was firebombed a few months later,[106] and Sikhs have been recipients of an unrelenting backlash ever since. The 2012 Wisconsin *gurdwara* massacre by a white supremacist resulted in the death of six worshippers.[107] To this day, American Sikhs continue to face physical attacks, discrimination in the workplace, harassment, racial profiling, bullying of children in schools, and have been barred from entry in public places.

The suffering of American has been depicted in Hollywood films. In Spike Lee's *Inside Man* (2006), a Sikh character played by turbaned and bearded Waris Ahluwalia is arrested at gunpoint, whilst being referred to as a 'fucking Arab'. Notably, actor Waris Ahluwalia became the subject of anti-Muslim hate in real life. A 2013 GAP campaign themed 'make love', modelled by the Sikh actor and model Quentin Jones, was defaced on a New York City subway platform: the word 'love' was replaced by 'bombs'. The graffiti also included the line 'stop driving taxis'.[108]

In Mira Nair's *The Reluctant Fundamentalist* (2012), a character refers to Sodhi's murder in Arizona, whilst another responds by saying 'it's really bad for Sikhs' and 'any beard and turban is a target'. In *Imperium* (2016) Daniel Radcliffe, who plays an undercover FBI agent tasked with infiltrating white supremacists, is briefed on (amongst others) Wade Michael Page, the neo-Nazi responsible for the Wisconsin Sikh *Gurdwara* massacre.

However, despite the efforts of directors like Spike Lee to highlight 'mistaken identity', the level of religious literacy amongst Americans, including senior officials has been woeful. When US presidential candidate Mitt Romney offered condolences to the friends and families of those mercilessly gunned down in Wisconsin in 2012, he inadvertently made reference to 'Sheikhs'.[109] A day after the massacre, the head of the US Air Force Academy Lieutenant General Michael Gould, superintendent of the Colorado Springs military school, a highly educated official, confused Sikhs with Muslims whilst addressing his subordinates. Remarkably, he referred to the killings having taken place in a 'Sikh Mosque'.[110] These two high-profile gaffes highlight an underlying problem, religious illiteracy, which makes the situation for Sikhs in America particularly problematic. In response to these misconceptions the year after Wisconsin, SALDEF published a study conducted in collaboration with Stanford University about post-9/11 'turban myths'.[111] A staggering 70 per cent of Americans could not identify a Sikh man in a turban as a Sikh, and almost half believed that 'Sikh was a sect of Islam'.

In an attempt to tackle this egregious level of ignorance, leading civil rights groups like SC have developed teaching resources for educators designed to tackle bullying in schools.[112] Since 2012 they have produced a number of reports including '"Go Home Terrorist:" A Report on Bullying of Sikh American Children'[113] and 'Say no to bullying: What can Sikh youth do?'.[114] Sikh children across the US have been shown to suffer disproportionately from bullying. Fifty per cent of Sikh children reported being bullied according to a SC survey, compared to 32 per cent of all American school children, and the figure for turbaned Sikhs was higher still at 67 per cent. Many said they were targeted because they were labelled 'terrorists'.[115] Educational outreach efforts extend beyond America's classrooms; both SC and SALDEF have worked to educate education law enforcement agencies and the Transportation Security Administration about the rights of Sikhs at airports and religious symbols like the *kirpan*.[116]

In 2016 SC created the Sikh Project, in collaboration with two British Sikh photographers Amit and Naroop.[117] It was America's first Sikh American photography exhibition in New York, featuring images of 38 Sikh men and women, highlighting the diversity within the community and 'embodying the beauty, resilience and perseverance of Sikh men and women 15 years after 9/11'.[118]

On the question of improving religious literacy, there have been other signs of progress in the US. On 4 January 2018, a popular game show, *Jeopardy*, included a series of questions about Sikhs. Professor Simran Jeet Singh told the authors:

> I was pleased to see 'Sikh' as a category on *Jeopardy*, especially given the immense popularity of the show. The glaring absence of Sikh representation in television is so stark that any positive representation at all has become cause for excitement and celebration. That Sikhs received sustained attention on the program reflects the continuing progress that Sikhs are making in American society. At the same time, it was disappointing to see that even some of the most informed people in America, Jeopardy contestants, know remarkably little about Sikhi (Sikhism). Yes, we are making progress, but we still have a very long way to go.

More significantly still, American Sikhs requested the first hate crime hearing in the Senate following the Wisconsin *gurdwara* massacre on 5 August 2012, with the aim of lobbying for separate hate crime monitoring for Sikhs. It was during this hearing on 19 September 2012, that 18-year-old Harpreet Singh Saini made history as the first Sikh to testify at a US Senate hearing. He gave an emotional tribute to his mother, Paramjit Kaur Saini, who was one of six worshippers murdered in Wisconsin. Saini told senators, 'I want to tell the gunman who took her from me: You may have been full of hate, but my mother was full of love. She was an American. And this was not our American dream.'[119] Saini subsequently wrote an opinion-editorial for *The New York Times* in which he said, 'After her death, I determined to make sure that her status as a victim of a hate crime would not go unrecorded'.[120]

The efforts of American Sikhs like Saini resulted in policy change when the FBI announced they would begin to separately track anti-Sikh hate (on a voluntary basis) in March 2015.[121] Movements like the National Sikh Campaign (hereinafter NSC) launched a 'We Are Sikhs' initiative to improve awareness of Sikhism and Sikhs in America, which became the recipient of the top 2018 PRWeek US award.[122] Reflecting on community efforts since 9/11, activist filmmaker and lawyer Valarie Kaur in *Colorlines* said, 'We are now telling our own stories and organizing on the ground and online. We are writing articles, making our own films, building new organizations. We are no longer victims or bystanders.'[123] Meanwhile other Sikhs, like software engineer and cartoonist (www.Sikhtoons.com) Vishavjit Singh, took an innovative approach to tackle racial stereotypes by dressing up as a Sikh Captain America with the trademark shield and 'A' on his turban.[124] Other creative approaches in the US include that of Los Angeles-based writer and activist, Sundeep Morrison. She dramatized the post-9/11 Sikh experience on stage with her powerful one-woman performance *Rag Head*,[125] the proceeds of which were denoted to the SC.

Hate crime figures released by the FBI in November 2018 for the previous year (2017) showed 7,175 hate crime incidents since 2016,[126] which represents a significant increase since 2001. In terms of hate directed at religious groups specifically, this rose by 23 per cent in 2017. Anti-Jewish incidents grew by 37

Figure 2.2 'Rag Head: An American Story', from one-woman show *Rag Head*.

Source: Copyright Ragni Agarwal (2018).

Note
Rag Head, which is about Sikhs in post-9/11 America, was written, performed and directed by Sundeep Morrison (www.sundeepmorrison.com).

per cent, and anti-Muslim hate was above historical averages. Anti-Sikh hate crime offences increased by 243 per cent. The total number of 'offences' was 24 for Sikhs, for anti-Islamic (Muslim) crime it was 314, and anti-Semitic crimes 976. To put these figures into context, one needs to reflect on the make-up of faith groups in the US, whilst reflecting on the issue of underreporting.

A 2016 Gallup report on the religious constitution of the US, estimated 2.1 per cent of the population was Jewish and 0.8 per cent Muslim, with other 'non-Christian religion' at 2.5 per cent.[127] In the same year, Brandeis University's American Jewish Population Project estimated the US Jewish population at 7.2 million,[128] and according to the Pew Research Center, the US Muslim population is approximately 3.45 million.[129] According to the SC, there are approximately 500,000 Sikhs in the US.[130] Therefore, it can be assumed that if American Sikhs had a similar population to Jews and Muslim in the US, hate crime incidents against Sikhs would be more prevalent.

Moreover, there remains concern that these figures may not capture all crimes, and underreporting remains a significant issue. For example, a vicious assault on an elderly Sikh in California in the summer of 2018 was categorized by the police as an 'attempted robbery', rather than a hate crime.[131] The high-profile murder of Srinivas Kuchibotla, a 32-year-old Indian engineer who was shot dead after being called a 'terrorist',[132] was missing from the FBI data, despite the gunman pleading to federal hate crime charges. Moreover, the FBI did not include a single hate crime murder in the state of Kansas for 2017.[133]

Reflecting on the FBI figures, the SC said:

> Due to systemic underreporting, there remains a significant gap between FBI hate crime data and the reality on the ground for Sikhs and other minority communities across the United States. According to a Bureau of Justice Statistics 2017 report, Americans experienced an average of 250,000 hate crimes per year from 2004–2015.[134]

They added, 'since the run up to the 2016 presidential election, the organization has averaged one hate-related legal intake every month and estimates that since 2001, Sikhs remain hundreds of times more likely to experience hate crimes than the average American'.[135] The SC's Legal Director Amrith Kaur stressed the importance of federal hate crime reporting becoming a mandatory requirement for all law enforcement agencies in order to address underreporting.

Sikh Americans have proven themselves to be a highly organized and an effective force for change. The acute backlash post-9/11 spawned the beginnings of a new generation of leadership, outside the traditional *gurdwara* setting. From filmmakers and writers through to academics, these young Sikhs, like Valarie Kaur and Professor Simran Jeet Singh (to name just two) were articulate, eloquent, media savvy and able to positively influence policy in the corridors of power, for the betterment of the community. In comparison with this significant effort and progress, British Sikhs have been less strategically effective, innovative and visionary than their American co-religionists. Perhaps this is partly because the backlash in Britain in the immediate aftermath of 9/11 was not as acute, and Sikhs were not being murdered like those in the US.[136]

The British Sikh experience in context

Whilst the British Sikh experience has been problematic, British Sikhs have fared better in the years after 9/11 compared to their American co-religionists, perhaps because they are often associated with the British Armed Forces, but also because of prominent turban-wearing Sikhs in the public eye. This includes individuals like the Glaswegian journalist/comedian Hardeep Singh Kohli; Sir Rabinder Singh, a Court of Appeal judge, and the first turbaned Sikh to enter the House of Lords; Lord Indarjit Singh, who has been a regular presenter on BBC Radio 4's *Thought for the Day*, as well as a founder member of the Interfaith Network for the United Kingdom; and Lord Suri in the House of Lords. In 2012, news of the first turbaned Sikh soldier, Jatinderpal Singh Bhullar, guarding Buckingham Palace was by and large positively received, reinforcing the position of Sikhs in the nation's collective consciousness as 'loyal' subjects to Queen and country. In line with Sikh tradition, Bhullar maintained his turban in place of the traditional bearskin for the Queen's guards.[137]

Two years later in 2014, the United Kingdom Punjab Heritage Association launched an exhibition *Empire, Faith & War: The Sikhs and World War One* in the Brunei Gallery at the School of Oriental and African Studies. Over 23,500 attended the exhibition[138] and there was significant coverage in the mainstream media. These kinds of initiatives have not just reminded the public of the Sikh contribution to the British Armed Forces, but also helped improve levels of religious literacy. Moreover, the armed forces have been commemorating 'Saraghari Day', to mark the sacrifice of 21 Sikhs who fought and died in a battle defending British interests in 1897 against 10,000 Afghan tribesmen.[139] Sikh military prowess, as defined by the posthumously decorated men of Saraghari, like the incredible contribution of Gurkhas to the British Army past and present, is considered by some as part of Britain's story.

As previously discussed, incidents where Sikhs have been targeted have on occasion been described as 'mistaken identity' attacks, and this description has been subject of some criticism by luminaries like Valarie Kaur.[140] The suggestion has been that if the protagonists had known their victim was Sikh rather than Muslim, they would not have targeted them. The authors see good reason to be critical of this definition because in many cases attackers do not really care whom they are targeting, difference being all that matters. However, as discussed, there are clear examples of individuals being attacked based on the assumption they are Islamic, making this disputed terminology in those specific instances perhaps more acceptable.

The authors believe in such instances that the terminology is therefore valid and innocuous in describing the motivation behind some attacks. After the 7/7 London bombings, young Sikhs travelling on London underground started wearing T-shirts that read, 'Don't Freak, I'm a Sikh', which speaks directly to the 'mistaken identity' issue. Katy Sian notes that the T-Shirt 'ironically illustrates the shared fate of both Muslims and Sikhs. The war on terror and the attendant panics seem to necessitate that both communities wear T-shirts that try in a humorous to allay the anxieties of the general population.'[141] T-shirts were also emblazoned with the words 'Don't panic, I'm not Islamic', but it is not clear if this was the initiative of young Sikhs, or others groups caught up in the negative reverberations of Islamism. Most recently there was a BBC drama, *The Informer*, in which following news of a terror attack, a father tells his son (a second-generation Muslim Pakistani), 'Don't be brave; tell them you're a Hindu', and 'Don't freak; I'm a Sikh'.[142]

Similarly, to correct misperceptions, a synonymous 2014 video by British fashion blogger Pardeep Singh Bahra, of Singh Street Style, attempted to dispel ignorance about the turban. It asks the audience to view the turban as a 'symbol against oppression'.[143] At the time of writing, the video had over 236,000 views.

With the emergence ISIS, the language of bigotry continued to evolve. The year 2016 saw the conviction for racially aggravated harassment of an ex-soldier for ten months for calling his Sikh neighbours 'ISIS bitches'. The court heard how Christopher Blurton would abuse his victims by hurling abuse from his garden and residence. This included the slurs, 'dirty Pakis', 'ISIS slags' and the threat that he would 'burn the holy Koran' and 'slice them up'.[144] Aside from the fact that the victims here were Sikh women, this, like the Mellhi and Dhanda cases, is yet another example where ethnicity is seemingly conflated with religiosity. All these hate crimes, be they violent attacks, slurs, graffiti or harassment, demonstrate how everyday prejudice has been shaped with global events reported on the 24-hour news cycle.

It is clear that the ripple effects of major world events relating to the activities of extremist Muslims are causing negative reverberations for Sikhs in the West. Jagdeesh Singh was attacked because of a hostage crisis involving a man held captive over two and a half thousands miles away in Iraq; Sikhs in Birmingham (and across the UK) were called 'bin Laden' after the twin towers attack, a pig's head being thrown in a former minister's driveway and Sikh women labelled 'ISIS bitches', all symptomatic of a new and troubling trend. As within the US, Sikhs in the UK have reacted to the backlash in a variety of ways, which can range from no longer wearing the turban, i.e. cutting their hair[145] or no longer wearing the turban in public. Some have chosen to style hair in a baseball cap,[146] which would stop the derogatory phrases that they were used to.

There is no British equivalent to the SALDEF 'turban myths' survey. However, all the incidents above highlight a serious lack of religious literacy amongst a subsection of the British public, who perceive all Muslims problematic, and those who resemble them, to be fair game for harassment, physical assault or verbal abuse. Notably, those that are mistaken for Muslims also include Britain's bearded hipsters, who have absurdly been mistaken for ISIS militants and physically attacked.[147] A conflation of religious symbols has also impacted white, black, Hispanic and other converts to Sikh tradition who wear turbans and beards, like members of the New Religious Movement founded by

Yogi Bhajan – Healthy, Happy, Holy Organization, or 3HO. Doris Jacobsh from the University of Waterloo, Ontario, notes:

> The tragic events of 9/11 have also had an effect on 3HO/Sikh Dharma relations with Punjabi American Sikhs. Those Sikhs who adhere to the outwards manifestation of Sikh identity, namely, the keeping of uncut hair and the accompanying turban, were particularly affected by the events of 9/11.[148]

It is short-sighted, therefore, to equate 'Islamophobia' in these instances with 'racism' per se, as this phenomenon is primarily related more to the conflation of religious symbols.Although the focus here is the post-9/11 backlash, the authors are cognizant of how Sikhs themselves (like other non-Muslims) are also fair game for Islamists, who consider all non-Muslims *kaffirs* or infidels. The most frightening example in recent years is the bombing of a Sikh temple by ISIS-influenced teenagers in Essen, Germany.[149]

Conclusion

The racism that Sikhs faced in the 1960s/1970s has evolved. The emergence of anti-Islam and anti-sharia politics by fringe groups in Britain like the EDL has been brought into the mainstream by political parties like UKIP, and the narrative has been problematic not only for Britain's Muslim community, but also those that one can describe as the 'Muslim-looking other'. This new wave of prejudice has been particularly problematic for Sikhs.

Sikhs have always faced marginalization and discrimination since arriving in Britain. During their history, they have stood up for their religious rights and been provided concessions under British law to maintain their religious symbols. There have been various iterations of discrimination since the arrival of the first set of migrants from the Indian subcontinent. In the 1960s far-right nationalist like the NF would have made no distinction between 'pakis' – be they Sikhs, Hindus or Muslims. However, since 9/11 Sikhs, like Muslims, have faced a new phase of hostility directed at them driven by suspicion and fear of aspects of Islam, and the behaviour of extremist Muslims. Sikhs who have maintained their religious identity with the *dastaar* and beard have been particularly vulnerable from 'mistaken identity' attacks, where they have been confused with Muslim extremists like Osama bin Laden and Ayman al-Zawahiri. Sikhs who do not wear outward symbols of their faith have also been targeted, due to what the authors describe as the *racialization of Islamophobia*. British Sikhs have had a serious problem but have fared better than their American co-religionists.

Despite a growing hostility to the 'Muslim-looking other', the British Sikh story has been essentially marginalized to the fringes of the broader Islamophobia debate. It is therefore unsurprising that Sikhs have been referred to as the 'invisible' victims of anti-Muslim hate. One would have expected the British authorities to have addressed the targeting of religious minorities in hate crime-related incidents with parity. However, as the authors discuss in Chapter 3, this has not been the case. Despite the attempted beheading of Dr Sarandev Singh Bhambra in 2015, the British government remarkably failed to acknowledge, let alone address, the Sikh issue.

Notes

1 The images of first bin Laden, followed by the Taliban, in the mainstream media further reinforced the association of beards and turbans with the 'enemy' and 'terrorism' per se. This in turn, fuelled hostility towards British Sikhs, who comprise the majority of turban wearers in Britain. Not many Muslim men wear turbans in Britain.
2 Hopkins et al., 'Encountering misrecognition'.
3 Ibid.
4 Awan and Zempi, *Islamophobia: Lived Experiences*.
5 I. Awan (2017). 'The non-Muslims experiencing Islamophobic attacks' *Newstatesman*. [online] Available at: www.newstatesman.com/politics/staggers/2017/10/non-muslims-experiencing-islamophobic-attacks [Accessed 17 December 2017].
6 E. Saner (2012). 'Why are Sikhs targeted by anti-Muslim extremists?' The *Guardian*. [online] Available at: www.theguardian.com/world/2012/aug/08/sikhs-targeted-anti-muslim-extremists [Accessed 8 October 2017].
7 F. Dawood (2016). 'Ugandan Asians dominate economy after exile'. BBC News. [online] Available at: www.bbc.co.uk/news/world-africa-36132151 [Accessed 11 October 2017].
8 *India Today* (2017). '32 years of Indira Gandhi assassination, anti-Sikh riots: All you need to know'. [online] Available at: http://indiatoday.intoday.in/story/indira-gandhi-assassination-death-anniversary-things-to-know-operation-blue-star/1/799136.html [Accessed 16 October 2017].
9 M. Abbott (2014). 'The Afghan Sikhs fleeing to the UK'. BBC News [online] Available at: www.bbc.co.uk/news/uk-england-29062770 [Accessed 8 October 2017].
10 BBC News (2012). 'Ugandan Asians advert "foolish"'. [online] Available at: www.bbc.co.uk/news/uk-england-leicestershire-19165216 [Accessed 5 January 2018].
11 *The Guardian* (2001). G2: 'Leicester's multicultural success'. [online] Available at: www.theguardian.com/uk/2001/jan/01/britishidentity.features11 [Accessed 5 January 2018].
12 Sidhu and Gohil, *Civil Rights in Wartime*.
13 *The Telegraph* (2007). 'Enoch Powell's "Rivers of Blood" speech'. [online] Available at: www.telegraph.co.uk/comment/3643823/Enoch-Powells-Rivers-of-Blood-speech.html [Accessed 8 January 2018]. Also see C. Schofield (2013). *Enoch Powell and the making of postcolonial Britain*. Cambridge: Cambridge University Press.
14 Ibid.
15 S. Heffer (2015). 'Paris is tragic proof that Enoch Powell was right about threats to our country'. *The Telegraph*. [online] Available at: www.telegraph.co.uk/news/uknews/terrorism-in-the-uk/12009577/Paris-is-tragic-proof-that-Enoch-Powell-was-right-about-threats-to-our-country.html [Accessed 6 October 2017].
16 C. Booker (2015). 'Enoch Powell and Tony Benn were right on Europe – it was a great deception'. *The Telegraph*. [online]. Available at: www.telegraph.co.uk/comment/11673377/Enoch-Powell-and-Tony-Benn-were-right-on-Europe-it-was-a-great-deception.html [Accessed 6 October 2017].
17 Ibid.
18 BBC News (2005). 'Sikh busmen win turban fight'. [online] Available at: http://news.bbc.co.uk/onthisday/hi/dates/stories/april/9/newsid_2523000/2523691.stm [Accessed 8 October 2017].
19 D. S. Tatla (2014) *The Sikh Diaspora*, London: Taylor & Francis.

20 Singh and Tatla, *Sikhs in Britain*.
21 Geoffrey Bindman QC (2008). 'The right to wear a turban'. *New Law Journal*. [online] Available at: www.newlawjournal.co.uk/content/right-wear-turban [Accessed 15 October 2017].
22 A. Gillan (2008). '"Proud to be Welsh and a Sikh". Schoolgirl wins court battle to wear religious bangle'. *The Guardian*. [online] Available at: www.theguardian.com/education/2008/July/30/schools.religion [Accessed 24 September 2018].
23 BBC News (2015). 'The pool of blood that changed my life'. [online] Available at: www.bbc.co.uk/news/magazine-33725217 [Accessed 8 October 2017].
24 Although there were a series of other high-profile race riots involving the Afro-Caribbean community, in particular Brixton (1981), for the purposes of this work the focus is on those involving Sikhs.
25 See 'Young Rebels – The Story of the Southall Youth Movement'. Available at: www.youtube.com/watch?v=OGWX233kHPg [Accessed 15 January 2019].
26 BBC News (2017). 'The immigrants "bussed" out to school'. [online] Available at: www.bbc.co.uk/news/uk-england-leeds-38689839 [Accessed 5 January 2018].
27 Olivier Esteves (2018). *The 'Desegregation' of English Schools: Bussing, Race and Urban Space, 1960s–80s*. Manchester: Manchester University Press. See respectively B. Purewal (no date). 'Indian Workers' Association (Southall): 60 years of struggles and achievements 1956–2016'. [online] www.iwasouthall.org.uk/writing.html [Accessed 20 October 2018]; 'Young Rebels – The Story of the Southall Youth Movement'. www.youtube.com/watch?v=OGWX233kHPg [Accessed 15 January 2019] and B. Purewal (2014). *Young Rebels: The Story of the Southall Youth Movement*. Booklet accompanying DVD.
28 Purewal, *Young Rebels*.
29 Ibid., p. 6.
30 UK Parliament (2017). Race Relations Act 1965. [online] Available at: www.parliament.uk/about/living-heritage/transformingsociety/private-lives/relationships/collections1/race-relations-act-1965/race-relations-act-1965/ [Accessed 8 October 2017].
31 Ibid.
32 Ibid.
33 National Archives (2010). Equality Act 2010. [online] Available at: www.legislation.gov.uk/ukpga/2010/15/section/9 [Accessed 8 October 2017].
34 P. Lewis (2010). 'Blair Peach killed by police at 1979 protest, Met report finds'. *The Guardian*. [online] Available at: www.theguardian.com/uk/2010/apr/27/blair-peach-killed-police-met-report [Accessed 8 October 2017].
35 YouTube (2009). Nick Griffin – Sikhs leave UK & Everybody is Happy. [online] Available at: www.youtube.com/watch?v=9gwFGeYF05E [Accessed 8 October 2017].
36 H. Siddique (2010). 'BNP would offer non-white Britons £50,000 to leave UK, says Nick Griffin'. *The Guardian*. [online] Available at: www.theguardian.com/politics/2010/apr/29/bnp-non-white-britons-resettlement-grants [Accessed 8 October 2017].
37 T. Wigmore (2016). 'What killed the BNP?' *Newstatesman*. [online] Available at: www.newstatesman.com/politics/staggers/2016/01/what-killed-bnp [Accessed 8 October 2017].
38 H. Siddique (2009). 'Sikh campaigner for BNP set to become party's first non-white member'. *The Guardian*. [online] Available at: www.theguardian.com/politics/2009/nov/20/sikh-man-bnp-member [Accessed 12 January 2018].
39 D. Casciani (2014). 'Who are the English Defence League?' BBC News. [online] Available at: http://newsbbc.co.uk/1/hi/8250017.stm [Accessed 8 October 2017].
40 ONS (2015). 'How religion has changed in England and Wales'. Visual.ONS. [online] Available at: https://visual.ons.gov.uk/2011-census-religion/ [Accessed 5 January 2018].

41 Ibid.
42 M. Howarth (2014). 'A child in Birmingham is now more likely to be a Muslim than Christian'. *Mail Online*. [online] Available at: www.dailymail.co.uk/news/article-2755654/The-changing-face-Britain-A-child-Birmingham-likely-Muslim-Christian.html [Accessed 5 January 2018].
43 O. Rudgard (2017). 'Muslim population of the UK could triple to 13m following "record" influx'. *The Telegraph*. [online] Available at: www.telegraph.co.uk/news/2017/11/29/muslim-population-uk-could-triple-13m-following-record-influx/ [Accessed 11 July. 2018].
44 H. Collier (2017). 'Activists clash with police as EDL and anti-fascist groups stage demos'. *Evening Standard*. [online] Available at: www.standard.co.uk/news/london/activists-clash-with-police-as-edl-and-antifascist-groups-stage-rival-protests-a3572441.html [Accessed 8 October 2017].
45 A. Gilligan (2013). 'Anti-fascists fuel the fire of hate'. *The Telegraph*. [online] Available at: www.telegraph.co.uk/journalists/andrew-gilligan/10122496/Anti-fascists-fuel-the-fire-of-hate.html [Accessed 19 October 2017].
46 F. Hamilton (2013). 'EDL chief Tommy Robinson quits after "neo Nazi hijack of group"'. *The Times*. [online] Available at: www.thetimes.co.uk/article/edl-chief-tommy-robinson-quits-after-neo-nazi-hijack-of-group-wgzzxthkxr3 [Accessed 8 October 2017].
47 Rebel Media (2017). Tommy Robinson, Shillman Fellow. [online] Available at: www.therebel.media/tommy_robinson [Accessed 8 October 2017].
48 BBC News (2018). 'Tommy Robinson banned from Twitter'. [online] Available at: www.bbc.co.uk/news/technology-43572168 [Accessed 14 September 2018].
49 Twitter (2017). Tommy Robinson on Twitter. [online] Available at: https://twitter.com/trobinsonnewera/status/426101533177307137 [Accessed 8 October 2017].
50 YouTube (2011). Guramit Singh of the EDL on BBC Look East discussing the upcoming Luton Demo on Feb 5th 2011. [online] Available at: www.youtube.com/watch?v=oOlzF05BzIQ [Accessed 8 October 2017].
51 Facebook (2017). English Defence League Sikh Division – EDL. [online] Available at: https://en-gb.facebook.com/EDLSikhs/ [Accessed 8 October 2017].
52 YouTube (2017). Tommy Robinson: Sikhs stand with Manchester bombing victims. [online] Available at: www.youtube.com/watch?v=qITyUwl8LxU [Accessed 8 October 2017].
53 YouTube (2013). Tommy Robinson praises Sikhs at Lee Rigby protest at Downing Street. [online] Available at: www.youtube.com/watch?v=Mf_hgM6SXXk [Accessed 7 January 2018].
54 J. Jhutti-Johal (2017). 'The problems and challenges going forward'. [online] Available at: https://blog.bham.ac.uk/cpur/2017/06/03/the-problems-and-challenges-going-forward [Accessed 16 October 2017]. For more information about the tensions between Sikhs and Muslims see K. P. Sian (2013). *Unsettling Sikh and Muslim Conflict: Mistaken Identities, Forced Conversions, and Postcolonial Formations*. Lanham, MD: Lexington Books.
55 Ibid.
56 Twitter (2017). Tommy Robinson on Twitter. [online] Available at: https://twitter.com/trobinsonnewera/status/933349630380859393 [Accessed 27 December 2017].
57 Facebook (2017). Britain First. [online] Available at: www.facebook.com/OfficialBritainFirst/photos/pb.300455573433044.-2207520000.1506699839./1460051730806750/ ?type=3&theater [Accessed 8 October 2017].
58 L. Dearden (2018). 'Britain First leaders jailed for anti-Muslim hate crime'. *The Independent*. [online] Available at: www.independent.co.uk/news/uk/crime/paul-golding-jayda-fransen-britain-first-leaders-guilty-religious-muslim-hate-crime-a8244161.html [Accessed 14 April 2018].

59 C. Chaplain (2017). 'Thousands of football fans gather for anti-extremism march'. *Evening Standard*. [online] Available at: www.standard.co.uk/news/london/football-lads-association-march-thousands-gather-in-central-london-in-antiextremism-protest-a3652981.html [Accessed 8 October 2017].

60 YouTube (2017). Mohan Singh Speaks Truth to!!HUGE!! crowd at the FOOTBALL LADS ALLIANCE. [online] Available at: www.youtube.com/watch?v=GZhyTOtElfg [Accessed 11 January 2018].

61 R. Mason (2015). 'Nigel Farage: British Muslim "fifth column" fuels fear of immigration'. [online] *The Guardian*. Available at: www.theguardian.com/politics/2015/mar/12/nigel-farag-british-muslim-fifth-column-fuels-immigration-fear-ukip [Accessed 8 October 2017].

62 Twitter (2017). For Britain (@ForBritainParty) on Twitter. [online] Available at: https://twitter.com/ForBritainParty [Accessed 16 October 2017].

63 P. Walker (2018). 'Gerard Batten drags Ukip further right with harsh anti-Islam agenda'. *The Guardian*. [online] Available at: www.theguardian.com/politics/2018/sep/21/gerard-batten-drags-ukip-further-right-with-harsh-anti-islam-agenda [Accessed 23 September 2018].

64 Sky News (2018). 'UKIP leader Gerard Batten links sexual grooming of girls to Islam'. [online] Available at: https://news.sky.com/story/ukip-leader-gerard-batten-links-sexual-grooming-of-girls-to-islam-11503909 [Accessed 23 September 2018].

65 BBC News (2010). 'Troop protest demonstrator denies Luton attack racist'. [online] Available at: http://news.bbc.co.uk/1/hi/england/beds/bucks/herts/8549767.stm [Accessed 8 October 2017].

66 C. Allen (2016). *Islamophobia*. London: Routledge.

67 Ibid.

68 BBC News (2001). 'Turbans and beards leave Sikhs vulnerable'. [online] Available at: http://news.bbc.co.uk/1/hi/england/1565146.stm [Accessed 8 October 2017].

69 *Financial Times* (2004). 'UK hostage Kenneth Bigley beheaded in Iraq'. [online] Available at: www.ft.com/content/aaa83c5a-192c-11d9-80e1-00000e2511c8 [Accessed 8 October 2017].

70 House of Commons, Select Committee on Home Affairs (2004). Minutes of Evidence. 'Examination of Witnesses (Questions 100–119)'. [online] Available at: https://publications.parliament.uk/pa/cm200405/cmselect/cmhaff/165/4111602.htm [Accessed 8 October 2017].

71 *Coventry Telegraph* (2004). 'Racist thugs attack dad'. [online] Available at: www.coventrytelegraph.net/news/coventry-news/racist-thugs-attack-dad-3143522 [Accessed 8 October 2017].

72 *Irish Examiner* (2017). 'Stabbed Sikh is blamed for attacks'. [online] Available at: www.irishexaminer.com/archives/2005/0715/ireland/stabbed-sikh-is-blamed-for-attacksbr-597560583.html [Accessed 10 October 2017].

73 Sidhu and Gohil, *Civil Rights in Wartime*.

74 S. Paterson (2015). '"Dangerous racist" inspired by Jihadi John who tried to behead a Sikh dentist in Tesco in revenge for Lee Rigby's murder is jailed for life'. *The Daily Mail*. [online] Available at: www.dailymail.co.uk/news/article-3230910/Dangerous-racist-inspired-Jihadi-John-tried-behead-Sikh-dentist-Tesco-revenge-Lee-Rigby-s-murder-jailed-life.html [Accessed 8 October 2017].

75 BBC News (2015). 'Life term for Rigby revenge attacker'. [online] Available at: www.bbc.co.uk/news/uk-wales-north-east-wales-34218184 [Accessed 8 October 2017].

76 Ibid.

77 Ibid.

78 E. Roberts (2015). '"An act of terror": Family of dentist attacked by machete-wielding man speak out'. *Wales Online*. [online] Available at: www.walesonline.co.uk/news/wales-news/an-act-terror-sikh-family-9528045 [Accessed 8 October 2017].

79 Network of Sikh Organisations (2015). 'Network of Sikh Organisations pushes BBC for on-air correction'. [online] Available at: http://nsouk.co.uk/network-of-sikh-organisations-pushes-bbc-for-on-air-correction/ [Accessed 8 October 2017].

80 H. Singh (2015). 'UK Sikhs remain invisible victims of "anti-Muslim" hate crime'. *International Business Times UK*. [online] Available at: www.ibtimes.co.uk/uk-sikhs-remain-invisible-victims-anti-muslim-hate-crime-1510588 [Accessed 25 November 2017].

81 S. Kern (2015). '"Britain Is the Enemy of Islam": One month of Islam in Britain'. Gatestone Institute. [online] Available at: www.gatestoneinstitute.org/5261/britain-enemy-islam [Accessed 8 October 2017].

82 Facebook page. 'Zak Ali'. On file.

83 Home Office (2016). 'National Action becomes first extreme right-wing group to be banned in UK'. GOV.UK. [online] Available at: www.gov.uk/government/news/national-action-becomes-first-extreme-right-wing-group-to-be-banned-in-uk [Accessed 8 October 2017].

84 The authors have had access to and have read a police statement (anonymous source) given by a Sikh victim regarding a complaint of racially aggravated harassment outside a London nightclub on 7 February 2015.

85 J. Staufenberg (2015). 'When a bouncer called this Sikh man a terrorist he had an inspiring response'. *The Independent*. [online] Available at: www.independent.co.uk/news/world/europe/british-sikh-punched-and-called-a-terrorist-by-polish-club-bouncer-a6760411.html [Accessed 8 October 2017].

86 M. Day (2015). 'Polish police tell British Sikh man "what do you expect after Paris attacks" after nightclub beating'. *The Telegraph*. [online] Available at: www.telegraph.co.uk/news/worldnews/europe/poland/12029627/Polish-police-tell-British-Sikh-man-what-do-you-expect-after-Paris-attacks-after-nightclub-beating.html [Accessed 8 October 2017].

87 YouTube (2017). Arsenal 2 Man City 2: We Need To Bring David Dein Back! [online] Available at: www.youtube.com/watch?v=Sr0pkjf0arc [Accessed 8 October 2017].

88 Sikhsindia.blogspot.co.uk (2009). 'Our shameful treatment of Britain's Sikh saviours'. [online] Available at: http://sikhsindia.blogspot.co.uk/2009/08/our-shameful-treatment-of-britains-sikh.html [Accessed 8 October 2017].

89 YouTube (2015). 80 year old Sikh man assaulted in Coventry UK by drunk woman DIES. [online] Available at: www.youtube.com/watch?v=v2XrCsoW-UE [Accessed 14 May 2019].

90 M. Molloy (2014). 'Coral Millerchip: Woman jailed for Coventry attack on Joginder Singh'. *Metro News*. [online] Available at: https://metro.co.uk/2014/05/10/coral-millerchip-woman-jailed-for-sickening-attack-on-frail-pensioner-in-coventry-4723259/ [Accessed 8 October 2017].

91 ITV News (2014). 'Sikh taxi driver had turban ripped off and burnt'. [online] Available at: www.itv.com/news/westcountry/story/2014-12-02/sikh-taxi-driver-had-turban-ripped-off-and-burnt/ [Accessed 8 October 2017].

92 *Huffington Post* (2014). 'Rapper posts racist message on Instagram'. [online] Available at: www.huffingtonpost.com/2014/03/28/joe-budden-sikh-instagram_n_5051917.html [Accessed 8 October 2017].

93 J. Jhutti-Johal (2017). 'Evidence for the Youth Select Committee – racist and religious discrimination from a Sikh perspective'. Byc.org.uk. [online] Available at: www.byc.org.uk/wp-content/uploads/2016/09/050-Jagbir-Jhutti-Johal.pdf [Accessed 8 October 2017].

94 *The Daily Caller* (2017). 'Cosmopolitan mag confuses a Sikh Cab driver for a Muslim'. [online] Available at: http://dailycaller.com/2017/05/23/cosmopolitan-mag-confuses-a-sikh-cab-driver-for-a-muslim/ [Accessed 8 October 2017].

95 Twitter (2016). Manpreet Mellhi on Twitter. [online] Available at: https://twitter.com/manpreetmellhi/status/797467133710049280 [Accessed 8 October 2017].

96   H. Singh (2015). 'Sikh lives matter in Britain too – whether Sikh or Muslim, racists don't discriminate'. *The Telegraph* [online] Available at: www.telegraph.co.uk/news/religion/11410809/Sikh-lives-matter-in-Britain-too-whether-Sikh-or-Muslim-racists-dont-discriminate.html [Accessed 9 October 2017].

97   P. Dhanda (2015). *My Political Race*. London: Biteback Publishing. [online] Available at: www.bitebackpublishing.com/books/my-political-race [Accessed 12 December 2017].

98   F. Perraudin (2018). 'Man arrested over fires at mosque and Sikh temple in Leeds'. *The Guardian*. [online] Available at: www.theguardian.com/uk-news/2018/jun/06/man-arrested-over-fires-at-mosque-and-sikh-temple-in-leeds [Accessed 11 July. 2018].

99   A. Watson (2018). 'Man arrested following firebomb attack on Leith Sikh temple'. *Edinburgh Evening News*. [online] Available at: www.edinburghnews.scotsman.com/news/crime/man-arrested-following-firebomb-attack-on-leith-sikh-temple-1-4791315 [Accessed 31 August 2018].

100   Blackburn, 'Yobs spray "die Muslims die" in graffiti'.

101   T. Stewart-Robertson (2015). 'Glasgow Sikh Gurdwara remains defiant after attack with sick Islamophobic graffiti and Nazi swastika'. *Daily Record*. [online] Available at: www.dailyrecord.co.uk/news/local-news/glasgow-sikh-gurdwara-remains-defiant-5512593 [Accessed 8 October 2017].

102   Saner, 'Why are Sikhs targeted'.

103   Ibid.

104   In 2016, a 21-year-old man was charged in Los Angeles, US, for spraying anti-ISIS graffiti on a *gurdwara*. This act of vandalism came in the aftermath of the San Barnardino shooting. In September 2017 a *gurdwara* in Los Angeles was vandalized with hateful messages that included one calling for the 'nuking' of Sikhs.

105   H. Singh (2016). 'It's time the Government ended its silence on Sikh hate crime victims'. *Coffee House*. [online] Available at: https://blogs.spectator.co.uk/2016/10/time-government-ended-silence-sikh-hate-crime-victims/ [Accessed 8 October 2017].

106   B. Daniel (2012). 'For Sikhs turban is a proud symbol and a target'. *The Washington Post*. [online] Available at: www.washingtonpost.com/national/on-faith/for-sikhs-turban-is-a-proud-symbol-_-and-a-target/2012/08/06/95d492aa-e012-11e1-8d48-2b1243f34c85_story.html?noredirect=on&utm_term=.365d7dd5eed6 [Accessed 15 October 2017].

107   M. Hughes (2012). 'Sikh temple massacre gunman was "white supremacist" Wade Michael Page'. *The Telegraph*. [online] Available at: www.telegraph.co.uk/news/worldnews/northamerica/usa/9457007/Sikh-temple-massacre-gunman-was-white-supremacist-Wade-Michael-Page.html [Accessed 8 October 2017].

108   M. Sidell (2013). 'GAP slams racist graffiti after ad featuring Sikh jewelry designer Waris Ahluwalia is vandalized with anti-Muslim slurs'. *The Daily Mail*. [online] Available at: www.dailymail.co.uk/femail/article-2513525/Gap-slams-racist-graffiti-ad-featuring-Sikh-Waris-Ahluwalia-vandalized.html [Accessed 5 January 2018].

109   *The Telegraph* (2012). 'Mitt Romney confuses "Sikh" with "sheikh" while paying tribute to Wisconsin temple shootings'. [online] Available at: www.telegraph.co.uk/news/worldnews/mitt-romney/9461305/Mitt-Romney-confuses-Sikh-with-sheikh-while-paying-tribute-to-Wisconsin-temple-shootings.html [Accessed 8 October 2017].

110   V. Kaur (2012). 'US military, open your doors to Sikhs'. [online] Available at: http://valariekaur.com/2012/08/the-washington-post-u-s-military-open-your-doors-to-sikhs/ [Accessed 8 October 2017].

111   Saldef.org (2013). 'Turban myths'. [online] Available at: http://saldef.org/policy-research/turban-myths/ [Accessed 8 October 2017].

112   F. Kai-Hwa Wang (2016). '15 years after 9/11 founding, the Sikh Coalition builds a "path forward"'. NBC News. [online] Available at: www.nbcnews.com/news/asian-america/15-years-after-9-11-founding-sikh-coalition-builds-path-n645646 [Accessed 15 September 2018].

113 Sikh Coalition (2014). '"Go home, terrorist": A report on the bullying of Sikh American school children.' [online] Available at: www.sikhcoalition.org/resources/go-home-terrorist-a-report-on-the-bullying-of-sikh-american-school-children/ [Accessed 15 September 2018].

114 Sikh Coalition (2016). 'Say no to bullying: What can Sikh youth do?' [online] Available at: www.sikhcoalition.org/resources/say-no-to-bullying-national-pamphlet/ [Accessed 15 September 2018].

115 Sikh Coalition (2014). National Report on School Bullying Released in Congress. [online] Available at: www.sikhcoalition.org/blog/2014/national-report-on-school-bullying-released-in-congress/ [Accessed 15 September 2018].

116 B. A. McGraw. (2016). *The Wiley-Blackwell Companion to Religion and Politics in the US*. West Sussex: Wiley-Blackwell, p. 436.

117 Kai-Hwa Wang, '15 years after 9/11 founding'.

118 Sikh Coalition (2016). The Sikh Project. [online] Available at: www.sikhcoalition.org/our-work/empowering-the-community/the-sikh-project/ [Accessed 15 September 2018].

119 H. Saini (2012). Testimony of Harpreet Singh Saini. Judiciary.senate.gov. [online] Available at: www.judiciary.senate.gov/imo/media/doc/9-19-12SainiTestimony.pdf [Accessed 22 September 2018].

120 H. Saini (2015). Opinion: 'There ought to be a law against hate'. *The New York Times*. [online]. Available at: www.nytimes.com/2015/07/27/opinion/there-ought-to-be-a-law-against-hate.html [Accessed 23 September 2018].

121 P. Mejia (2015). 'FBI to track hate crimes against Hindus, Sikhs, Arab Americans'. *Newsweek*. [online] Available at: www.newsweek.com/fbi-track-hate-crimes-against-hindus-sikhs-arab-americans-317563 [Accessed 15 September 2018].

122 *Hindustan Times* (2018). '"We Are Sikhs" campaign wins top US public relations award'. [online] Available at: www.hindustantimes.com/world-news/we-are-sikhs-campaign-wins-top-us-public-relations-award/story-gKKdUkb3AtzKct6ffMMs2H.html [Accessed 15 September 2018].

123 D. Iyer (2016). 'In our own words: Reflections on the 15th anniversary of 9/11'. *Colorlines*. [online] Available at: www.colorlines.com/articles/our-own-words-reflections-15th-anniversary-911 [Accessed 15 September 2018].

124 A. Ahmad (2015). 'Captain America dons a turban'. BBC News. [online] Available at: www.bbc.co.uk/news/magazine-30941638 [Accessed 15 September 2018].

125 Broadway World (2018). 'RAG HEAD Returns To The Stage'. [online] Available at: www.broadwayworld.com/los-angeles/article/RAG-HEAD-Returns-To-The-Stage-20180822 [Accessed 23 August 2018].

126 Federal Bureau of Investigation (2018). 2017 'Hate crime statistics'. [online] Available at: https://ucr.fbi.gov/hate-crime/2017 [Accessed 14 November 2018].

127 Gallup (2016). 'Five key findings on religion in the US'. [online] Available at: https://news.gallup.com/poll/200186/five-key-findings-religion.aspx [Accessed 13 November 2018].

128 Brandeis University (2016). American Jewish Population Project. [online] Available at: http://ajpp.brandeis.edu/aboutestimates.php [Accessed 13 November 2018].

129 B. Mohamed (2018). 'A new estimate of US Muslim population'. Pew Research Center. [online] Available at: www.pewresearch.org/fact-tank/2018/01/03/new-estimates-show-u-s-muslim-population-continues-to-grow/ [Accessed 13 November 2018].

130 Sikh Coalition (2018). 'Sikhs implore action & accountability in response to new FBI hate crime stats'. [online] Available at: www.sikhcoalition.org/press-release/sikhs-implore-action-accountability-response-new-fbi-hate-crime-stats/ [Accessed 13 November 2018].

131 M. Haag (2018). 'Police chief's son charged in attack on Sikh man in California'. *The New York Times*. [online] Available at: www.nytimes.com/2018/08/09/us/sikh-man-attacked-california.html [Accessed 14 September 2018].

132 C. Fuchs (2018). 'Hate crimes spiked in 2017. Community advocates think there's even more'. NBC News. [online] Available at: www.nbcnews.com/news/amp/ncna938551 [Accessed 24 November 2018].

133 Ibid.

134 Sikh Coalition (2018). 'Sikhs implore action and accountability in response to new FBI Hate Crime stats'.

135 Ibid.

136 Whilst in Toronto for the Parliament of the World's Religions in November 2018, Hardeep Singh met Professor Simran Jeet Singh, Jaideep Singh, co-founder of SALDEF, Amrith Kaur, Legal Director of SC and other American Sikhs. It is clear from discussions that the challenges and environment that American Sikhs continue to face is different from the UK context. For example, American Sikhs have taken a robust approach by prosecuting hate crime and the SC has led in this regard. There also appear to be mixed views on the 'We Are Sikhs' campaign, and this may be in part related to (Democratic or Republican) political affiliation.

137 R. English (2012). 'Sikh soldier makes history as he guards Buckingham Palace wearing turban instead of traditional bearskin'. *Mail Online*. [online] Available at: www.dailymail.co.uk/news/article-2246410/Sikh-soldier-makes-history-guards-Buckingham-Palace-wearing-turban-instead-traditional-bearskin.html [Accessed 8 October 2017].

138 Empire, Faith & War: The Sikhs and World War One (2016). In conversation with the IWM. [online] Available at: www.empirefaithwar.com/blog-entries/harbakhsh-grewal-in-conversation-with-the-imperial-war-museum [Accessed 8 October 2017].

139 Ministry of Defence (2015). 'Armed Forces commemorate the Battle of Saragarhi'. GOV.UK. [online] Available at: www.gov.uk/government/news/armed-forces-commemorate-the-battle-of-saragarhi [Accessed 8 October 2017].

140 V. Kaur (2012). 'Two Sikh American activists: Let's retire "mistaken identity"'. OnFaith. [online] Available at: www.onfaith.co/onfaith/2012/08/10/two-sikh-american-activists-lets-retire-mistaken-identity/10590 [Accessed 8 October 2017].

141 Sian, 'Losing my religion'.

142 E. Cumming (2018). 'BBC One's "Informer" is as nonsensical as "Bodyguard" – episode one review'. *The Independent*. [online] Available at: www.independent.co.uk/arts-entertainment/tv/reviews/informer-bbc-episode-one-review-plot-cast-paddy-considine-bodyguard-a8586371.html [Accessed 18 October 2018].

143 YouTube (2014). Don't Freak, I'm Sikh. [online] Available at: www.youtube.com/watch?v=Bug3TrH3pWo [Accessed 8 October 2017].

144 T. Mann (2016). 'Christopher Blurton called his Sikh neighbours "ISIS slags" – jailed'. *Metro News*. [online] Available at: http://metro.co.uk/2016/09/18/ex-soldier-jailed-for-racially-abusing-sikh-neighbours-and-calling-them-isis-bitches-6135147/ [Accessed 8 October 2017].

145 Virendra Kalra noted how the verbal and physical attacks have made the community sanction their behaviour. Kalra, 'Locating the Sikh pagh'.

146 J. Puar and A. Rai (2002). 'Monster, terrorist, fag: The War on Terrorism and the production of docile patriots'. *Social Text*, 20(3), pp. 117–148.

147 Twitter (2015). The *Sunday Sport* on Twitter. [online] Available at: https://twitter.com/thesundaysport/status/670693059097686017?lang=en [Accessed 24 October 2015].

148 D. Jakobsh (2008). '3HO/Sikh Dharma of the Western Hemisphere: The forgotten new religious movement?' *Religion Compass*, 2(3), pp. 385–408.

149 H. Singh (2016). 'The Islamist war against Sikhs is arriving in Europe'. *Coffee House*. [online] Available at: https://blogs.spectator.co.uk/2016/09/islamist-war-sikhs-arriving-europe/ [Accessed 9 October 2017].

3   UK – do Sikhs count?

Introduction

Racism targeting Sikhs was experienced in the 1960s onwards, when immigrants from the Indian subcontinent (particularly the Commonwealth countries) came to settle in the UK to work. The events post-9/11 highlight how Sikhs remain victims of prejudice, but how it has evolved (alongside racism per se) into a phenomenon rising from an anti-Islam or anti-Muslim sentiment. Whilst it is evident that 'Islamophobia' is having an impact on Muslim communities, it must be equally acknowledged that it is also having an impact on those perceived to be Muslim – or 'the Muslim-looking other'.

The attempted beheading of Sikh dentist Dr Sarandev Singh Bhambra by a neo-Nazi influenced by 'Jihadi John' in January 2015 is one of the most egregious cases in Britain to date. This new wave of hatred towards the Sikh community has become increasingly ignored, evidenced by the government's 'Abrahamic-centric' policy approach in tackling religiously motivated hate, something that became apparent with the publication of the HO's four-year hate crime action plan 'Action against hate' (2016), which failed to address Dr Bhambra's case. In light of the evidence of attacks on Sikh individuals and places of worship this raises some legitimate questions for policymakers, journalists and legal professionals. Why is anti-Islam sentiment, which affects those perceived to be Muslim or the 'Muslim-looking other', ignored, and why does one of Britain's most visible minorities fail to feature in this important policy area? Why is hate crime not tackled even-handedly? The authors evaluate the reasons for Sikhs becoming subsumed and essentially marginalized within the broader Islamophobia debate, and how British Sikhs have responded to what has been a glaring policy blind spot.

Policy agenda

When one thinks of race hate crime monitoring and the policy agenda it is clear that it has been guided by historical events. The primary focus of influential British think tanks, the police, media and more importantly the British government itself, has been anti-Muslim and anti-Jewish hatred.

Anti-Semitism is often described as 'the oldest hatred', and Holocaust Memorial Day provides an annual reminder of the genocide committed by, amongst others, the Nazis. Although anti-Semitism has in the past been associated predominantly with the far right – groups like NA – in the current UK political climate it is a phenomenon also seen on the left as evidenced by the Labour Party. In 2016 the leader of the Labour Party Jeremy Corbyn launched the Chakrabarti inquiry.[1] Despite the inquiry, the controversy within the Labour Party continues, candidates like Nasreen Khan being dropped for offensive Facebook posts.[2]

Recent high-profile cases and convictions highlight the serious nature of modern-day anti-Semitism. In 2016, Joshua Bonehill-Paine was jailed at the Old Bailey for publishing anti-Semitic blogs directed at MP Luciana Berger.[3] International events like the war in Gaza in 2014 resulted in a sharp increase in reports of anti-Semitic incidents in the UK.[4] More troubling still, a 2017 survey by the Campaign against Anti-Semitism (hereinafter CAA) showed one-third of British Jews had considered leaving the UK in light of increasing anti-Semitism.[5] According to a CAA spokesperson, 2017 was 'likely to be the worst year on record for anti-Semitic crime'.[6] Jew hate comes not only from the far right and far left, but according to another survey, also from a minority within the British Muslim community.[7] The anti-Semitism crisis in the Labour Party hit a new high in 2018, with the intervention of the former Chief Rabbi, Lord Sachs, who accused the Labour leader of being an anti-Semite, which was dismissed by Labour as an 'absurd and offensive' charge.[8] This intervention came following Labour's refusal to adopt the International Holocaust Remembrance Alliance (hereinafter IHRA) definition of anti-Semitism.

The issues affecting British Jews exist outside the arena of mainstream politics. For example, there is a culture of anti-Semitism in a number of British University campuses. In 2018, in the realm of education, Judaism was left off a NUS survey of religions (six months after the same omission was made in a previous questionnaire), causing anger amongst Jewish students.[9] Former NUS leader Malia Bouattia was condemned by the Home Affairs Select Committee for referring to Birmingham University as a 'Zionist outpost'.[10]

Whilst the rise of anti-Semitism is due to factors including the politics of the Middle East and sympathies with the Palestinian cause from the hard left, anti-Muslim attacks have occurred due to a fear of 'the other' and retaliation for Islamic terror attacks on the West. Other factors however have also contributed to the Islamophobia narrative. These include the question around compatibility of Sharia law with British values, British-born *jihadists* joining ISIS, sexual 'grooming gangs' as in Rochdale and Rotherham, FGM, the migration problem particularly in light of the Syrian crisis, and the rhetoric of some UKIP politicians describing Islam as a 'death cult'.[11]

A study of views and attitudes amongst British Muslims was conducted in a 2016 ICM poll commissioned for a Channel 4 documentary, 'What British Muslims Really Think'. The extensive survey indicated that 86 per cent of British Muslims said they felt a strong sense of belonging to Britain. Moreover,

88 per cent suggested that Britain was a good place for Muslims to live and 78 per cent said they were keen to integrate into British life.[12] However, these more positive aspects were overshadowed with views on homosexuality, equality and blasphemy. For example, some of the worrying statistics from the extensive ICM poll include: 52 per cent of Britain's Muslims think homosexuality should be illegal, 39 per cent think a woman should always obey her husband, and 18 per cent sympathize with those who take part in violence against those who insult the prophet.[13]

These views are in conflict with the values espoused by Western liberalism, which champions gay rights, women's equality, and in Britain's case, abolition of ancient blasphemy laws, (an amendment was passed to the Criminal Justice and Immigration Act (2008), ruling out prosecutions for blasphemy and blasphemous libel in England and Wales).[14] Reflecting on some of the conservative views from the poll, the former chief of the EHRC Trevor Phillips, who presented the documentary, said, 'Everyone who has pinned their hopes on the rise of reforming and liberal British Muslim voices are in for a disappointment'. He went on, 'These voices are nowhere near as numerous as they need to be to make an impact.'[15]

This has meant that the Muslim community has had significant attention from government because of these negative attitudes shown up by PREVENT.[16] The community has also recognized that some of these beliefs and their consequences, which elicit fear in the general population, have strengthened anti-Muslim/anti-Islam sentiment amongst the far right, and have inevitably led to an increase in religiously motivated hate and Islamophobia in the UK. The negative perception of Islam has been the subject of significant speculation, research and media coverage. In a Pew study from 2017 on European attitudes towards Islam across ten countries, 28 per cent of British respondents (the lowest percentage) said they held an 'unfavorable view of Muslims' in their country, compared with 72 per cent in Hungary (the highest percentage), and 69 per cent (second highest) in Italy.[17] This is evidenced by the rise in hate crimes against Muslims in Britain ranging from non-violent incidents to violent crimes: from leaving a bacon sandwich outside a mosque,[18] to the 2017 Finsbury Park attack, which resulted in 11 worshippers injured and one dead.[19]

Anti-Muslim attacks on individuals are a real and serious problem. Whilst anti-Semitism is generally frowned upon, what is clear with Islamophobia is that it has become normalized and 'passed the dinner party test' or become socially acceptable to openly express prejudice against Muslims.[20]

It is also important to highlight that it is notably Muslim women with visible Islamic clothing like the *hijab* who are reportedly more likely to be victims of 'street level' anti-Muslim attacks.[21] This worrying and disturbing trend, however, is no different in the authors' view from the targeting of turbaned Sikhs, or attacks on orthodox Jews wearing the *kippah*, hats or other head coverings. It should also be noted that Sikh women, particularly initiated Sikh women who wear the turban or keep their hair covered at all times with a *dupatta/chunni* (long scarf), have been mistaken for being Muslim.

Government focus on Muslims and Jews

The government provides considerable apparatus and funding to Muslims and Jews in tackling religiously motivated hate crime. APPGs committed to specifically tackling Islamophobia[22] and anti-Semitism[23] have been established, with cross party support. There is an APPG on British Jews[24] and an APPG on British Muslims,[25] which address the issue of hate crime. There is also a cross-governmental Anti-Muslim Hatred Working Group, whose agenda priorities amongst others include 'tackling the far right and counter jihadists', 'anti-Muslim bullying in schools' 'Muslim literacy in the media' and a 'public transport awareness campaign to encourage reporting of anti-Muslim hatred incidents'.[26] This particular group works closely with ministers at the Ministry for Housing, Communities & Local Government (hereinafter MHCLG) and reports directly to them,[27] due to the government's serious concerns around the issue and its impact on the community. The government's concerns about potential attacks on Muslims was highlighted after the Finsbury Mosque attack when Prime Minister Theresa May promised to provide extra police resources to mosques in the run up to Eid.[28]

Alongside these APPGs the government has invested in research and reporting mechanisms for the Jewish and Muslim communities. For example, the Conservative–Liberal Democrat coalition government in 2012 helped launch Tell MAMA, the Muslim hate crime monitor, with £395,000 in initial start-up grant funding.[29] In 2013, the government decided not to renew funding for the group.[30] However, state funding appears to have been later reinstated, as Tell MAMA received a government grant of £182,000 for 2015–16,[31] whilst in the intervening period the Big Lottery fund provided them with £255,450,[32] over two years from October 2013. In December 2018, Baroness Burt of Solihull said the government had agreed to give Tell MAMA £2.5 million to 'help with its work in encouraging reporting of Islamophobic and anti-Muslim incidents and supporting victims'.[33]

The government had previously provided significant funding to projects dedicated to Islam. For example, MHCLG, as part of its Integration Projects and Work Streams, funded research to the sum of £76,000 for 'contextualising Islam'.[34] The organization behind Tell MAMA, Faith Matters, had previously received significant government funding for projects like 'Living Islam out Loud', 'Mosques Directory Compilation' and 'Caring for Converts'.[35]

At the same time, with reports of increasing hatred towards British Jewry, the government continued its prioritization of tackling anti-Semitism. This has translated into tangible results. In December 2016, the government announced it would formally adopt the IHRA working definition of anti-Semitism to 'take fresh steps in the fight in hatred against Jews'.[36] In the same year, the then Home Secretary Amber Rudd pledged £13.4 million for the protection of every Jewish college, school, nursery and synagogue in Britain.[37] The Community Security Trust (hereinafter CST), established in 1994, is a charity that protects British Jews and works with the HO. According to the centre-right think tank Policy

Exchange government, funding for the CST first began in 2010 when Michael Gove, then Secretary of State for Education, committed £2 million per year to protect Jewish state schools.

The CST helped in the creation of Tell MAMA,[38] which is now part of a coalition of minority organizations working with police, government and academia to encourage the reporting of hate crime. This includes True Vision, a website owned by the National Police Chiefs' Council (hereinafter NPCC), which allows reporting on the five protected characteristics of race, religion, sexuality, disability and gender orientation.[39] Since 2015, the police have put in place hate crime data-sharing agreements with both the CST and Tell MAMA in response to what the NPCC say is: 'the increased community tension threat levels experienced by Jewish and Muslim communities in the UK'.[40] Since 2015 there have been data-sharing agreements on anti-Semitism and Islamophobia across all police forces in England and Wales.[41]

There is no separate hate crime category for any other faith group: remarkably, this also includes Britain's majority religion, Christianity, despite growing concerns about anti-Christian attacks.[42] There has been no equivalent funding in place for Sikhs, Hindus or other non-Abrahamic faiths in terms of setting up dedicated hate crime monitoring platforms, or nationwide protection for schools and places of worship. Even though it is evident that Sikhs have been victims of anti-Muslim sentiment since 9/11, the British state's prioritization is clear when it comes to tackling religiously motivated hate, with its strong focus on Jews and Muslims to the detriment of other faith groups.

Since 2012, November has been marked as Islamophobia Awareness Month,[43] and in 2017 a Transport for London (hereinafter TfL) campaign during National Hate Crime Awareness Week was launched across the London transport network, in partnership with the police and Tell MAMA.[44] The campaign included a scheduled visit to East London Mosque.[45] Whilst the TfL campaign is to be commended, one of Sadiq Khan's pledges to London's 125,000-strong[46] Sikh community in the run-up to the mayoral election was 'Some crimes where Sikhs are targeted are wrongly recorded by the police as Islamophobic incidents due to mistaken identity. If I'm mayor I will make sure crimes against Sikhs are properly recorded [as] hate crime[s].'[47] However, specific measures to tackle the Sikh 'mistaken identity' issue by City Hall are still thin on the ground. Although the authors requested an update on Sadiq Khan's pre-election pledge, and whether or not the TfL campaign had included a *gurdwara* visit, as of August 2018 no confirmation was provided by City Hall.

However, a core commitment within 'Action against hate' (2016) did include a £2.4 million government fund for a 'places of worship: security scheme'. This was open to all religious communities, bar synagogues, which as previously discussed are funded separately. From 2016, churches, *gurdwara*s, mosques and temples were open to apply to secure funding to improve security measures, like the installation of CCTV.[48]

Unexpectedly, during the first round of bidding for the security scheme in 2016, most applicants were in fact Christians, rather than Muslims, as had been expected.

There were 225 churches that applied, 36 mosques, 11 *gurdwara*s and three other places of worship, and no *gurdwara*s were successful. Although the bids came in following the *jihadist* murder of Father Jacques Hamel in Rouen, France, many of the successful church applicants used funds to enhance security against the threat of Satanists and witches, rather than Islamists.[49] In December 2017, the HO informed the authors that four *gurdwara*s[50] (out of roughly 300 in Britain)[51] were amongst the places of worship reported to have been successful (by then) in the first and second round of bidding combined.[52] During the first round in 2016, 45 churches, 12 mosques and one Hindu temple had been successful, but no *gurdwara*s.

By October 2018 the government announced that a further 45 places of worship – 22 mosques, 12 Sikh *gurdwara*s, nine churches and two Hindu temples – would receive nearly £800,000 for improvements.[53]

Why were/are Sikhs 'invisible' to government?

Having considered some of the policies and initiatives that have been put in place to curb Islamophobia and anti-Semitism, what is clear is that other faith groups who have a distinct identity, particularly Sikhs, have been largely ignored.

For example, after the murder of Balbir Singh Sodhi in the aftermath of the 9/11 terror attacks in the US, there was concern about similar targeting of British Sikhs, which led umbrella organizations like the NSO, led by Lord Singh, to act and fill the void. On 10 December 2001, Lord Indarjit Singh wrote to then Prime Minister Tony Blair:

> Going back to the events of September 11 and their aftermath, Sikhs as Britain's most visible minority, became Britain's most vulnerable community in the public backlash against Osama Bin Laden. This arose from the fact that more Sikhs than Muslims in the UK wear turbans. School children in particular, have been subjected to hostile comment and playground violence. Sikhs have fully supported the government's frequently stated warning that innocent British Muslims should in no way be blamed for the events of September 11. All here today have, on a number of different platforms, expressed our support for the British Muslim community. Sikhs have noted with concern, considerably less government or media support for Sikhs, innocent victims of mistaken identity.

He went on:

> Although the British Sikh population is thought to number about half a million, there is not a single turbaned Sikh in Parliament, or in religious broadcasting in the BBC or in Independent religious broadcasting. No wonder it's difficult to get a Sikh view heard. It also explains the ignorance about Sikhs and Sikhism shown in the attacks on Sikhs and desecration of Sikh places of worship following the events of September 11.

Aside from sympathy and condemnation for the attacks on British Sikhs, nothing tangible appeared to materialize from this initial request for government support.[54] The then Prime Minister's office did, however, suggest that preventing attacks on Sikhs and catching culprits was a policing priority, but this was seemingly empty rhetoric rather than a commitment to make a difference in real terms.[55]

Whilst Lord Singh did try to raise the issue, there are a number of factors that are likely to have contributed to this situation. These include under-reporting of hate crime, religious illiteracy and lack of representation. Lack of parliamentary representation and political advocacy are arguably the most important. Sikhs have been in parliament since before 9/11. The late Piara Singh Khabra (Labour) was the first Sikh MP, elected in 1992 in Southall and Ealing. Khabra passed away in 2007. Parmjit Singh Dhanda (Labour) served as MP for Gloucester between 2001 and 2010. Marsha Singh (Labour) served in Bradford West from 1997–2012. Between 2004 and 2005 Parmjit Singh Gill was Leicester South's MP for the Liberal Democrats and between 2010 and 2015, Paul Uppal (Conservative) held Wolverhampton South West – the seat historically held by Enoch Powell. So, between 2001 and 2012, there had at best been up to four Sikh MPs, from 2012–15 only one, and from 2015, until the 2017 election of Tanmanjeet Singh Dhesi (Slough) and Preet Kaur Gill (Edgbaston), there were none. Dhesi became the first turbaned Sikh MP, and Gill the first Sikh woman to be elected into parliament, and both have been vocal about the issue.

During his tenure Khabra signed a 2004 Early Day Motion (hereinafter EDM) 1540 titled 'Mr Nick Griffin and Islamophobia',[56] however this was written in the context of comments made by the former BNP leader on BBC *Newsnight*, which were considered to be 'a gross insult to the Muslim population of the United Kingdom'.

Individuals like Jagdeesh Singh, gave evidence to the Home Affairs Committee in late 2004 providing a personal account of suffering hate crime.[57] A year on, following the London bombings, Rob Marris, MP for Wolverhampton South West and Chair of the APPG for British Sikhs (which was set up in 2005),[58] tabled an EDM titled 'London bombings and attacks on Sikhs' that read as follows:

> That this House notes the deep sadness, the condolences and the concerns of the UK Sikh community following the London bombings on 7th July; condemns all the subsequent attacks on minority communities, including those on Sikh Gurdwaras (temples), for example those in Leeds, in Erith and in Merton; recalls and condemns the several attacks suffered by the visible UK Sikh community and by other minority communities following the New York atrocity of 11th September 2001; and so urges the Home Secretary, chief constables and local authorities to take very seriously and investigate thoroughly any such attacks, whether experienced by the UK Sikh community or by any other minority communities.[59]

Although this EDM received 54 signatures and was co-sponsored by the current Labour leader Jeremy Corbyn, there were no specific policies subsequently proposed, debated or implemented to address the growing disquiet amongst British Sikhs. EDMs have often been referred to as 'parliamentary graffiti', and form no substitute for direct communication with ministers, which often elicit clear responses.

Parmjit Singh Dhanda gave evidence (referring to the pig's head incident) to a parliamentary inquiry into electoral conduct in 2013. He also gave evidence in relation to racism he had experienced in public life, and said he did not want to make 'a big deal' about the pig's head incident back in 2010, because he did not want the people of Gloucester to be tarnished, nor did he want the incident to define what he was remembered for. He said it was, 'a low ebb, but I wanted to get on with life as my overarching goal was to protect my wife and children'.[60] The wider societal impact of Islamophobia on Sikhs was not explored at the time.[61] Perhaps if Dhanda had been a Muslim, the incident may have received significantly more airtime, commentary from prominent columnists, and subsequently been the subject of considerable lobbying efforts by organizations like Tell MAMA, or the likes of Baroness Warsi. This was an important opportunity to get the issue on the government's agenda. However, his disturbing story did receive a bit more prominence following promotion and launch of his 2015 political memoir *My Political Race*.[62]

Government interest has been lacking and indicates a broader pattern of political indifference to Sikhs, and the 'Muslim-looking other' on the subject of Islamophobia. This was further compounded by the lack of genuine advocacy by Sikh MPs and others, but most importantly, the Sikh community itself on such an important issue, which meant that the community voice was simply not heard. Alongside the lack of advocacy, what is evident is that in comparison to Jews (and later Muslims), Sikhs did not have the existing apparatus in place to take on such a complicated task. This involved not only working with government departments and understanding the modus operandi of the civil service, but also liaising with police authorities and improving levels of religious literacy, whilst communicating the Sikh experience to individual MPs/ministers and sharing their predicament with sympathetic journalists.

There were also no government-funded projects in place designed to improve 'Sikh literacy in the media' or anti-bullying campaigns to support Sikh schoolchildren, or public awareness campaigns on public transport to address anti-Sikh hate. There was no sense (even as recently as 2016 and 2018) that Whitehall had even grasped the extent of the problem, let alone that it had any plans in place to mitigate the backlash against one of Britain's most visible minorities.

As a result, the community has taken responsibility to inform the state about the discrimination and prejudice that has affected them since 9/11. Community groups like the Sikh Federation UK (formerly the International Sikh Youth Federation, hereinafter SFUK), established in 2003, and the secretariat for the APPG for British Sikhs took up the issue. Following the attack of 7/7, it was reported:

The first reported hate crime took place in Erith, Kent: a Sikh gurdwara (place of worship) was firebombed. Since then the Sikh Federation (UK), a lobby group, which represents more than 150 Sikh organisations, has recorded five further attacks on gurdwaras and two serious assaults on Sikh individuals. And as Jagtar Singh, of the Federation's national executive council, points out, there is a huge problem of under-reporting, particularly in the case of less serious attacks. 'For every crime reported to the authorities, we estimate another 30 to 40 that go unreported.'[63]

Jagtar Singh went on to say how the 'the turban wearing Sikh community is under siege'.[64]

United Sikhs, which emerged in the post-9/11 period, focused primarily on legal cases related to religious symbols,[65] and another group, SCUK, was officially launched in 2011.[66] The latter was involved in setting up a hate crime reporting website called Sikh Aware UK in April 2017, but at the time of writing, with the exception of an insignificant social media presence and a press release marking its launch, there is little else to report about Sikh Aware UK.[67] Notably, it was not the recipient of government funding like Tell MAMA. Another website, Stay Safe, was also set up in 2017 by Tarsem Singh but remains unaffiliated to any one organization.[68] Other groups took initiatives attempting to quantify the problem. In 2016, the SN published a report titled 'UK Sikh Survey 2016', in which it was reported that that 'over 100,000 hate crimes against Sikhs aged 16 and over in the last 12 months',[69] and led to a further startling claim that:

> more than 1 in 5 or 21% of those taking part in the survey have personally experienced race hate crime i.e. verbal or physical abuse in the last 12 months.[70]

This claim was rebutted because the report equates the percentage of responders to the percentage of Sikhs in the UK. To get from 21 per cent of the sample to a population estimate, it appears that the report has taken 21 per cent of the population (around 430,000). However, the sample does not include people under 16 (about 20–25 per cent), so the wrong population figure is being used. Nevertheless, 21 per cent is a very high figure, and it may be distorted by non-response bias (those not experiencing it may be more likely to be indifferent to taking part). But even if the estimate is twice as big as it should be, that is still a lot compared to government figures released for 2015–16 and 2017–18, and the authors acknowledge the issue of underreporting.

CS,[71] in their British Sikh Report (2017), looked at anti-Sikh incidents, amongst other things. From just over 2,000 responses it reported:

> 13% of all respondents said they had been victims of hate crime, and this was similar in all age groups and for men and women. When asked if they had experienced hate crimes in Britain, over 60% said yes. About half of these experiences had been before the year 2001: 12% between 2001 and

2010, and 9% between 2011 and 2015. In these recent periods, those aged 20–34 were more likely to be victims.[72]

However, what is clear is that whilst there is growing community activism and engagement, there was and still is no joined up working within the community that would/could achieve a maximum impact at an earlier stage.

Police monitoring

Linked to the issue of attempts by groups to quantify the size of the problem facing the community was inertia from police forces, who did not see Sikhs as a priority group. From a policing perspective, things had not really moved forward from the time of evidence provided by Jagdeesh Singh in 2004 to a Select Committee on Home Affairs in 2004. Although, at the time, the MET had acknowledged the wider impact of hate crime targeting Muslims, Sikhs and Hindus, they write,

> The Jewish and Muslim communities within London have been identified as being at the greatest risk from terrorist activity and related hate crime. This is not to understate risks held by other ethnic groups all of which are monitored by the MET (Metropolitan Police Service) as a matter of course.[73]

So one of the '*most visible*' and '*most vulnerable*' faith communities in the aftermath of 9/11 (Lord Singh's words to former Prime Minister Tony Blair, emphasis added) was simply not seen as a policing priority. Comments by the former Detective Police Sergeant Gurpal Virdi that some police officers did not know the difference between the Taliban and turbaned Sikh Londoners post-9/11, were also not acknowledged in the MET's evidence.

Recognition of anti-Sikh hate crime in political debates

With the recent exception of positive steps taken by the community to ascertain figures and engage parliamentarians, Sikhs lacked a share of voice with those in the corridors of power, which meant they were unable to influence public policy. To confirm the lack of visibility of discussions on hate crime targeting Sikhs in government circles, online audits using the key word search 'Islamophobia' in Hansard (transcripts of parliamentary debates) over two one-year periods, August 2014–August 2015 and August 2016–August 2017, were conducted. The earlier period was chosen because it included the months directly after the attempted murder of Dr Bhambra. The results paint an interesting, but unsurprising picture.

Between 2014 and 2015 there were in total 18 debates in which the word 'Islamophobia' was included somewhere in the title or raised by individual contributors (or both) in either the House of Commons or the House of Lords. Islamophobia is referred to either in general terms, or more specifically with reference to Muslims. Of the debates, all with the exception of one refer to the suffering of Sikhs or other non-Muslim victims. The exception was on 25 June 2015, during a 'Communities: Young Muslims' debate tabled by Muslim peer Baroness Afshar, in which she asked the government what measures had been put into place to tackle 'Islamophobia and stigmatisation on (sic) young Muslims'.[74]

Lord Singh of Wimbledon intervened in this debate and commented:

> My Lords, is the Minister aware that ever since 9/11 there has been a huge increase in the number of attacks on Sikhs and Sikh places of worship in cases of mistaken identity? The most recent case was a machete attack on a young Sikh dentist in Wales, which was described on 'Newsnight' as Islamophobia. Does the Minister agree that hate crime is hate crime against any community, and that it should be tackled even-handedly, irrespective of the size of the community?[75]

The second Hansard audit from August 2016–August 2017 identified a total of 25 debates in which 'Islamophobia' was included somewhere in the title or raised by individual contributors (or both). It revealed that of the 25 debates, not one raised Islamophobia affecting the Sikh or other non-Muslim communities. However, in a commons debate on 'terror attacks', Seema Malhotra MP said on 22 June 2017, 'We know that there is a ripple effect of hate crime that carries on afterwards, and that reaches much wider and affects other communities'.[76] Given the significant Hindu and Sikh demographic in her constituency of Feltham and Heston in Northwest London,[77] Seema Malhotra should have expanded on which communities specifically suffered this 'much wider' backlash. In another debate on 'visible religious symbols', on 15 March 2017 Chuka Umunna MP said, 'Islamophobia is not only widespread but rampant'; whilst in this debate Rob Marris MP does mention Sikhs, he does so only in the context of the problems they face in wearing religious symbols in France and Belgium.[78] What is abundantly clear is that the problem Seema Malhotra hints at in 2017, the *racialization of Islamophobia*, was either still unknown to lawmakers, or not viewed as a policy priority – or worse still, was an indication that Sikhs (and others) had failed in effectively raising their concerns with politicians and the media, which was indirectly a result of a lack of statistical evidence, because anti-Sikh attacks were not being separately measured as a statistic by UK police forces, and hence the problem was never quantified. This obstacle made it difficult to move forward with policymakers.

It can be argued that Sikhs ended up in this situation due to the disjointed activities of vying groups leading to an overall disorganized approach. What is clear is that when it came to hate crime, a community who had previously shown successful activism shaping the motorcycle helmet campaign and the right for a boy, Gurinder Singh Mandla, to wear the turban to school in *Mandla v. Dowell-Lee*, suffered from what some would describe as political indifference. The reality was that politicians who cynically offer promises to voting groups in the run-up to elections are of course more likely to try and curry favour with those with more influence at the ballot box. As means of illustration, if one uses the 2011 census, note how the 'religious affiliation' of 4.8 per cent of those in England and Wales was Muslim, and less than 1 per cent Sikh.[79] One may be able to make the assumption that when the former Labour leader Ed Miliband said cynically that if Labour were to be elected (in 2015) he would make 'Islam-ophobia' an aggravated criminal offence, this was clearly with the intention of winning the Muslim vote. If Sikhs had constituted a larger vote bank and had successfully lobbied on the issue, politicians would have taken more serious steps to help assuage Sikh concerns.

Community challenges government indifference since 2016

Perhaps another reason Sikhs did not lobby on the issue as effectively as Muslims or Jews relates to the doctrinal concept of *chardi kala*, a worldview that even in times of adversity, Sikhs should remain steadfast, and in 'high spirits'. In the darkest periods of Sikh history, this stoical ethos replaced victimhood and a sense of doom with hope and everlasting optimism. This occurred despite periods of terrible persecution, not only under India's Mughal invaders, but also during the Congress Party-led Sikh genocide in 1984. In an article reflecting on the 'victimization' theme following the 2012 Wisconsin temple massacre, Pro-fessor Simran Jeet Singh refers to this foundational principle when he writes:

> Traditionally, the Sikh community does not lament periods of persecution and hardship but instead celebrates the contributions and sacrifices made by the community members and greater society living within those moments.[80]

The publication of the government's four-year hate crime action plan 'Action against hate' (2016) and even the latest 'Action against hate' 'refresh' (2018)[81] demonstrated that the suffering of Sikhs and other non-Abrahamic faiths had become a long-term policy blind spot. Despite the attack on Dr Bhambra in 2015, his case remarkably did not even get a mention in the plan. Nor was it, 15 years on from 9/11, deemed necessary to address the issue of Islamophobia dir-ected at Sikhs or 'the Muslim-looking other', or the disclosure of the breakdown of 'Islamophobic hate crime' statistics showing high numbers of non-Muslim victims in London. One would have assumed the government would address the wider picture, given Amber Rudd's introduction to the report in which she announced: 'Hate crime of any kind, directed against any community, race or religion has absolutely no place in our society.' This opening gambit, however, provided a false impression of inclusivity, because when one read the plan in full, the government appeared to take the myopic view that only Abrahamic faiths suffer bigotry.[82]

To the community it was surprising that the 'Action against hate' (2016) plan had failed to include them when groups like NSO, SCUK, SFUK and CS had engaged with government officials before its publication. Prior to publication FOI requests to the MET showed that 28 per cent of victims of so-called 'Islamophobic hate crime' recorded in London during 2015 were in fact non-Muslim or of no recorded faith.[83] The NSO's Director, Lord Singh, wrote to express his concerns to the then minister Greg Clarke from the Department for Communities and Local Government (now MHCLG). Greg Clarke responded on 25 February 2016, confirming they were aware of the issue and that religious hate crime would be disaggregated by police forces from April 2017, giving clarity around which faith groups suffer. However, post-April 2017, this disaggregated breakdown was only still obtainable via FOI requests. The minister sent a copy of the correspondence to the HO, and reference was made to development of 'Action against hate' (2016). The NSO subsequently wrote to the minister on 1 April 2016, but aside from a delayed acknowledgement on 26 May 2016, which read 'I am sure our Hate Crime team could potentially explore with you', no meeting or consultation regarding Sikh concerns ever materialized.[84]

In January 2017, the NSO submitted evidence to the Home Affairs Committee inquiry into hate crime and its violent consequences, stating:

> The cross-governmental four-year hate crime strategy – *Action Against Hate* (2016) – focuses solely on Abrahamic faiths. The report categorically fails to acknowledge the suffering of Sikhs, Hindus or other non-Abrahamic faith victims. There are 45 examples of the suffering of Muslims, Jews and Christians – but not one from non-Abrahamic communities. The report outlines a number of taxpayer-funded projects designed to challenge Islamophobia and anti-Semitism, but none for Hindus or Sikhs. The existing 'Abrahamic-centric' strategy is causing significant disquiet amongst Britain's Sikh and Hindu communities.[85]

From around 2016, British Hindu community representatives such as Satish K. Sharma, from the National Council of Hindu Temples, also joined the Sikh protest.[86]

'Action against hate' (2016) also outlined the Government's five-prong strategy: prevention, response, reporting, support and better understanding. Under 'prevention', it says that hate crime is to be prevented through 'challenging the beliefs and attitudes' that underlie it.[87] Specifying educational settings, it stated this was to include a 'new programme to equip teachers to facilitate conversations about "difficult topics" and carry out a new assessment of the level of anti-Muslim, anti-Semitic, homophobic, racist and other bullying in schools'. This 'prevention' element involves working with the Anne Frank Trust and Streetwise, which run educational programmes.

There was no reference to Sikh boys who had been bullied due to their long hair, when there should have been. After all, tackling bullying in schools should not just be the preserve of Muslims and Jews. What about young Sikh boys being picked on for their *patka* (traditional headdress for boys), or those referred to by their classmates as 'terrorist', as illustrated in the case of a schoolboy in

America on a bus, who filmed his abusers in a video that went viral on YouTube.[88] The SFUK ratcheted up the pressure, by saying that despite increased levels of discrimination, British Sikhs had become 'invisible to the government since 9/11'.[89]

Pointing out this clear bias and his disappointment at the government's approach, Lord Singh of Wimbledon told ministers that the government itself needs to improve its religious literacy. On 14 September 2016, in a House of Lords debate, further to a question tabled on hate crime, Lord Singh said:

> My Lords, I thank the Minister for her response but it does not address my concerns over the narrow and biased thinking in a report that details 45 examples of hate crime against Abrahamic faiths but not a single example of the many, well-documented mistaken-identity hate crimes suffered by Sikhs and others – and this in a report emanating from a department with specifically designated officers to consider hate crime against the Jewish and Muslim communities but not anyone else. Would the Minister agree that that omission is more due to ignorance than deliberate discrimination? Would she further agree that those who preach the need for religious literacy should first themselves acquire some basic religious literacy, and apologise to those they have offended in such a way?[90]

The Minister's response was far from satisfactory; in short suggesting that the responsibility, when it came to religious literacy, lay at the door of the media.

To placate growing disquiet after the launch of the report, the former Home Secretary Amber Rudd organized an impromptu visit to the UK's biggest *gurdwara*, Sri Guru Singh Sabha, Southall. Her office subsequently issued a press statement titled 'Amber Rudd meets Sikh community to discuss hate crime'.[91] The Home Secretary said:

> The Sikh community plays an important role in the diverse Britain that works for everyone and I was delighted to visit the Sri Guru Singh Sabha Gurdwara and hear about the important work taking place to unite the community.

She went on:

> Hate crime has absolutely no place in our society and it is vital we protect those who follow this peaceful religion. That is why I've made over £3 million available to protect places of worship and for community projects to combat hatred, and I'd urge all gurdwaras and Sikh groups to consider whether this funding could help them.[92]

Whilst the visit was a commendable gesture, the security element for places of worship was something already incorporated into government initiatives outlined under 'security funding' in the hate crime action plan, and as previously discussed, some *gurdwaras* did benefit. Amber Rudd referred to an additional £900,000 for innovative community projects, and although two Sikh groups applied for this funding (the NSO and CS), neither succeeded in the first round of bidding. The reality was that, in terms of policy, absolutely nothing had changed.

Amber Rudd's visit, however, demonstrates that the government had realized their error, and furthermore noted that isolating Sikh (and Hindu) voters was not a risk worth taking. In a further belated step to assuage growing concerns, Communities Secretary Sajid Javid (the current home secretary) subsequently announced an extra £375,000 funding to support communities with the prevention and reporting of hate crime, on 26 January 2017. Aside from funds for Polish, Roma and Traveller communities, this included a token £25,000 for Sikhs and Hindus to report hate crime through True Vision, the police reporting portal.[93] This was something specifically requested in evidence submitted to the inquiry into hate crime and its violent consequences by the NSO. At the time of writing, almost a year on, there has regrettably been no progress with this initiative.

In October 2017, Preet Gill MP challenged the Home Secretary directly as to why her department had ignored Sikhs a second time in the Race Disparity Audit, going on to suggest that a draft copy of 'Action against hate' (2016) had in fact included reference to Bhambra's case that was allegedly redacted by No. 10 Downing Street. Gill, who remains an active member of the SFUK's sister organisation SN,[94] was subsequently praised by the SFUK, who accused the government of 'clear institutional racism'.[95] Notably, a few months prior to this in July 2017, Slough's MP Tanmanjeet Singh Dhesi took the opportunity during his maiden speech to raise 'mistaken identity' attacks (one resulting in the murder of an American Sikh). He stressed his personal commitment in tackling the politics of hate and division, including Islamophobia.[96]

What became clear by 2016 was that Sikhs were playing catch-up primarily because the focus on Islamophobia affecting British Muslims had a long and well-established history. Influential bodies and think tanks were amongst those who played a pivotal role in actively pushing the Muslim agenda forward. As far back as 1997, the Runnymede Trust Commission on British Muslims and Islamophobia published its seminal report entitled *Islamophobia: A Challenge for Us All*. It was commissioned by Trevor Phillips (then chairperson of the Runnymede Trust), and there is no doubt that the report popularized the phrase 'Islamophobia', which has since become synonymous with any criticism of Islam, legitimate or otherwise.[97] In the years following the report, the debate around Islamophobia gained significant traction across the public and political sphere, and has been the subject of significant media attention. However, the term is problematic, given a consensus on its definition has not been universally agreed since the 1997 report, and it does not demarcate legitimate criticism of aspects of Islam. Nevertheless, it has percolated into the public vernacular. In the report's introduction the Commission's Chair Professor Gordon Conway (vice-chancellor of the University of Sussex), writes:

We did not coin the term Islamophobia. It was already in use among sections of the Muslim community as a term describing the prejudice and discrimination, which they experience in their everyday lives. For some of us on the Commission it was a new term, a rather ugly term, and we were not sure how it would be received by readers of our document. However, it is evident from the responses we received that Islamophobia describes a real and growing phenomenon – an ugly word for an ugly reality.

Sikhs were not featured in the Runnymede report, and this is primarily because the Sikh issue only became pronounced a few years after its publication, particularly following Balbir Singh Sodhi's murder and significant violence against Sikh Americans post-9/11. The report did suggest that 'Hindu and Sikh leaders have important roles to play in combating Islamophobia in their own communities'. As discussed, the issue of sexual 'grooming gangs' has become particularly polarizing in this regard.

Two Sikh groups from the Midlands, SYUK and SAS, have been accused of Islamophobia for pointing to the specific heritage of those convicted in sexual grooming gang cases, and for their unsubstantiated accusations that Muslim/Pakistani men are targeting and grooming Sikh girls and women. The former group, SYUK, have faced external and internal criticism for their involvement with Tommy Robinson. That said, the Runnymede authors do not elaborate on the specific causes of Islamophobia amongst Hindu and Sikhs at the time. Furthermore, an equitable approach does not appear to have been considered, as there is no mention of the importance of Muslim leaders playing a role in combating hatred of *kaffirs*, a derogatory term for non-Muslims.[97]

Revised Runnymede report (2018)

The Runnymede Trust, to their credit (unlike the government's hate crime action plan), did at least later acknowledge Sikh suffering by including a case study in their twentieth-anniversary report, entitled *Islamophobia: Still a Challenge for Us All*. A London-based British barrister called Jasvir Singh says:

As a Sikh man who wears a turban I experience a hyper-visibility. Over the years, various national or global events have precipitated an intensification of abuse directed at me. Most recently I found myself the target of a high level of abuse following the 2016 Brexit referendum. Much of the abuse levelled at me takes on an Islamophobic tinge. Abuse took place both online and on the street as I attempted to go to work. As I walked past people, they would make monkey sounds. I was left unsure of how to react. Not knowing if responding would provoke further abuse or put me at further risk. Online, following a tweet I sent commenting on the incidents of South Asians being attacked after the referendum I faced a barrage of abuse. This included comments such as 'Once you niggers fuck off back to curry land …' and people calling me Taliban or Bin Laden. It felt the same as the environment after the London bombings.[98]

He went on to say that when he had been targeted in street hate crime incidents, he did not take the position 'I'm not Muslim – don't attack me'. This was his way of expressing solidarity with all victims of hatred.[100] A similar approach was taken by Amandeep Sidhu, the co-founder of SC in America, who writes that the nuanced approach he and his colleagues took in the aftermath of 9/11 was to say:

> we are Sikh, this is what Sikhs believe in, the Sikh religion in an independent religion from northern India, separate and distinct from Islam – and by the way, it is *not OK* to direct anger and frustration at innocent Muslims, Arabs, and South Asians.[101]

The leader of the Canadian New Democratic Party (hereinafter NDP), Jagmeet Singh, appeared to have also applied principles rooted in Sikh teachings, when dealing with an anti-Muslim protestor during his leadership campaign. In a video that went viral in September 2017, an angry woman is seen heckling the turbaned and bearded Sikh politician. She is seen in footage saying, 'when is your *sharia* going to end', and 'we know you're in bed with the Muslim brotherhood'.[102] Jagmeet Singh, who was widely lauded for the way he handled the delicate situation, did not inform the woman he was Sikh and not Muslim, but responded by saying 'we welcome you, we love you, we support you'.[103]

It later transpired that the heckler, Jennifer Bush, knew Jagmeet Singh was a Sikh, but was protesting against his support of M103, an 'anti-Islamophobia' motion passed by Ottawa in 2017.[104] Referring to the incident, Jennifer Bush told Rebel Media, 'what we really need to do is research his votes and policies, what he wears on his head and what his religion states, is very different to what he actually stands for'. Opponents, like Conservative politicians, believe that M103[105] is a slippery slope towards curtailing Canada's free speech.[106]

As evidenced by the latest Runnymede report and recent studies conducted by Hopkins et al. (2017), and Awan and Zempi (2017), Sikhs have been given some acknowledgement from an academic perspective under the umbrella of non-Muslim victims of Islamophobia. However, the overall research continues to predominantly focus on the suffering of Muslim communities.

The most significant attempt to define Islamophobia since the 1997 Runnymede report came in late 2018. The APPG on British Muslims launched the Islamophobia Defined report, announcing a proposed working definition following two years of consultation:

> Islamophobia is rooted in racism and is a type of racism that targets expressions of Muslimness or perceived Muslimness.[107]

The report considered written and oral evidence submitted by the NSO, and in doing so acknowledged both the *racialization of Islamophobia* and 'mistaken identity'.[108] However, a notable intervention in the debate came from Sara Khan, the Lead Commissioner for Countering Extremism, who said it is important to recognize that Muslims like her are also targeted by their own community because they 'don't have a "Muslimness" that other Muslims find acceptable'.[109]

Sexual grooming gangs, 'mistaken identity' and Islamophobia

Grooming gangs have operated across towns and cities in the UK, and in Rotherham alone, it is estimated there were 1,500 victims,[110] mainly white working-class girls. In 2012 following the convictions of men in Rochdale, Muslim groups accused the EDL of exploiting the issue, and use of the term 'Muslim paedos' was highlighted in this specific context.[111]

In 2018, a survivor of a Rotherham grooming gang wrote an article in which she said the abuse by these gangs has both a racial and a religious motivation, and that this is not covered by existing hate crime definitions.[112] She acknowledged the APPG definition for Islamophobia as outlined in Islamophobia Defined, and made it clear that it is not Islamophobic to speak up against experiences like hers. She said:

> As grooming victims, my friends and I were called vile racist names such as 'white trash' and 'kaffir girl' as we were raped. Our Sikh and Hindu friends who were also targeted by Muslim Pakistani gangs were disparagingly called 'kaffir slags'.[113]

Although these are difficult conversations, policymakers have a duty to promote parity for all victims of religious and racial hatred and must seriously consider such issues alongside Islamophobia and anti-Semitism. Although the proposed Islamophobia definition suggests that individuals are targeted for expressions of 'Muslimness' or 'perceived Muslimness', the article by the Rotherham victim suggests that she and others were targeted because of 'non-Muslim hate' or hate against 'those with a perceived lack of Muslimness'. If the government fails to address these issues, there is a danger that they open the space for the far right to hijack the debate, and in doing so, will allow them to smear the majority law-abiding British Pakistani Muslim community.

The issue of Islamophobia and 'mistaken identity' has also been impacted by the definition of sexual grooming gangs by the media as 'Asian'. In Britain, all South Asians – those with parents or grandparents from India, Pakistan, Bangladesh or Sri Lanka – are considered part of the 'Asian' umbrella. Use of this vague terminology in the media does nothing to promote cultural or religious literacy amongst the public, or to encourage the understanding of differences between Muslims, Hindus, Sikhs and others. In December 2018, a man was fined £180 by a court in Nottinghamshire for calling an Indian Sikh man a 'Muslim paedo'.[114] This incident serves to illustrate how Britain's sexual grooming gang phenomenon has resulted in prejudice against Muslims, and those perceived to be Muslims – or the 'Muslim-looking other'.

The Times' chief investigative reporter Andrew Norfolk, who investigates child sexual exploitation, told the authors:

> we kept using the headline 'Asian' in those early days, but every time we did this, we got complaints from Hindus and Sikhs, and from my perspective this was a valid complaint. There was the odd white person, Hindu or the odd individual Sikh involved in the gangs, but they were overwhelmingly Pakistani men, or Bangladeshi or Kurdish men, often involving families – uncles and nephews.

Norfolk said *The Times* increasingly focused on the specificity of the perpetrators (supported by statistics) from around January 2011, and things then became problematic. He said:

> From the word go, the same coalition of Islamist groups and the left, were both screaming 'Islamophobia' and 'racist', when what we were highlighting was a clear trend in criminality. It was difficult for the first few months. I got to my forties without ever being accused of being racist. I'm pleased we kept going, despite the denial from police and social services. Rotherham changed things, after a year of writing countless stuff – they launched an independent inquiry.

Norfolk said a Sikh family from the West Midlands had contacted him following concerns for their daughter, but he said 'honour issues' often made it harder for Sikh girls to speak out, and for decades no one wanted to listen to white working-class girls either. What was clear from these discussions was that whilst one should continue to discuss genuine cases of hate crime, one must remain cognizant of illiberal efforts to accuse individuals raising important issues with the false and malicious charge of 'racist' or 'Islamophobe'.[115]

Media representation and discussion

Whilst it was clear that the focus on anti-Sikh hate was thin on the ground in the political sphere, amongst prominent race relations think tanks and academia, it was even more so in the mainstream media. This despite the presence of high-profile Sikh born journalists – the likes of the BBC's Anita Rani, Sathnam Sanghera of *The Times* and Hardeep Singh Kohli, to name but a few. There was ignorance amongst journalists about the suffering of non-Muslims (such as Sikhs) from Islamophobia in the first instance, but even when it was known, Sikh stories were subsumed within the broader Islamophobia debate in media reports. To highlight this, the authors looked at stories in the media from both the UK and US around the theme of religious literacy, because religious illiteracy can fuel hate crime. They also looked for examples of where images resembling Sikhs have been used inappropriately to talk about anti-Muslim hate, without even acknowledging Sikhs.

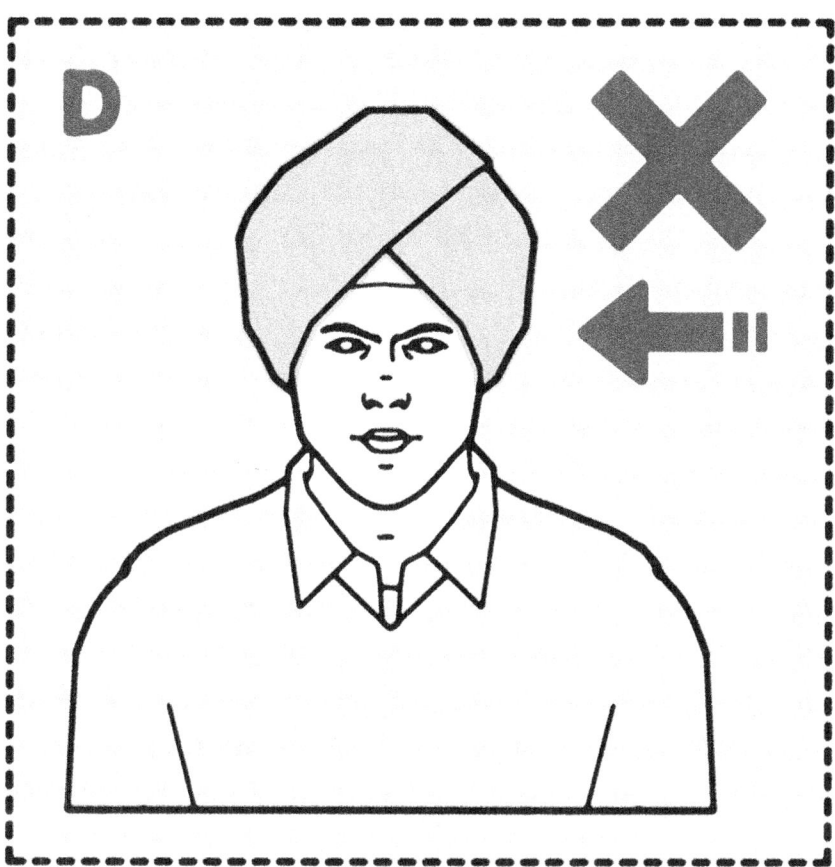

Figure 3.1 'Wear appropriate clothing'.
Source: Copyright Son of Alan/Folio (2016).

The Guardian best illustrates the latter on 16 August 2016 with the incorrect use of an image resembling a Sikh turban used to illustrate an article titled, 'The perils of "flying while Muslim"'.[116]

This misplaced artwork was picked up on by an observant Kate Mansey, the Deputy Features Editor at *The Mail on Sunday*. Kate Mansey told the authors:

> When I spotted the story in *The Guardian*, I thought it was brilliantly written and very informative. Sometimes, however, the captions and artwork that accompany stories are not subjected to such rigorous checks. It struck me as odd that a passenger with a Sikh turban was used to depict a story about Muslims. I took to Twitter to express my surprise. For me, this was another example of how those of the Sikh faith are often confused with

Figure 3.2 Kate Mansey's tweet, 9 August 2016.
Source: Copyright @KateMansey.

Muslims. No doubt, it is a source of annoyance for Sikh people, but it also shows a wider misunderstanding of religion in our society. The point of the article in *The Guardian* was that, of course, we should not prejudice all Muslims by assuming they are terrorists. Indeed. But nor should we assume all people with darker skin are Muslims. The key, surely, to building a more tolerant society is to educate children – and adults – about different religions. Perhaps no surprise then that this was one of my most widely shared and 'liked' tweets.

After complaints and retweets of Mansey's original tweet, the image was subsequently removed from the top of the article, being replaced lower down under a paragraph discussing the SC's app (FlyRights) to highlight and report discrimination whilst flying. The image description however remained 'wear appropriate clothing', with no clarification around its resemblance to a Sikh turban.[117] This was one of the rare occasions where a member of a national newspaper's editorial team advocated on social media on behalf of British Sikhs, and, at least on this occasion, made a difference.

Kate Mansey's insightful view on the importance of improving religious literacy is something echoed by Hopkins et al. as previously discussed, and also highlighted by Lord Singh of Wimbledon in a House of Lords debate.

Whilst national media demonstrated religious illiteracy, so did local media. In the *Slough Express*, a Sikh family who had become victims of hate crime in the aftermath of the 7/7 London bombings were ignorantly described as Muslim in an article titled, 'Neighbour accused of race hate threats to kill family'. A response to the editor in the subsequent edition of the newspaper on 13 January 2006 under the heading 'Sikhs are just as likely to be attacked', read as follows:

> Your article on race hate threats to kill a family was very misleading. It looks like the man accused of threatening to kill a Muslim family post 7/7 wasn't the only one to get his religious identity confused. Your reported seems to have made the very same mistake. Tejinder Bhogal unambiguously is a Sikh name. As there is a large Sikh population in Slough, I feel that such a mistake by the local newspaper could only be damaging for the Sikh community who are likely to be attacked by race hate gangs post 9/11 and 7/7 because they wear turbans and stand out from the crowd. Sikhs are a proud people who have served in two great wars for Great Britain against despots like Hitler. Isn't it time that the media got it right? Perhaps we should all go to Blockbuster and hire a copy of *The English Patient* to remind ourselves of the unique Sikh identity?[118]

Despite these examples, it could still be argued that ignorance about Sikhs and Sikhism in the US media was, and still is, in fact far worse than in the UK.[119]

For all the reasons discussed, it is by no means surprising that the British media's coverage of hate crime has continued to be focused primarily on Jews and Muslims. For the former, coverage increased following reaction to British and American foreign policy on Israel, an example being President Trump's declaration that Jerusalem is the capital of the Jewish state, which fuelled anti-Semitic attacks by Muslim immigrants in Europe,[120] as well as the ongoing anti-Semitism problem in the Labour Party. For Muslims, there is heightened coverage, especially in the aftermath of Islamic terror attacks, where left-leaning publications in particular focus their attention on 'spikes' in hate crime against Muslims, sometimes at the expense of exploring the reasons why someone would choose to become a *jihadist* in the first instance.[121]

A few news headlines from 2017 help illustrate what has now become a predictable trend in the aftermath of Islamic terror attacks: 'Islamophobic hate crimes jump fivefold after London Bridge terror attack',[122] 'Anti-Muslim hate crime surges after Manchester and London Bridge attacks',[123] 'Anti-Muslim hate crimes increase fivefold since London Bridge attacks'[124] and 'Shocking figures reveal spike in anti-Islam hate crime in London'.[125] Alongside these news articles, there has been a significant level of commentary on anti-Muslim hate and opinion-editorial pieces from community activists, writers and journalists from within the British Muslim community, and outside it.

In 2013 Baroness Warsi, who has undoubtedly been a champion in the battle against anti-Muslim prejudice, highlighted how the coverage on Muslims since 9/11 was largely negative and was having an impact on how Muslims, or 'the

Muslim-looking other', was perceived and treated. According to a survey by Chris Allen, 74 per cent knew 'nothing or next to nothing about Islam', whilst 64 per cent said what they did know had been knowledge 'acquired through the media'.[126] Warsi said that some journalists, 'albeit a small cohort', were willing to write about Islamophobia, naming Peter Oborne, Mehdi Hasan, Ian Birrell and Oliver Wright.[127]

In addition, there have also been dedicated documentary programmes focusing on Muslim victims of Islamophobia, like Channel 4's 'My Week As A Muslim'[128] in 2017, although it courted some controversy because of 'brownfacing' a white woman to look Muslim, and BBC Three's 'United States of Hate: Muslims under Attack' the year before.[129] In order to tackle inaccurate press coverage on Muslims, a small group of dedicated activists in the Muslim community, such as Miqdaad Versi from the Muslim Council of Britain, have developed an expertise in making complaints related to breaches of the Editors' Code of Practice, which is regulated by the Independent Press Standards Organisation (hereinafter IPSO). IPSO covers most of the print media. Activists like Miqdaad Versi have achieved some level of success in obtaining corrections to inaccurate or misleading stories about Muslims in the British press.

Sikhs in the media

According to Sikh teachings, the term *dharam* refers to spiritual wisdom, righteous living and responsibility towards God and creation. It is a term that expresses the sense of 'duty' and 'way of life' that a Sikh aspires towards, which promote solidarity, harmony and cohesion. Guru Gobind Singh said:

ਮਾਨਸ ਕੀ ਜਾਤਿ ਸਬੈ ਏਕੈ ਪਹਚਾਨਬੋ

Manas ki jaat sabhe ekai pehcahnbo.

Recognise the whole human race as one.[130]

Recognizing the Divine Light (*jot*) dwelling within all of God's creation – from minute creatures to human beings – promotes and advocates for an egalitarian and pluralistic outlook to society. This worldview came from day one with Guru Nanak's very first sermon, 'There is no Hindu, there is no Muslim'. Many of the other teachings focus on performing good deeds that centre on the three fundamental principles: *naam japna* (recitation of God's name); *kirat karna*, or *dharam di kirat karni* (earning an honest living); and *vand chakana* (selfless service involving giving to those in need). These teachings have enabled the successful integration of Sikhs into British society as demonstrated by:

> high levels of educational attainment, their substantial number in professions such as law, medicine and accountancy, and their election as mayors

and members of parliament, as well as the recognition of individuals by the honors, conferred by the monarch, of the CBE, OBE and MBE.[131]

It is unsurprising therefore that Sikhs have not become recipients of negative press coverage as a faith group per se. The actions of a few individuals on the thorny issue of 'interfaith marriage',[132] and stories relating to SYUK associating itself with Tommy Robinson, have been the recent exception.[133] When a Birmingham-based Sikh TV channel, Sikh Channel, aired SYUK video on sexual grooming titled 'Misused Trust' it became subject of a complaint to Ofcom. The channel was accused of encouraging victims of sexual grooming to take vigilante action.[134] Groups such as SYUK have also brought a negative light on the community due to their narrative around sexual grooming.

However, Sikhs did not have the attention or advocacy of Oxbridge educated journalists like Oborne or Hasan, newspaper editors or academics when on the receiving end of anti-Muslim backlash. Nor were there any dedicated mainstream documentaries focusing specifically on the Sikh problem. It was through the efforts of grassroots organizations like the Basics of Sikhi (founded by the late Jagraj Singh) that the wider public were provided with an education on Sikhism through street dialogue or *parchaar*, which became widely disseminated via YouTube.

In a 2016 BBC documentary, 'The Selfless Sikh: Faith on the Frontline', which followed Ravi Singh (Khalsa Aid) on a humanitarian mission supporting persecuted Yazidis in Northern Iraq, he briefly spoke about his identity and said, 'a lot of people identify with the beard and turban in a negative way because of what ISIS are doing'.[135] However, this small segment on 'mistaken identity' was the rare exception, and clearly showed that misidentifying Sikhs as Muslim extremists was not just a Western phenomenon.

The Sikh issue was largely hidden collateral damage, and aside from the occasional article and mention (often after tragedies like Wisconsin),[136] there was little focus on Sikh suffering. Very few online articles looked to address the British government's biased approach. A 2017 piece 'Why isn't the Government doing more to tackle anti-Sikh discrimination?'[137] in *Vice*, and another (the year before) 'It's time the Government ended its silence on Sikh hate crime victims'[138] in *The Spectator*, were among the exceptions.

When it came to religious literacy, if the public knew little about Islam, they also knew little about Sikhism, or Sikh articles of faith. Ignorance about Sikh identity was after all fuelling hate crime in Britain, as evidenced with the examples of violence meted out against Jagdeesh Singh in Coventry and Hardip Singh in Dublin. It is clear that the 'Sikh voice' as *Newsweek*'s Orlando Crowcroft puts it,[139] did not receive the media profile it deserved, and this affected the public's understanding of Sikh identity. Moreover, conflation of race with religion was causing also causing problems for unorthodox Sikhs, like Manpreet Mellhi and Parmjit Singh Dhanda. Sikhs and other minority faiths faced marginalization due to increased interest in Islam in the years following 9/11. This is evidenced by a breakdown of programming from the BBC's

Religion and Ethics department, obtained by Ashish Joshi in 2008, which revealed that between 2001 and 2008, the BBC made 41 dedicated television documentaries on Islam, compared with just five on Hinduism and one on Sikhism.[140] This resulted in complaints from Sikhs and Hindus about a pro-Muslim bias. The one programme on Sikhs was rather unhelpfully called 'Sikhs and the City',[141] an inconvenient pun on *Sex and the City*.

Looking back, the BBC's disproportionate focus on Islam at the time is likely to have had a knock-on effect in promoting religious illiteracy around Sikhism in those critical years post-9/11. The reality was that the Twin Towers attack had spawned a disproportionate, almost obsessional focus on Islam, relegating other faiths into the lower rungs of commissioning priority. A Cardiff University study by Justin Lewis et al. showed how news stories about Muslims increased dramatically over the period between 2000 and 2008, suggesting this was due to 9/11 and 7/7, but also 'as a product of a wider preoccupation with Islam and British society'.[142] In any case, a more equitable approach by the BBC and the news media in general may have been an antidote to propagation of the danger-ous misconception that Sikh turbans and beards were synonymous with the attire and ideology of Osama bin Laden. It is also worth noting in the case of tabloids at least, sensationalism sells. So news stories about a generally law-abiding British Sikh community would probably not have been as profitable as coverage of a minority of Muslims who had been controversially described as 'a fifth column', 'the enemy within', 'home grown extremists' or more recently with the emergence of ISIS, 'jihadi brides'.

Audit on 'Islamophobia' in the UK national newspapers

Methodology

Having highlighted the general stories on Sikhs in the media, in order to learn whether anti-Sikh hate crime was reported in the media, an analysis of UK national newspapers, searching for articles that included reference to the word 'Islamophobia' (anywhere in the text), was conducted. It was done via Nexis. com, a comprehensive news and business information online research tool. To refine their search criteria, the authors chose to exclude documents with fewer than 500 words, newswires and group duplicates as well as websites. They then analysed whether the articles that included the key search word 'Islamophobia' mentioned Sikhs, and if not, whether there was (1) a general reference to Islamo-phobia or (2) a specific reference in the context of Muslim communities. To help illustrate the context, an article with specific reference to Islamophobia specifi-cally affecting Muslim communities included one titled: 'I'm a Muslim woman, Mr Cameron: here's what your radicalisation speech means to me', published in *The Guardian* on 24 July 2015. On the other hand examples of a general refer-ence to Islamophobia includes articles such as 'Totalitarianism in the age of Trump: lessons from Hannah Arendt' published in *The Guardian* on 1 February 2017, which mentions Islamophobia in passing, without a specific reference to

Muslims. This was done this to see whether observable trends could be established: did the majority of coverage on 'Islamophobia' provide a specific reference to Muslims, or examples of anti-Muslim hate crime?

Each article was read in detail, with a second reviewer to ensure a robust research framework was implemented. Each article was also reviewed to see if 'anti-Semitism' had also been mentioned, to see if any clear trends in coverage could be established. For example, how often are attacks on Jews thought of within the discourse of anti-Muslim attacks? For consistency, the audit was conducted within the same time frames as the Hansard audit discussed earlier, so as to incorporate the period before and after the attempted beheading of Dr Sarandev Singh Bhambra. The two periods were August 2014 to August 2015, and August 2016 to August 2017.

The audit included articles from UK national newspapers including *The Guardian, The Observer, The Independent, I-Independent Print Ltd, The Sun, The Daily Mirror, The Sunday Mirror, The Daily Telegraph, The Sunday Telegraph, The Times, The Sunday Times, The Daily Mail, The Mail on Sunday, The Express, The Sunday Express*. The articles included news, opinion, features and letters to the editor. As the sample size for the Sunday papers was small, data for *The Guardian* were merged with those of its sister paper *The Observer*, and likewise for *The Daily Telegraph* with *The Sunday Telegraph*, *The Times* with *The Sunday Times* and *The Daily Mirror* with *The Sunday Mirror*. This provided the authors with the following nine categories:

- *The Guardian*
- *I-Independent Print Ltd*
- *The Independent*
- *The Daily Mail*
- *The Daily Mirror*
- *The Express*
- *The Sun*
- *The Telegraph*
- *The Times*

There are some caveats to take into consideration. In particular the methodology employed with the key word search does not allow that mention of 'Islamophobia' may not always be the same thing as complete coverage of the subject matter. For example, it is possible to report on a fire bombing of a mosque without using the word 'Islamophobia'. The same would also apply to the authors' secondary analysis on 'anti-Semitism'. An attack on a Jew or synagogue may not necessarily be reported on with use of the word 'anti-Semitism', and thus some coverage of the issue may have been missed.

Results

Of all the UK national newspapers, the vast majority of articles containing the word 'Islamophobia' in the 2014–15 period were published in *The Guardian* (40 per cent) followed by *The Times* (19.4 per cent) and *The Independent* (15.6 per cent). The majority of these articles for all three publications referred to Islamophobia in the specific context of Muslim communities. Remarkably, there was no mention of Sikhs throughout the whole 2014–15 timeframe. However, an article in *The Independent* on 23 January 2015 referred to the case of Dr Sarandev Singh Bhambra, but referred to him as a 'young Asian dentist' rather than a Sikh.[141]

During the 2016–17 period there was again no mention of Sikhs; however, an article in *The Times* on 26 January 2017, titled 'Goths and travellers get government cash to fight hate crime', referred to the government's decision to fund these groups to monitor and help with hate crime. Sikhs, joined by Hindus had also lobbied for support with reporting hate crime through the NPCC's online hate crime portal True Vision, and this was mentioned albeit in brief.

Again, for this period the vast majority of articles containing the word 'Islamophobia' were published in *The Guardian* (53 per cent), followed jointly by *The Times* (14 per cent) and *The Independent* (14 per cent). The majority of articles in all three of these publications referred to Islamophobia specifically in the context of Muslim communities. During the 2014–15 period, 17.5 per cent of the articles also referred to anti-Semitism, whilst during 2016–17, 11.2 per cent also mentioned anti-Semitism.

Content of articles

Most articles reporting on 'Islamophobic hate crime' statistics failed to acknowledge non-Muslim victims, but it is understood that the fault cannot be assigned to the media itself, because authorities do not break down figures issued to the press. *The Guardian*'s consistently high level of coverage on Islamophobia during both audit periods is by no means surprising. It has a reputation for raising minority rights, sees itself as a champion for the underdog, and the coverage on Islamophobia with reference to Muslims fits its ideological alignment with the Labour Party and liberal left. There were no articles in *The Guardian* during this period that mentioned Sikhs in the context of Islamophobia. Although *The Times* published the second highest number of articles on the subject during the first audit period (joint second in the second audit), it is disappointing that only one article in *The Times* referred to Sikhs and Hindus, and even then, it did not discuss or raise the *racialization of Islamophobia*, or 'mistaken identity'.

The audit also highlights another problem, and that is how the vague word 'Asian' is problematic outside of the context of sexual grooming gangs. The article in *The Independent* on 23 January 2015 referring to Dr Sarandev Singh Bhambra as a 'young Asian dentist' rather than a Sikh shows how even when Sikhs suffered, they have remained invisible due to vague terminology. It is difficult to imagine *The Guardian* reporting on a hate crime against a Muslim as anything other than 'anti-Muslim' or 'Islamophobic'. It would also be unusual

Table 3.1 UK national newspaper audit on 'Islamophobia' (2014–15)

National newspaper*	No. of articles that mention Islamophobia	General reference to Islamophobia	Specific reference to Muslim communities
The Guardian (1)	106/262 **(40%)**	17/34 **(50%)**	89/228 **(39%)**
The Times (2)	51/262 **(19.4%)**	5/34 **(14.7%)**	46/228 **(20.2%)**
The Independent (3)	41/262 **(15.6%)**	5/34 **(14.7%)**	36/228 **(15.7%)**
The Telegraph	23/262 (8.7%)	3/34 (8.8%)	20/228 (8.7%)
The Daily Mail	16/262 (6.1%)	2/34 (5.8%)	14/228 (6.1%)
I-Independent Print Ltd	10/262 (3.8%)	1/34 (2.9%)	9/228 (3.9%)
The Express	9/262 (3.4%)	0/34 (0%)	9/228 (3.5%)

Note
* There were a small number of articles in other publications like *The Daily Mirror* and *The Sun*; however, these were not included in the table. One article had no mention of 'Islamophobia' but came up in the audit due to a related hyperlink.

Table 3.2 UK national newspaper audit on 'Islamophobia' (2016–17)

National newspaper*	No. of articles that mention Islamophobia	General reference to Islamophobia	Specific reference to Muslim communities
The Guardian (1)	175/328 **(53%)**	52/96 **(54%)**	123/232 **(53%)**
The Times (2)	46/328 **(14%)**	9/96 **(9.4%)**	37/232 **(15.9%)**
The Independent (2)	46/328 **(14%)**	17/96 **(17.7%)**	29/232 **(12.6%)**
The Telegraph	18/328 (5.4%)	5/96 (5.2%)	13/232 (5.6%)
The Daily Mail	17/328 (5.1%)	4/96 (4.2%)	13/232 (5.6%)
The Sun	10/328 (3%)	3/96 (3.1%)	7/232 (3%)
I-Independent Print Ltd	9/328 (2.7%)	2/96 (2.1%)	7/232 (3%)

Note
* There were a small number of articles in other publications like *The Daily Mirror*, however these were not included. There were six articles that had no mention of 'Islamophobia' but came up in the audit due to a related hyperlink.

Table 3.3 Number of articles that also mention 'anti-Semitism'

Audit year(s) of UK National newspaper articles	No. of articles that mention 'Islamophobia' (total)	No. of articles that include mention of 'anti-Semitism' no./%
2014–15	262	46 **(17.5%)**
2016–17	328	37 **(11.2%)**

for a journalist to report on an attack on a Jew as one directed against a 'Caucasian'. Why is this then any different for British Sikhs?

These results, as with the Hansard audit, indicate a general indifference to the suffering of Sikhs, as compared with Muslims and Jews. As the authors have already observed, this trend is by no means unique to UK national newspapers, but rather is a systematic issue. It is multifactorial, stemming from subjectivity in police recording (discussed in more detail below), the significant lobbying success of British Muslims/Jews, and a specific focus on Islam in the mainstream media after 9/11.

Over both audit periods, a significant number of articles also mention 'anti-Semitism'. For 2014–15, this came to 17.5 per cent of articles, and for 2016–17, the figure was 11.2 per cent (Table 3.3). Attacks on Jews are often thought of when it comes to the discourse on anti-Muslim hate crime, whereas even though Sikhs suffer Islamophobia, they are left out. This is by no means surprising given the significant intra-faith efforts by Muslim and Jewish groups in jointly tackling hate crime, but also because many news reports rely on official police statistics, which are only available for Jews and Muslims. So it can be concluded that a significant number of stories on Islamophobia against Muslims also refer to anti-Semitic attacks within the same column inches.

In short, the audit paints a bleak picture for Sikhs and highlights how, despite Sikhs being victims of race hate crime, their post-9/11 Sikh experience in Britain has remained on the fringes of the broader political discourse around Islamophobia.

Inaccurate coverage of religion in the media

When religion is discussed, questions about accuracy in reporting are evident, and increasingly an issue, especially when it comes to Islam, but also Sikhism. In 2015, IPSO received 12,278 enquiries and complaints, increasing to 14,455 in 2016. Although the authors must be careful not to extrapolate too much from this dataset, another useful indicator of a disproportionate media focus on Islam is the number of complaints about reporting on the Muslim community adjudicated by IPSO to final published resolution.

Between 2016 and 2018 there were approximately 23 such cases adjudicated by IPSO that reached a final decision, of which seven constituted a breach of the editor's code. Whilst inaccurate coverage of the Muslim community has been clearly observed and corrections made, during the same period there were no final decisions or published resolutions on complaints related to coverage of the Sikh community. According to IPSO, they may well have received Sikh related complaints, but they did not reach the stage of a final decision, and were thus not published on their website. This may have been because complaints were rejected as third-party complaints (complaints by people not affected by the article concerned) or because they were complaints against publications, which IPSO does not regulate and are thus considered outside its remit.[144] However, IPSO told the authors they were aware of complaints related to use of the word 'Asian' (it is not clear if this was related to descriptions of those convicted in sexual grooming cases), and these complaints not necessarily being from Sikhs or Hindus. It is clear however, that the Muslim community regularly engages with the media, and IPSO, to correct any perceived inaccuracies and potential breaches of the Editor's Code.[145]

The media has an important role in helping improve levels of religious literacy for all faiths, and therefore they must continue to be held accountable for misleading or inaccurate coverage. The Muslim community has taken a lead here. Journalists not covering religion as a speciality would also benefit from accurate religious coverage by colleagues. This is the reason that both the government's Anti-Muslim Hatred Working Group and projects flowing from 'Action against hate' (2016) chose to specifically work on 'Muslim literacy in the media', and to collaborate with IPSO to devise training for journalists 'for a better understanding of Islam'[146] respectively. This is also why Bolton MP Yasmin Qureshi launched the APPG for Religion in the Media in 2016.[147] Its *raison d'être* is stated as being:

> To foster a better understanding and representation of religion in the media as religion is a prime motivator of individuals and the community. Also, to aim for a seventh public purpose for the BBC in charter renewal, namely to promote religious literacy.[148]

Again, Sikhs did not have government assistance in framing or delivering structured projects in this critical area, so organizations like the NSO took their own initiative to develop a 'journalists' guide to Sikhism' with IPSO, scheduled to be published in spring 2019. Others, like the Sikh Press Association (hereinafter SikhPA), took positive steps in building relationships with the mainstream media in order to ensure that Sikh stories were covered, and reported accurately. They set up campaigns such as Langar Week, inviting all to participate in Sikhism's institution of the free kitchen or *langar* across *gurdwara*s in Britain and across the world. In doing so, they promoted a better understanding of Sikh ethos by informing others what *langar* stands for – their summary 'Fighting Hunger, Equality in Action and Teaching Compassion'.[149]

Additionally, the SikhPA have grasped the nettle of anti-Sikh hate on several occasions. In 2016 during a broadcast titled 'Sikhs targeted in Islamophobic attacks', they told BBC Asian Network that even though non-Muslims were targeted for their appearance, many did not report incidents to the police.[150] This was echoed by a number of respondents interviewed by the authors: one said that he 'did not report because most times the argument has to be made that a hate crime even occurred and this is time consuming', and another, 'what is the point in engaging in the process if you no [sic] in the end it will not be recorded as such'. A third respondent commented that they had a 'lack of confidence that anything will come of it', but also said that others may not report because of a 'lack of familiarity with the processes'.

Flaws in reporting hate crime figures in the news

As previously suggested, the reporting of hate-crime statistics by journalists was problematic because journalists on tight deadlines do not have time to access the actual breakdown of 'Islamophobic hate crime' figures from forces like the MET, which do not routinely make them available. Thus, many wrongly assumed that the category only covers crimes against Muslims. Headlines like 'Shocking figures reveal spike in anti-Islam hate crime'[151] implied that Muslims were the only victims recorded in the 'Islamophobic hate crime' category. Hence, non-Muslim victims remained invisible. Inaccurate reporting also inflated the perception of crime rates against Muslims beyond the reality. In the case of Sikhs, if they could not quantify the problem in the first place, how could they possibly go about improving it? Some sections of the media therefore inadvertently did a disservice to the wider communities facing the backlash to Islamism.

However, it is important to note that the issue lay further upstream with a lack of transparency and accurate breakdown of figures from authorities issuing hate crime figures such as the MET in the first instance. As previously discussed, the authors already knew through FOI, that 28 per cent of victims of 'Islamophobic hate crime' recorded by the MET in 2015 were non-Muslims or of no recorded faith, and this included Sikhs. Subsequent FOI disclosures from the MET showed that 25 per cent of the total 1,227 victims of 'Islamophobic hate crime' recorded in London between January and December 2016 were either non-Muslims or of unknown faith.[152] For the 2016–17 financial year the MET disclosed that 28 per cent of 1,267 crimes were either non-Muslims or of unknown faith.[153] The non-Muslim component comprised Christians, Hindus, Jews, Sikhs, Buddhists, Atheists and Agnostics.[154] Charles Moore, the former editor of *The Telegraph* and *The Spectator* makes the following observations on the FOI disclosures:

> What to make of this? That morons wanting to upset Muslims cannot even identify their victims accurately? I bet that is quite often the case, though anecdote suggests that anti-Christian attacks – which are not recorded as such – are rising. But it comes back to the thorny question of what counts as a hate crime. As with child abuse claims, this is solemnly recorded as being a crime just because the victim, or anyone else, reports it as such to the police. No corroboration is required. The question then arises, 'Do these figures have any value at all?'[155]

So when reflecting on headlines like 'Anti-Muslim hate crimes increase fivefold since London Bridge attacks',[156] as well as the contents of such articles (which fail to mention non-Muslim victims), it is important to realize that they are simply not a true reflection of the reality on the ground. Such reporting also fails to acknowledge the complexity involved in capturing hate crime statistics. The complexity lies in how hate crime is defined. For example, the MET say 'an Islamophobic offence is any offence which is perceived as Islamophobic by the victim or any other person, that is intended to impact upon those known or perceived to be Muslim'.[157] Therefore, as Charles Moore observed, this subjectivity means that in some cases, victims are not even contacted, and the feelings of 'any other person' are relied upon as evidence.

Notably, the formulation of this peculiar test dates back to the Macpherson Report following the death of black teenager Stephen Lawrence back in 1999. However, who is this 'any other person' whose subjective input the police might rely upon?

Looking into this in more detail, the authors can establish whom the police categorize as 'any other person'. The College of Policing's 'Hate Crime Operational Guidance', sheds further light. Section '1.2.4 Other Person' explains that this may be a police officer, a family member, a witness, 'civil society organisations who know details of the victim, the crime or hate crimes in the locality, such as a third-party reporting charity', a 'person from within the group targeted with the hostility', a professional who supports a victim or 'someone who has knowledge of hate crime in the area – this could include many professionals and experts such as the manager of an education centre used by people with learning disabilities who regularly receives reports of abuse from students'.[158] Rather remarkably, the previous section, '1.2.3 Perception-based recording of hate crime', says, 'the victim does not have to justify or provide evidence of their belief, and police officers or staff should not directly challenge this perception'.[159] Therefore, no evidence base for this element is required at all and the police, if they choose to investigate, should not question the victim's belief.

Indeed, although from April 2017 it became mandatory for all police forces to disaggregate religious hate crime, these statistics can still only be obtained through FOI (for example, they are not broken down on the MET's hate crime or special crime dashboard), and thus the status quo for the reporting press remains unchanged. This means the perception of hate crime against Muslims will continue to be inflated, and non-Muslim victims (like Sikhs) remain invisible. The MET has more than 900 specialist members of staff dedicated to investigating hate crime (along with domestic abuse), and the number of officers was recently increased by 30 per cent.[160] It is difficult to understand why, with this level of resource, the MET are unable to publish the breakdown on their special crime dashboard for the public to view. Having analysed the reporting and breakdown of the Sikh experience it is clear that in terms of police reporting and recording, the British Sikh experience is in contrast to the American one. Following years of lobbying, in 2015 the FBI started to separately monitor hate crime against Sikhs, Hindus and Arabs (although on a voluntary basis).[161] In this respect, Britain is still lagging behind the US.

Conclusion

When it comes to hate crime it is clear from the perspective of historical events, police reporting categories, the current political discourse and media focus that anti-Semitism and Islamophobia are clear areas of priority, and there continues to be a significant commitment of public resource and political momentum behind this, and understandably so due to the numbers of attacks that are revealed by reporting figures and research.

Sikhs, however, have largely been absent from this national conversation, and government initiatives to tackle Islamophobia and anti-Semitism need to be extended to Sikhs and other non-Abrahamic faiths. The British government has recently begun to acknowledge hate crime affecting Sikhs following the publication of its 2016 'Abrahamic-centric' hate crime action plan and its recent 'Action against hate' 'refresh' report (2018). However, at the same time it is also true that there remains no separate category for 'anti-Sikh' attacks in police recording and monitoring. This all needs to change so that data sets can be improved and the real depth of the problem can be ascertained. There needs to be a concerted effort by the government and the community to engage in constructive dialogue to ensure that this happens. Further suggestions will be explored in the conclusion.

Notes

1 Shami Chakrabarti (2016). *Shami Chakrabarti Inquiry Report*. [online] Available at: https://labour.org.uk/wp-content/uploads/2017/10/Chakrabarti-Inquiry-Report-30June16.pdf [Accessed 15 January 2018].

2 BBC News (2017). 'Labour nominee dropped "for anti-Semitism"'. [online] Available at: www.bbc.co.uk/news/uk-england-leeds-42009240 [Accessed 18 November 2017].

3 D. Gayle (2017). 'Man who harassed MP Luciana Berger online is jailed for two years'. *The Guardian*. [online] Available at: www.theguardian.com/uk-news/2016/dec/08/man-joshua-bonehill-paine-harassed-mp-luciana-berger-online-jailed-two-years [Accessed 19 November 2017].

4 L. Dearden (2014). 'Israel–Gaza conflict: Anti-Semitic incidents "up 500%" in UK since'. *The Independent*. [online] Available at: www.independent.co.uk/news/uk/home-news/israel-gaza-conflict-anti-semitic-incidents-up-500-in-uk-since-start-of-bombardment-of-gaza-9681324.html [Accessed 28 December 2017].

5 S. Paterson (2017). 'One third of British Jews have considered quitting the UK because of anti-Semitic hate crimes reveals shock new survey'. *The Daily Mail*. [online] Available at: www.dailymail.co.uk/news/article-4806578/One-British-Jews-considered-quitting-UK.html [Accessed 18 November 2017].

6 L. Dearden (2017). 'Anti-Semitic attacks hit record high in UK'. *The Independent*. [online] Available at: www.independent.co.uk/news/uk/home-news/anti-semitic-hate-crime-attacks-british-jews-assaults-uk-incidents-record-high-cst-research-a7861721.html [Accessed 18 November 2017].

7 S. Daisley (2017). 'Britain has an anti-Semitism problem. Here are the numbers that prove it'. *Coffee House*. [online] Available at: https://blogs.spectator.co.uk/2017/09/britain-has-an-anti-semitism-problem-and-now-we-have-the-numbers-to-prove-it/ [Accessed 23 November 2017].

8 *The Economist* (2018). 'A senior British rabbi takes the fight to Jeremy Corbyn'. [online] Available at: www.economist.com/erasmus/2018/08/29/a-senior-british-rabbi-takes-the-fight-to-jeremy-corbyn [Accessed 16 September 2018].

9 D. Sugarman (2018). 'NUS president makes video apology after Judaism left off student survey'. *The Jewish Chronicle* [online] Available at: www.thejc.com/news/uk-news/nus-president-shakira-martin-makes-video-apology-after-judaism-left-off-student-survey-1.451497 [Accessed 15 January 2018].

10 R. Pells (2016). 'MPs have accused the NUS president of "outright racism"'. *The Independent*. [online] Available at: www.independent.co.uk/news/education/nus-president-malia-bouattia-anti-semitism-parliament-home-affairs-select-committee-israel-a7363591.html [Accessed 16 January 2018].

11 P. Walker (2017). 'Ukip MEP's "death cult" remarks spark new Islamophobia row'. *The Guardian.* [online] Available at: www.theguardian.com/politics/2017/apr/29/ukip-new-islamophobia-row-death-cult-remarks-gerard-batten-paul-nuttall [Accessed 18 November 2017].

12 Channel 4 (2016). 'C4 survey and documentary reveals what British Muslims really think'. [online] Available at: www.channel4.com/info/press/news/c4-survey-and-documentary-reveals-what-british-muslims-really-think [Accessed 17 January 2018].

13 Ibid.

14 M. Beckford (2008). 'Blasphemy laws are lifted'. *The Telegraph.* [online] Available at: www.telegraph.co.uk/news/1942668/Blasphemy-laws-are-lifted.html [Accessed 17 January 2018].

15 J. Delingpole (2016). 'Trevor Phillips's documentary on Muslims was shocking – but not surprising'. *The Spectator.* [online] Available at: www.spectator.co.uk/2016/04/why-do-we-pretend-that-all-muslims-are-sweet-smiley-and-integrated/ [Accessed 27 November 2017].

16 PREVENT is one of the government's strands of its counter-extremism policy, launched by the Labour government in 2003.

17 M. Lipka (2017). 'Muslims and Islam: Key findings in the US and around the world'. Pew Research Center. [online] Available at: www.pewresearch.org/fact-tank/2017/08/09/muslims-and-islam-key-findings-in-the-u-s-and-around-the-world/ [Accessed 22 November 2017].

18 J. Curtis (2016). 'Man jailed for leaving a bacon sandwich outside a mosque is found dead in prison halfway through his 12-month sentence'. *The Daily Mail* [online]. Available at: www.dailymail.co.uk/news/article-4075328/Man-jailed-leaving-bacon-sandwiched-outside-mosque-dead-prison-half-way-12-month-sentence.html [Accessed 20 November 2017].

19 V. Dodd and J. Grierson (2017). 'Finsbury Park attack suspect was probably "self-radicalised"'. *The Guardian.* [online] Available at: www.theguardian.com/uk-news/2017/jun/21/finsbury-park-mosque-attack-two-victims-in-critical-care [Accessed 20 November 2017].

20 D. Batty (2011). 'Lady Warsi claims Islamophobia is now socially acceptable in Britain'. *The Guardian.* [online] Available at: www.theguardian.com/uk/2011/jan/20/lady-warsi-islamophobia-muslims-prejudice [Accessed 10 October 2018].

21 H. Agerholm (2017). 'Women "bearing brunt" of Islamophobic attacks in the UK'. [online] *The Independent.* Available at: www.independent.co.uk/news/uk/home-news/uk-islamophobia-attacks-women-bearing-brunt-hate-crimes-a8036581.html [Accessed 19 December 2017].

22 House of Commons (2015). Register of All-Party Groups as at 30 July 2015: Islamophobia. [online] Available at: https://publications.parliament.uk/pa/cm/cmallparty/register/islamophobia.htm [Accessed 17 November 2017].

23 Twitter (2017). APPG Antisemitism (@APPGAA) on Twitter. [online] Available at: https://twitter.com/APPGAA?ref_src=twsrc%5Egoogle%7Ctwcamp%5Eserp%7Ctwgr%5Eauthor [Accessed 17 November 2017].

24 APPG on British Jews (2014). Home – All-Party Parliamentary Group on British Jews. [online] Available at: http://appgbritishjews.org.uk/ [Accessed 28 November 2017].

25 APPG on British Muslims (2017). Homepage of the APPG on British Muslims. [online] Available at: https://appgbritishmuslims.org/ [Accessed 28 November 2017].

26 Ministry of Housing, Communities & Local Government (2017). Anti-Muslim Hatred Working Group. GOV.UK. [online] Available at: www.gov.uk/government/groups/anti-muslim-hatred-working-group [Accessed 7 December 2017].

27 Ministry of Housing, Communities & Local Government (2017). Draft Terms of Reference for the Anti-Muslim Hatred Working Group. [online] Available at:

www.gov.uk/government/uploads/system/uploads/attachment_data/file/571139/
AMHWG_-_terms_of_reference.pdf [Accessed 28 November 2017].

28 P. Walker (2017). 'Theresa May promises to protect mosques after Finsbury Park
attack'. [online] *The Guardian*. Available at: www.theguardian.com/uk-news/2017/
jun/19/theresa-may-to-chair-cobra-meeting-after-finsbury-park-terror-attack
[Accessed 20 November 2017].

29 House of Commons (2014). Hansard Written Answers for 30 April 2014 (pt 0001).
[online] Available at: https://publications.parliament.uk/pa/cm201314/cmhansrd/
cm140430/text/140430w0001.htm [Accessed 17 November 2017].

30 Gilligan, 'Muslim hate monitor to lose backing'.

31 DLCG FOI response on file dated 5 January 2016.

32 Ibid.

33 Hansard. HL Deb (20 December 2018) Islamophobia vol. 794 col. 1937. [online]
Available at: https://hansard.parliament.uk/Lords/2018-12-20/debates/2F954D45-
1962-4256-A492-22EBF6AEF8F0/Islamophobia   (Accessed: 31   December
2018).

34 University of Cambridge (2009). *Contextualising Islam in Britain*. [online]
Available at: www.cam.ac.uk/research/news/contextualising-islam-in-britain-report-
released [Accessed 28 November 2017].

35 Information obtained from FOI responses (on file) from the then Department for
Communities and Local Government provides a breakdown of funding to various
faith groups.

36 Ministry of Housing, Communities & Local Government, and Prime Minister's
Office (2016). 'Government leads the way in tackling anti-Semitism'. GOV.UK.
[online] Available at: www.gov.uk/government/news/government-leads-the-way-in-
tackling-anti-semitism [Accessed 20 November 2017].

37 Hope, 'Amber Rudd pledges £13.4million'.

38 Community Security Trust (2017). Protecting our Jewish Community: Other Communities. [online] Available at: https://cst.org.uk/about-cst/other-communities
[Accessed 18 November 2017].

39 True Vision (2017). 'Stop homophobic, transphobic, racial, religious and disability
hate crime'. [online] Available at: www.report-it.org.uk/home [Accessed 24 December 2017].

40 NPCC (2015). 'Police agree data sharing protocols with the Community Security
Trust and TELL MAMA'. National Police Chiefs' Council [online] Available at:
https://news.npcc.police.uk/releases/police-agree-data-sharing-protocols-with-the-
community-security-trust-and-tell-mama [Accessed 24 December 2017].

41 BBC News (2015). 'Anti-Muslim crimes get own category'. [online] Available at:
www.bbc.co.uk/news/uk-34511274 [Accessed 16 November 2017].

42 H. Singh (2017). 'Is Britain becoming a Christianophobic country?' *Coffee House*.
[online] Available at: https://blogs.spectator.co.uk/2017/11/is-britain-becoming-a-
christianophobic-country/ [Accessed 24 December 2017].

43 National Union of Students (2017). It's Islamophobia Awareness Month @ NUS
connect. [online] Available at: www.nusconnect.org.uk/articles/it-s-islamophobia-
awareness-month [Accessed 24 November 2017].

44 Transport for London (2017). TfL and the police join forces to combat hate
crime. [online] Available at: https://tfl.gov.uk/info-for/media/press-releases/2017/
october/tfl-and-the-police-join-forces-to-combat-hate-crime [Accessed 24 November
2017].

45 Ibid.

46 London Datastore (2018). 'Population by Religion, Borough'. Office for National
Statistics (ONS) [online] Available at: https://data.london.gov.uk/dataset/percentage-
population-religion-borough [Accessed 3 July. 2018].

47 H. Singh (2015). 'UK Sikhs remain invisible victims'.

48 Home Office (2017). 'Places of worship: Security funding scheme'. GOV.UK. [online] Available at: www.gov.uk/guidance/places-of-worship-security-funding-scheme [Accessed 23 November 2017].

49 A. Taher (2016). 'Churches used £2.4m government grant to fend off witches and Satanists'. *Mail Online*. [online] Available at: www.dailymail.co.uk/news/article-3886006/Church-cash-fend-jihadis-witches-Hundreds-government-funding-protect-against-pagans-Halloween.html [Accessed 22 November 2017].

50 Email from Home Office Press Office on file dated 8 December 2017.

51 BBC News (2013). 'Homeless and hungry Sikh temples'. [online] Available at: www.bbc.co.uk/news/uk-england-21711980 [Accessed 28 November 2017].

52 *Asian Voice* (2017). 'Applications open for government-funded security at places of worship'. [online] Available at: www.asian-voice.com/News/UK/Applications-open-for-government-funded-security-at-places-of-worship [Accessed 24 November 2017].

53 L. Dearden (2018). 'Hostility to men could become hate crime under government plans'. *The Independent*. [online] Available at: www.independent.co.uk/news/uk/crime/hate-crime-men-misogyny-misandry-age-women-laws-review-law-commission-action-plan-rise-a8585236.html [Accessed 17 October 2018].

54 Sikh Spirit (2001). 'Blair condemns attacks on British Sikh community'. [online] Available at: www.sikhspirit.com/khalsa/nso011211.htm [Accessed 22 November 2017].

55 Ibid.

56 UK Parliament (2004). Early day motion 1540 – Mr Nick Griffin and Islamophobia. [online] Available at: www.parliament.uk/edm/2003-04/1540 [Accessed 18 November 2017].

57 House of Commons, Select Committee on Home Affairs, (2004). Minutes of Evidence. 'Examination of Witnesses (Questions 100–119)'.

58 BBC News (2005). 'UK Parliament launches Sikh group'. [online] Available at: http://news.bbc.co.uk/1/hi/uk_politics/4675079.stm [Accessed 28 November 2017].

59 UK Parliament (2005). Early day motion 645 – London bombings and attacks on Sikhs. [online] Available at: www.parliament.uk/edm/2005-06/645 [Accessed 23 November 2017].

60 Interview with Parmjit Singh Dhanda conducted by Hardeep Singh, on file (2018).

61 APPG Inquiry into Electoral Conduct (2013). Report of the All-Party Parliamentary Inquiry into Electoral Conduct. [online] Available at: https://files.graph.cool/cj3e6rg8y906h0104uh8bojao/cj4muuuz500250145fwnqvzat [Accessed 23 November 2017].

62 H. Singh (2015). 'Sikh lives matter in Britain too'.

63 *Guardian, The* (2005). 'Shivani Nagarajah talks to non-Muslim Asians about feeling under siege'. [online] Available at: www.theguardian.com/world/2005/September/05/religion.July7 [Accessed 25 November 2017].

64 Ibid.

65 United Sikhs (2009). Press release: 'UK school bans kirpan forcing Sikh out of school'. [online] Available at: www.unitedsikhs.org/PressReleases/PRSRLS-08-10-2009-00.html [Accessed 26 November 2017].

66 Steve Brine (2011). 'Launch of the Sikh Council UK'. [online] Available at: www.stevebrine.com/news/launch-sikh-council-uk [Accessed 1 May 2019].

67 Sikh Aware UK (2017). About Us. [online] Available at: https://sikhaware.co.uk/about-us/ [Accessed 29 November 2017].

69 The Sikh Network, 'UK Sikh Survey 2016', p. 5. Jhutti-Johal queried this figure in a blog post titled 'Research on the Sikh community in the UK is essential to better inform policy, but surveys must be improved'. [online] Available at: http://blogs.lse.ac.uk/religionglobalsociety/2017/01/research-on-the-sikh-community-in-the-uk-is-essential-to-better-inform-policy-but-surveys-must-be-improved/ [Accessed 30 April 2019].

70 The Sikh Network, 'UK Sikh Survey 2016', p. 9.
71 CS has been writing reports based on surveys of British Sikhs that have been launched in parliament since 2013. These have included pertinent questions on current issues.
72 British Sikh Report 2017, p. 29.
73 House of Commons, Select Committee on Home Affairs (2004). Written Evidence. '24.Memorandum submitted by the Metropolitan Police Diversity Directorate'. [online] Available at: https://publications.parliament.uk/pa/cm200405/cmselect/cmhaff/165ii/165we25.htm [Accessed 24 November 2017].
74 Hansard. HL Deb (25 June 2015) Communities: Young Muslims vol. (unknown) col. 1697. [online] Available at: https://publications.parliament.uk/pa/ld201516/ldhansrd/text/150625-0001.htm#15062547000429 [Accessed: 24 November 2017].
75 Ibid.
76 Hansard. HC Deb (22 June 2017) Terror Attacks vol. 626 col. 211. [online] Available at: https://hansard.parliament.uk/commons/2017-06-22/debates/D00D2537-BD22-4E4D-8E65-FE170E02848A/TerrorAttacks [Accessed: 26 November 2017].
77 ONS data on file: According to the 2011 census, 10.3 per cent of the population of the London Borough of Hounslow is Hindu and 9 per cent is Sikh – amongst the highest proportions for each respective faith group nationally.
78 Hansard. HC Deb (15 March 2017) Visible Religious Symbols: European Court Ruling vol. 623 col. 419. [online] Available at: https://hansard.parliament.uk/commons/2017-03-15/debates/599884E8-6E05-41C0-8FD3-B6F5A6E1F45F/VisibleReligiousSymbolsEuropeanCourtRuling [Accessed: 26 November 2017].
79 ONS (2011). 'Religion in England and Wales 2011'. [online] Available at: www.ons.gov.uk/peoplepopulationandcommunity/culturalidentity/religion/articles/religioninenglandandwales2011/2012-12-11 [Accessed 2 December 2017].
80 S. Singh (2012). 'Revisiting the victim narrative'. [online] Available at: http://archive.jsonline.com/news/opinion/revisiting-the-victim-narrative-dq818fg-184769641.html/ [Accessed 18 January 2018].
81 The 'refresh' (Action against hate: The UK government's plan for tackling hate crime – 'two years on') did provide a case study of a *gurdwara* that had received £8,000 for CCTV in 2018 from the Home Office funding scheme to protect places of worship.
82 As mentioned in an article by Hardeep Singh in *The Spectator* in late 2016, from a Sikh perspective 'Action against hate' may well have been described as a 'damp squib'. Singh, 'It's time the Government ended its silence on Sikh hate crime victims'.
83 C. Moore (2016). 'Is it Islamophobic to record "Christianophobic" hate crimes?' *Coffee House*. [online] Available at: https://blogs.spectator.co.uk/2016/02/is-it-islamophobic-to-record-christianophobic-hate-crimes/ [Accessed 28 November 2017].
84 Email communication on file from Mark A. Hall (Policy Analyst, Dharmic, Sikh and Bahá'í Faith Engagement/Remembering Srebrenica, Faith Engagement Team) and Hardeep Singh (Network of Sikh Organisations) dated 26 May 2016.
85 UK Parliament (2017). Written evidence – Network of Sikh Organisations. [online] Available at: http://data.parliament.uk/writtenevidence/committeeevidence.svc/evidencedocument/home-affairs-committee/hate-crime-and-its-violent-consequences/written/45945.html [Accessed 19 November 2017].
86 H. Singh (2016). 'It's time the Government ended its silence on Sikh hate crime victims'.
87 Home Office (2016). Action against hate. [online] Available at: www.gov.uk/government/uploads/system/uploads/attachment_data/file/543679/Action_Against_Hate_-_UK_Government_s_Plan_to_Tackle_Hate_Crime_2016.pdf [Accessed 30 December 2017].
88 BBC News (2015). 'The Sikh boy labelled a "terrorist" by his classmates'. [online] Available at: www.bbc.co.uk/news/blogs-trending-31695234 [Accessed 30 December 2017].

89 H. Sherwood (2016). 'Sikhs in UK are "invisible to government" despite hate crime increase'. *The Guardian.* [online] Available at: www.theguardian.com/world/2016/nov/25/sikhs-in-uk-are-invisible-to-government-despite-hate-increase [Accessed 28 November 2017].

90 Hansard. HL Deb (14 September 2016) Hate Crime vol. 774 col. 1457. [online] Available at: https://hansard.parliament.uk/lords/2016-09-14/debates/AAC3CAC3-78CC-4B7F-B50C-FFB58FBD7244/HateCrime [Accessed: 8 October 2017].

91 Home Office (2016). 'Home Secretary visits Britain's biggest gurdwara'. GOV.UK. [online] Available at: www.gov.uk/government/news/home-secretary-visits-britains-biggest-gurdwara [Accessed 2 December 2017].

92 Ibid.

93 Ministry of Housing, Communities & Local Government (2017). 'New hate crime package to target groups at need'. GOV.UK. [online] Available at: www.gov.uk/government/news/new-hate-crime-package-to-target-groups-at-need [Accessed 19 November 2017].

94 The Sikh Network (2017). Cllr Preet Kaur Gill. [online] Available at: www.thesikhnetwork.com/team/cllr-preet-kaur-gill/ [Accessed 28 November 2017].

95 Lamiat, Sabin (2017). 'Crimes against Sikhs left out of Tory action plan'. *Morning Star* [online] Available at: www.morningstaronline.co.uk/a-5172-Crimes-against-Sikhs-left-out-of-Tory-action-plan [Accessed 28 November 2017].

96 Hansard. HC Deb (18 July 2018). Drugs Policy vol. 627 col. 748. [online] Available at: https://hansard.parliament.uk/commons/2017-07-18/debates/733C6229-49D0-4559-8F59-5F1244C2DE13/DrugsPolicy [Accessed: 5 December 2017].

97 Trevor Phillips, who commissioned the original Runnymede report, admitted he had 'got almost everything wrong' on Muslim immigration. On publication of the 2016 ICM Poll results featured in the C4 documentary 'What British Muslims Really Think', Phillips said that followers of Islam in the West were creating 'nations within nations'. R. Kassam (2016). 'UK Equalities Chief who popularised the term "Islamophobia" admits: "I thought Muslims would blend into Britain … I should have known better"'. *Breitbart.* [online] Available at: www.breitbart.com/london/2016/04/10/thought-europes-muslims-gradually-blend-britains-diverse-landscape-known-better/ [Accessed 30 November 2017]. This dramatic change in opinion resulted in his 2017 nomination for the controversial satirical 'Islamophobe of the year' award from the Islamic Human Rights Commission, which, Phillips told *The Sunday Times,* had 'painted a target on the back of people on the list'. See Nicholas Hellen (2017). 'Islamophobia award "puts target on back" of former Equalities Chief Trevor Phillips'. *The Times* [online] Available at: www.thetimes.co.uk/edition/news/islamophobia-award-puts-target-on-back-of-former-equalities-chief-5j3swc7dg [Accessed 30 November 2017]. Other nominees included Dame Louise Casey, who was responsible for the eponymous comprehensive review into opportunity and integration. See L. Casey (2016). *The Casey Review: A Review into Opportunity and Integration.* GOV.UK [online] Available at: www.gov.uk/government/publications/the-casey-review-a-review-into-opportunity-and-integration [Accessed 22 December 2017]. Previous nominees of 'Islamophobe of the year' included the journalists at Charlie Hebdo, who two months prior to their nomination had been shot dead by an Islamist gunman. See V. Richards (2015). '"Insensitive" or "tongue in cheek"? Murdered Charlie Hebdo staff given award – for Islamophobia'. *The Independent.* [online] Available at: www.independent.co.uk/news/world/europe/charlie-hebdo-murdered-staff-given-islamophobe-of-the-year-award-10100317.html [Accessed 30 November 2017]. Trevor Phillips is not alone in facing this kind of reaction. It is important to note that the accusation 'Islamophobia' can be used to shut down legitimate debate on aspects of Islam or the behaviour of a minority of Muslims. Some prominent journalists have also run into difficulty.

98 Conway, *Islamophobia: A Challenge for Us All.*

 99 Farah and Khan, *Islamophobia: Still a Challenge*.
100 Ibid.
101 Sidhu and Gohil, *Civil Rights in Wartime*.
102 R. Kalvapalle (2017). 'Jagmeet Singh speaks out about anti-Islam heckling incident: "Hate doesn't pick and choose"'. *Global News*. [online] Available at: https://global-news.ca/news/3732571/jagmeet-singh-racist-heckler-statement/ [Accessed 16 January 2018].
103 Ibid.
104 YouTube (2018). Jagmeet Singh 'heckler': Her side of the story. [online] Available at: www.youtube.com/watch?reload=9&v=rfaqa1aCudA [Accessed 31 January 2018].
105 M103 – on systemic racism and religious discrimination – was a private member's motion introduced by Canadian MP Iqra Khalid representing Mississauga (Erin Mills. Mississauga, Ontario). Text of motion:

> That, in the opinion of the House, the government should: (a) recognize the need to quell the increasing public climate of hate and fear; (b) condemn Islamophobia and all forms of systemic racism and religious discrimination and take note of House of Commons' petition e-411 and the issues raised by it; and (c) request that the Standing Committee on Canadian Heritage undertake a study on how the government could (i) develop a whole-of-government approach to reducing or eliminating systemic racism and religious discrimination including Islamophobia, in Canada, while ensuring a community-centered focus with a holistic response through evidence-based policy-making, (ii) collect data to contextualize hate crime reports and to conduct needs assessments for impacted communities, and that the Committee should present its findings and recommendations to the House no later than 240 calendar days from the adoption of this motion, provided that in its report, the Committee should make recommendations that the government may use to better reflect the enshrined rights and freedoms in the Constitution Acts, including the Canadian Charter of Rights and Freedoms.
>
> (Available at: www.ourcommons.ca/Parliamentarians/en/members/ Iqra-Khalid(88849)/Motions [Accessed 9 May 2019])

106 *Global News* (2017). 'House of Commons passes anti-Islamophobia motion M-103'. [online] Available at: https://globalnews.ca/news/3330776/anti-islamophobia-motion-m-103-approved/ [Accessed 31 January 2018].
107 C. Allen (2018). 'Why UK's working definition of Islamophobia as a "type of racism" is a historic step'. *The Conversation* [online]. Available at: https://the conversation.com/why-uks-working-definition-of-islamophobia-as-a-type-of-racism-is-a-historic-step-107657 [Accessed 27 November 2018].
108 The authors of Islamophobia Defined wrote: 'Let us be clear, the aim of establishing a working definition of Islamophobia has neither been motivated by, nor is intended to curtail, free speech or criticism of Islam as a religion.' This nevertheless has and continues to be a contentious area.
109 S. Khan (2018). 'We are still ignoring victims of anti-Muslim prejudice'. *Huffington Post UK*. [online] Available at: www.huffingtonpost.co.uk/entry/islamophobia-extremism-hate-crime-racism_uk_5c0566e8e4b066b5cfa475a3 [Accessed 3 December 2018].
110 L. Dearden (2018). 'More than 420 Rotherham grooming gang suspects being investigated in "unprecedented" operation'. *The Independent*. [online] Available at: www. independent.co.uk/news/uk/crime/grooming-gangs-rotherham-suspects-victims-girls-rape-uk-nca-prosecutions-a8609511.html [Accessed 5 December 2018].
111 M. Taylor and H. Siddique (2012). 'Muslim leaders warn of far right exploitation of Rochdale child sex case'. *The Guardian*. [online] Available at: www.theguardian. com/uk/2012/may/11/far-right-rochdale-sex-case [Accessed 6 November 2017].

112 E. Hill (2018). 'As a Rotherham grooming gang survivor, I am scared by racism and hate crime in Brexit Britain'. *The Independent*. [online] Available at: www.independent.co.uk/voices/brexit-deal-racism-hate-crime-rotherham-grooming-gang-child-sex-abuse-islamophobia-definition-a8666416.html [Accessed 5 December 2018].

113 Ibid.

114 R. Malcolm (2018). 'West Bridgford man fined for "Muslim peado" comment towards Sikh man'. *Nottingham Post*. [online] Available at: www.nottinghampost.com/news/local-news/west-bridgford-man-fined-muslim-2264283 [Accessed 3 December 2018].

115 It is worth noting that whilst the current debate on 'grooming gangs' has revolved primarily around convictions of men targeting white girls across Britain, on 23 April 2013 seven Sikhs were jailed for a 'revenge attack' at the Muslim-run Moghul Durbar restaurant in Leicester, because they suspected a Sikh girl was being sexually assaulted on the premises. BBC News (2013). 'Seven jailed for "revenge attack"'. [online] Available at: www.bbc.co.uk/news/uk-england-leicestershire-22315118 [Accessed 17 January 2018]. When the police began an investigation, it transpired their suspicions proved to be well founded. Six men were jailed on 30 August 2013 for paying or offering to pay a 'vulnerable and damaged' 16-year-old Sikh girl for sex. BBC News (2013). 'Six jailed over child prostitution'. [online] Available at: www.bbc.co.uk/news/uk-england-23896937 [Accessed 17 January 2018]. In fact, there has been a history of violence between a section of Sikh and Pakistani Muslim communities in Britain, in areas like the West Midlands, Slough and West London. In a letter to Labour colleagues, Fiona Mactaggart (former MP for Slough), writes that when she stood for election in 1997, the town 'was a troubled place, rival gangs of Sikh and Muslim youth were trying to kill each other on our streets'. M. Smith (2017). 'Labour MP Fiona Mactaggart quits because she is "bored of political squabbles"'. *The Mirror*. [online] Available at: www.mirror.co.uk/news/politics/labour-mp-fiona-mactaggart-steps-10261079 [Accessed 22 January 2018]. In 2018, members of a 20-strong grooming gang in Huddersfield were jailed, and there were two Sikhs amongst them: Amere Singh Dhaliwal and Raj Singh Basran. Dhaliwal caused the most outrage within the Sikh community because at the time of the trial, he appeared as a turban-wearing, initiated Sikh. Some members of the community falsely suggested he was a Muslim who had converted to Sikhism. They made this claim to deflect negative attention away from the Sikh community, but also to strengthen their narrative that Muslim men were adopting the Sikh identity to harm the community. Much of the narrative being promoted by some groups is very Islamophobic, particularly when it comes to Britain's grooming gang problem. L. Dearden (2018). 'Huddersfield grooming gang convicted of abusing vulnerable girls'. *The Independent*. [online] Available at: www.independent.co.uk/news/uk/crime/huddersfield-child-abuse-ring-sex-trial-court-grooming-tommy-robinson-reporting-restrictions-a8592176.html [Accessed 20 October 2018]. This tension between Sikhs and Muslim is also discussed K.P. Sian (2013), *Unsettling Sikh and Muslim conflict: Mistaken Identities, Forced Conversions, and Postcolonial Formations*.

116 H. Khaleeli (2016). 'The perils of "flying while Muslim"'. *The Guardian*. [online] Available at: www.theguardian.com/world/2016/aug/08/the-perils-of-flying-while-muslim [Accessed 6 December 2017].

117 Ibid.

118 On file response to editor written by Hardeep Singh, 13 January 2006.

119 Although it is by no means the only example, it is difficult to forget the egregious Fox News interview following the 2012 Wisconsin temple massacre, where a distraught Sikh was ignorantly asked by an ill-informed interviewer if the community had previously faced any 'anti-Semitic acts' when he should have asked about 'anti-Sikh attacks'. In such situations it is important that organizations like the

British-based Sikh Press Association formed in 2015, ensure that there is correct reporting of Sikh affairs, and publication of accurate stories that help to educate others about the Sikh ethos.

120 *VICE News* (2017). 'Trump's Jerusalem decision is reigniting anti-Semitism in Europe'. [online] Available at: https://news.vice.com/story/trumps-jerusalem-decision-is-reigniting-anti-semitism-in-europe [Accessed 18 December 2017].

121 The authors have conducted a Nexis audit of national newspaper articles that clearly shows left-leaning publications like *The Guardian* dedicating significant attention to 'Islamophobia', be it news, opinion or features.

122 T. Batchelor (2017). 'Islamophobic hate crimes jump fivefold after London Bridge terror attack'. *The Independent*. [online] Available at: www.independent.co.uk/News/uk/crime/london-bridge-attack-latest-rise-islamophobic-hate-crimes-borough-market-stabbing-terror-police-a7777451.html [Accessed 7 December 2017].

123 A. Travis (2017). 'Anti-Muslim hate crime surges after Manchester and London Bridge attacks'. *The Guardian*. [online] Available at: www.theguardian.com/society/2017/jun/20/anti-muslim-hate-surges-after-manchester-and-london-bridge-attacks [Accessed 7 December 2017].

124 V. Dodd and S. Marsh (2017). 'Anti-Muslim hate crimes increase fivefold since London Bridge attacks'. *The Guardian*. [online] Available at: www.theguardian.com/uk-news/2017/jun/07/anti-muslim-hate-crimes-increase-fivefold-since-london-bridge-attacks [Accessed 7 December 2017].

125 C. Chaplain and M. Bentham (2017). 'Shocking figures reveal spike in anti-Islam hate crime in London'. *Evening Standard*. [online] Available at: www.standard.co.uk/news/crime/shocking-figures-reveal-spike-in-antiislam-hate-crime-across-london-with-25-more-offences-reported-a3660501.html [Accessed 12 September 2018].

126 Ministry of Housing, Communities & Local Government (2013). 'Tell MAMA' (Measuring Anti-Muslim Attacks) speech. GOV.UK. [online] Available at: www.gov.uk/government/speeches/tell-mama-measuring-anti-muslim-attacks-speech [Accessed 7 December 2017].

127 Ibid.

128 A. Lusher (2017). 'Channel 4 mocked for blacking up white woman to disguise her as Muslim'. *The Independent*. [online] Available at: www.independent.co.uk/arts-entertainment/tv/news/my-week-as-a-muslim-channel-4-documentary-black-up-brownface-row-white-woman-islamophobia-racism-a8016911.html [Accessed 11 December 2017].

129 BBC, Media Centre (2016). 'United States of hate: Muslims under attack'. [online] Available at: www.bbc.co.uk/mediacentre/proginfo/2016/21/united-states-of-hate [Accessed 11 December 2017].

130 Guru Gobind Singh, Akaal Ustat, *Dasam Granth*, Ang 17. [online] Available at: www.searchgurbani.com/dasam-granth/index/chapter/en [Accessed 1 May 2019].

131 Eleanor Nesbitt (2016) 'Sikh diversity in the UK: Contexts and evolution', in K. Jacobsen and K. Myrvold (2016). *Sikhs in Europe*. London: Routledge.

132 H. Grewal (2016). 'Interfaith marriage is not the battle young Sikhs should be fighting'. *The Independent*. [online] Available at: www.independent.co.uk/voices/if-young-sikhs-opposing-interfaith-marriage-are-just-asserting-their-religious-identity-here-are-the-a7296631.html [Accessed 8 December 2017].

133 A. Lusher (2017). 'Influential Sikh youth group associating with far-right EDL founder Tommy Robinson'. *The Independent*. [online] Available at: www.independent.co.uk/news/uk/home-news/sikh-youth-uk-muslim-film-university-tommy-robinson-edl-scx-groomers-islamophobia-racism-a8002526.html [Accessed 8 December 2017].

134 A. Bassey (2017). 'Sikh TV accused of encouraging vigilantes to target groomers'. *Birmingham Mail*. [online] Available at: www.birminghammail.co.uk/news/

midlands-news/birmingham-sikh-tv-channel-accused-13468017 [Accessed 24 December 2017].

135 BBC (2016). 'The selfless Sikh: Faith on the frontline'. BBC One. [online] Available at: www.bbc.co.uk/programmes/b0834s76 [Accessed 19 December 2017].

136 Saner, 'Why are Sikhs targeted'.

137 N. Chester (2017). 'Why isn't the Government doing more to tackle anti-Sikh discrimination?' *Vice*. [online] Available at: www.vice.com/en_uk/article/ezmyam/why-isnt-the-government-doing-more-to-tackle-anti-sikh-discrimination-89 [Accessed 10 December 2017].

138 H. Singh (2016). 'It's time the Government ended its silence on Sikh hate crime victims'.

139 Interviews with Orlando Crowcroft conducted by Hardeep Singh on file.

140 B. Farmer (2008). 'BBC favours Muslims, complain Hindus and Sikhs'. *The Telegraph*. [online] Available at: www.telegraph.co.uk/news/religion/2703863/BBC-favours-Muslims-complain-Hindus-and-Sikhs.html [Accessed 8 December 2017].

141 BBC, Press Office (2004). 'Sikhs and the City'. [online] Available at: www.bbc.co.uk/pressoffice/pressreleases/stories/2004/08_august/13/sikhs.shtml [Accessed 8 December 2017].

142 Centre for the Study of Islam in the UK (2008). 'The role of the media'. [online] Available at: http://sites.cardiff.ac.uk/islamukcentre/rera/online-teaching-resources/muslims-in-britain-online-course/module-4-contemporary-debates/the-role-of-the-media/ [Accessed 17 December 2017].

143 C. Milmo (2015). 'Rise in abuse on British Muslim schoolchildren following Paris attacks'. *The Independent*. [online] Available at: www.independent.co.uk/news/education/education-news/british-muslim-school-children-suffering-a-backlash-of-abuse-following-paris-attacks-9999393.html [Accessed 2 January 2018].

144 IPSO data on file on the complaints to published resolution from the Muslim and Sikh community respectively between 2016 and 2017.

145 SikhPA have also begun to challenge and report inaccurate reporting on the Sikh community. For example, see SikhPA (2018). 'Sikh Press Association v. *The Times*'. [online] Available at: www.ipso.co.uk/rulings-and-resolution-statements/ruling/?id=03484-18 [Accessed 23 May 2019].

146 Ministry of Housing, Communities & Local Government, Home Office and Ministry of Justice (2016). Hate crime action plan 2016 to 2020. GOV.UK. [online] Available at: www.gov.uk/government/publications/hate-crime-action-plan-2016 [Accessed 7 December 2017].

147 Yasmin Qureshi (2016). 'APPG launch to tackle religion in the media'. [online] Available at: www.yasminqureshi.org.uk/appg_launch_to_tackle_religion_in_the_media [Accessed 8 December 2017].

148 House of Commons (2017). Register of All-Party Parliamentary Groups as at 29 March 2017: Religion in the Media. [online] Available at: https://publications.parliament.uk/pa/cm/cmallparty/170329/religion-in-the-media.htm [Accessed 18 December 2017].

149 Sikh Press Association (2016). 'LangarWeek 2016, 3–9 October'. [online] Available at: www.sikhpa.com/campaigns/langarweek/ [Accessed 17 December 2017].

150 BBC (2016). 'Sikhs targeted in Islamophobic attacks'. Asian Network Reports – BBC Asian Network. [online] Available at: www.bbc.co.uk/programmes/p03jvnkk [Accessed 10 December 2017].

151 Chaplain and Bentham, 'Shocking figures reveal spike in anti-Islam hate crime'.

152 C. Moore (2017). 'The SNP's feat is to make non-Scots equate them with the Scottish people'. *The Spectator*. [online] Available at: www.spectator.co.uk/2017/03/the-snps-feat-is-to-make-non-scots-equate-them-with-the-scottish-people/ [Accessed 7 December 2017].

153 FOI on file disclosed on 14 November 2017 by David Edwards Information Rights Unit.
154 Ibid.
155 Ibid.
156 Dodd and Marsh, 'Anti-Muslim hate crimes increase fivefold'.
157 Melanie Phillips (2017). 'Hate crime through the Looking Glass'. MelaniePhillips. com. [online] Available at: www.melaniephillips.com/hate-crime-looking-glass/ [Accessed 10 December 2017].
158 College of Policing (2014). Crime Operational Guidance [online] Available at: www.college.police.uk/What-we-do/Support/Equality/Documents/Hate-Crime-Operational-Guidance.pdf [Accessed 10 December 2017].
159 Ibid.
160 Metropolitan Police (2017). Statement on hate crime in London. [online] Available at: http://news.met.police.uk/news/statement-on-hate-crime-in-london-245032 [Accessed 27 December 2017].
161 Mejia, 'FBI to track hate crimes'.

Conclusion

Given the UK context, it is clear that despite becoming targets for attack, Sikhs in the UK, like those in the US, have been largely 'invisible' to policymakers, and this is evident in how race hate crimes against them seem to have gone ignored. Whilst Chapter 2 considered the history of attacks on Sikhs in the UK and how Sikhs have become 'invisible victims' of the post-9/11 rise in hate crime, Chapter 3 considered media coverage, government discussions of Islamophobia and police reporting categories to highlight how the current political discourse and media focus mean that both anti-Semitism and Islamophobia are clear areas of priority, to the detriment of other communities that are experiencing similar problems (although perhaps not at the same level). This conclusion draws on the analysis of the previous chapters and the recommendations of respondents on how to tackle the problem directed at both the Sikh community and the government.

There is a discourse globally about religious/racial hate crime that is focused predominantly on Islamophobia and anti-Semitism. This dominant discourse ignores how Islamophobia has affected other communities due to 'mistaken identity'. A 48-year-old father of two sons who also wore turbans said:

> Whenever you hear of a terrorist attack has a Sikh you stop, pause and think could something happen to you, and what should you do differently to avoid bringing negative attention to oneself. Media and government always respond by addressing the fears of the Muslim community, rightly so, but they should recognize that Sikhs are also affected and need support and guidance due to their visible identity which many can't distinguish from Bin Laden.

The Sikh community globally has been affected because the Sikh turban or *dastaar*, a symbol of faith that holds religious significance, has been conflated with the Islamic identity of those who are engaged in extremism and use a head covering similar to a turban. For example, Ayatollah Khomeini wore a *dulband*; Yasser Arafat, the former Palestinian leader, and Osama bin Laden wore the *kaffiyeh*. Whilst the turban/headdress worn by such figures varies from the Sikh turban because of the way it is tied, it is evident that not many people are aware of this and mistake turban-wearing Sikhs for Muslims.

Sikhs, particularly in the US, have encountered intimidation since 9/11 because people confused 'the long beards and turbans worn by many Sikh men as a representation of Islam. Others viewed it simply as an opportunity to attack individuals they perceived as being "un-American".'[1] What is clear is that attacks on Sikhs in the US have continued ever since 9/11, and have intensified recently, perhaps in response to the rise of the alt-right in America, which has become emboldened by President Trump's election.

Sikhs in the UK have also encountered the same treatment. In the UK, attacks have been occurring on Sikh places of worship, but more importantly, on turban-wearing Sikh men. There has been a rise in attacks on Sikhs since the EU referendum on 23 June 2016 and the spate of Islamic terror attacks thereafter including two targeting parliament.

The reasons for these attacks in the UK resonate with research that has been produced in the US pointing out that 'the term "Islamophobia" has come to refer to racialized bigotry, discrimination, policies and practices directed towards a range of groups, Muslim and otherwise'.[2] Media analysis of race hate crime attacks in the US and UK identify how, through racialization, Sikh identity has become conflated with Muslim identity. Sikhs have become the 'Middle Eastern-looking'[3] or the 'Muslim-looking other', and, as Kwan explains, 'leaves Arabs, Muslims, and South Asians enormously vulnerable'.[4]

Underreporting

Whilst the authors did not hear much about attacks on British Sikhs in the past, there appears to be a concerted effort by the community in recent years to highlight the issue. Two ways in which the community has raised the visibility of this issue are posting stories on social media, and reporting incidents to the police.

The latest Home Office figures show a 17 per cent increase in hate crimes in the year 2017/2018.[5] It is difficult to claim that this rise in attacks is something new because the authors cannot compare with past figures due to underreporting and the unavailability of official statistics recording such attacks on the Sikh community separately.

Underreporting in the past is still an issue, and it is clear from academic studies and policy studies looking at the work of organizations such as Tell MAMA (2014)[6] that there are many who would not report a race hate crime in the first instance. This was echoed by the Sikh respondents, who had encountered or had been victims of race hate crime. Sikh turban-wearing men's lived experiences may vary, but when it came to how they might deal with a hate crime a common theme emerged – apathy in reporting hate crime incidents. The reticence in reporting can be attributed to several reasons, which also apply to other communities who may be affected by 'mistaken identity' but do not report incidents. For example, one 32-year-old turban-wearing engineer described how in 2012:

I was attacked by some young boys who when running passed me pushed me and purposefully tried to pull my turban off and called me 'Paki' among other things. I just ignored them. I didn't want to provoke them because I was on my own and was worried things could escalate. I was left shaken, but I didn't report it. What were the police going to do? Nothing, I wasn't hurt so why would they waste their time on me.

Another 26-year-old turban-wearing banker highlighted how he was verbally abused on a bus on his way home from a night out:

I was sitting, minding my own business when these guys got on and all at once started verbally abusing me. They called me all sorts of derogatory names – they called me 'Bin Laden' and were disrespectful to my turban. I just ignored them, but they just carried on. What hurt most was that nobody stepped in to stop them. Whilst I was upset by what had happened, I didn't report it to the police because what would they have done? I just didn't have the heart or energy to go through the process of telling the police and then waiting for them to investigate when they are probably busy with other more serious issues.

A 35-year-old turban-wearing woman commented how in 2015:

I was walking with my daughter to the park when somebody shouted 'Hey you, what you hiding under that hat? You should all go back home'. They continued to make further comments, which shocked me. I was hurt because the person shouting couldn't tell that I was a Sikh. I didn't report it because while my feelings were hurt I hadn't been physically assaulted so what could the police do?

A 28-year-old male postgraduate student respondent said:

We shouldn't respond with hostility or even differentiating ourselves from others. Instead, just ignore it and let the abusers think that they haven't won because we haven't been affected by their words.

Another 44-year-old male Sikh teacher with *Mona* (cut hair) asked:

I wonder how many of our gursikh *bibian* (ladies) who wear the *dastaar* and *chunni* (scarf) have suffered from attacks. I guess there have been some, but I don't think they will report it.

Another respondent who had been a victim of the common 'Osama' jibe whilst coming out of a London underground station but chose not to report the incident to the police commented:

Most turban wearing Sikh men have been called 'Osama bin Laden'. I think generally Sikhs tend to ignore this and take a lot more than others will because they have this warrior mentality, but at the same time let things slide, whereas I think other communities might start you know reporting such things, ... I think Sikhs are a bit more hesitant.

Another respondent told the authors he thought people might be put off reporting hate crime because it is so time consuming, and 'because it's going to end up eating my time and energy and mental peace'. It was interesting that some felt that it was too burdensome and difficult to report due to the impact of austerity measures:

I think generally it's not easy these days with lots of police stations closing down and the fact that when you go to a police station after waiting about half an hour you might walk away anyway, because of the waiting and knowledge that nothing will be done that's the problem I think.

A 33-year-old turban-wearing businessman said:

I am not sure police will take seriously a Sikh reporting a verbal attack. They are more concerned about attacks on the Muslim and Jewish community. I think other people who may be vulnerable to attack; especially those that are from the LGBT community probably also feel the same as Sikhs.

Others highlighted how they felt that the police would just pay 'lip service', listen but not take them seriously, that their complaint would be dismissed and that they would not be supported. One elderly man said he did not report the verbal abuse he had received after the Charlie Hebdo affair because he was worried about being accused of wasting police time and getting into trouble himself. Such perceptions lead to dissatisfaction and reluctance to report, which stems from a frustration that there is not enough police resource and hence the police are not interested in such issues. Concerns about being a low priority are given some validation by the story of a Sikh taxi driver from Bristol whose turban was ripped off and burnt. He said in an ITV interview that 'the officers told him to move on'.[7] Members of the Muslim community also echo this sentiment of not being taken seriously.[8]

A 21-year-old male university Sikh student who had cut hair but had experienced what he defined as racism said:

The media is vilifying the brown Muslim community, and as a result all brown people are targeted. We are all dragged into these attacks due to the colour of our skin. It is neither fair nor right, but it shows how when fears are spread it is essential that we all work together to get the right narrative out. However, a lot of us who have never had to deal with the police are probably weary of approaching them and worry about the impact such an incident can have on your record even though you are the one who has been attacked.

Whilst the authors agree that recorded numbers of hate crime offences motivated by religious bias against Sikhs are low it can be assumed, as advocates argue, that the figures are not a true representation of what is happening on the ground for the reasons mentioned above. Many Sikhs do not report because as one young man said:

> While there is a sense of vulnerability after being attacked verbally, which I have on several occasions, I think there is a Sikh sense of resilience coming from '*Chardi Kalla*'. You walk away from the incident and just get on with things.

Whilst the authors are aware that their qualitative data have limitations because of the small sample size, it is clear from the above that valuable information was gained. When cross-referenced with other academic research a similarity in terms of experiences and views of victims and community members was evident. For example, from the qualitative research, it was clear that how individuals perceived an attack varied from respondent to respondent, and this perception varied, due to not only generational differences, but also socio-economic background. This is also true for how victims cope with attacks, which can range from verbal abuse and harassment, through to physical assaults and criminal damage. From the interviews, it was clear that there was a variety of coping methods that Sikh men would employ that had an impact on their identity. One of the most common response of the young Sikh men was that they would replace the turban with a baseball cap, or tie up their hair in a 'man bun' if going out.

A 43-year-old turban-wearing factory worker said:

> When we were growing up we all experienced racism due to the colour of our skin. The police never did anything then, so why would they do anything now because we are being attacked due to our skin and religious identity. We have to deal with the issues ourselves as individuals and learn how to ensure that our identity does not open us up for attack. For me, whilst I don't like doing it I downplay my turban wearing identity in some places. For example, I did this the second time I went to the States after 9/11. On my first trip in 2015, I felt very uncomfortable with my identity. On my second trip in 2017 I never wore my turban – just a baseball cap and I had no problems.

None of the young men the authors spoke to had considered cutting their hair or shaving their beard. What was most interesting was that most respondents said that if they were younger and at school, they probably would have cut their hair to avoid attacks and discrimination.

Difference between a 'hate crime' and a 'hate incident' preventing reporting

Another very important reason for why there may be an underreporting of attacks is that individuals may not fully understand the difference between a 'hate crime' and a 'hate incident', which in turn has meant that the attacks on the Sikh community remain invisible and the recognition that was needed by policy-makers was lacking. A hate crime occurs when someone breaks the law by hurting another person because of prejudice against a group that they belong to. Thus, a hate crime is not normally caused by something someone says, but more because of a person's identity, otherwise known as a 'protected characteristic'. A hate crime can include verbal abuse, intimidation, threats, assault and bullying.

A hate incident is any kind of prejudice or bias against a protected characteristic that is not a criminal offence. A hate incident can start as a micro-aggression; subtle behaviour that is directed at someone who belongs to a group with a pro-tected characteristic. Micro-aggressions can include everyday insults, offensive and hurtful words, slurs, degrading language, snubs, insults and online hate.

Thus, the difference between a 'hate crime' and a 'hate incident' is complex. Although they are separate and distinct, some insults may well be categorized as hate crime if they relate to characteristics protected under the Equalities Act (2010). Data analysed from the longitudinal Understanding Society Project (pooled from 2011 to 2015) by Richard Norrie and David Goodhart showed how 12.4 per cent of adults claimed to have been insulted in the last 12 months.[9] In the case of insults directed solely at religion, 3.6 per cent of Muslims had been insulted on grounds of their religion as had 3.3 per cent of Sikhs.[10] Furthermore, the study data (although dated) support the authors' observations, made through structured interviews, that insults are more likely to occur in public spaces like streets and parks. Furthermore, as reflected in the research, it is clear that visual markers are a driver for attacks, and therefore it is unsurprising that turbaned Sikhs the authors spoke with were more likely to face insults in the public space than those without turbans.

EU referendum

There appears to be a concerted effort by the community to air the issue of attacks on British Sikhs since the EU referendum. As highlighted previously, this is evidenced in the Home Office report *Hate Crime, England and Wales, 2017 to 2018*,[11] which recorded the number of hate crimes between April 2017 and March 2018 as 94,098 – a rise of 17 per cent. Seventy-six per cent were classified as 'race hate'. Where the perceived religion of the victim was recorded, 2 per cent of religious hate crime offences were targeted against Sikhs (117 offences).

It is difficult to claim that this rise in attacks is something new, because the authors cannot make comparisons with past figures due to underreporting and unavailability of official statistics recording such attacks on the Sikh community separately, but what is clear is that Vote Leave-linked prejudice[12] following the EU referendum made some Sikhs speak up against racial and religious discrimination,[13] highlighting that attacks on Sikhs and their places of worship are becoming more prominent, whether by posting stories on social media or by reporting incidents to the police.

Just in 2018 alone, there have been two attacks on *gurdwara*s (Leeds,[14] and Edinburgh[15]) that have received much media and social media coverage, and there was the very public assault on Ravneet Pal Singh, a turbaned Sikh man outside Portcullis House that caused an outcry amongst the usually placid British Sikh community and brought the issue to the public's attention.[16] On 22 February 2018 Ravneet Pal Singh, an environmentalist from an organization called EcoSikh, had been queuing up outside Portcullis House to meet Tanmanjeet Singh Dhesi MP when a man attacked him saying 'Muslim go home', and tried to remove his turban. Ravneet Pal Singh, an Indian national, and his organization took to social media to express their outrage. No doubt, this was the last thing the Indian environmentalist would have expected outside the mother of all parliaments.

The attack on Ravneet Pal Singh outside the British Parliament was in fact a watershed moment. First, it was immediately reported to the MET, who told the authors, 'the incident is being treated as a hate crime as the victim had his turban grabbed prior to the assault'. Tanmanjeet Singh Dhesi MP also took up the case and put out a video that was shared widely on social media and WhatsApp, condemning the attack. He issued a statement in which he said, 'I felt embarrassed that he would be left with a personal scar from his visit whilst also giving him a negative perception of our country'.[17] With Ravneet's posting on social media and Tanmanjeet Singh's video, the attack became a major news story in the British press with articles published in *The Independent*,[18] *Huffington Post*[19] and the *Evening Standard*.[20] *Asian News International* in India tweeted the story to 2.3 million followers, and the story made it into *The Indian Express*[21] and *The Tribune*[22] amongst others.

Not leaving it there, on 26 February 2018 Tanmanjeet Singh Dhesi MP made a point of order[23] to the Speaker of the House of Commons, in which he said:

> I was disgusted on Wednesday when someone, consumed with hatred, tried to pull off the turban of one of my Sikh guests, as he queued up outside our Parliament buildings, and shouted 'Muslim, go back home.' It has been brought to the Government's attention on previous occasions that the hate crime action plan to properly record and monitor hate crimes completely ignores Sikhs. The Sikhs regard the turban as a crown on their heads. Indeed, Mr Speaker, when you presided over the launch of the National Sikh War Memorial campaign, for which I am extremely grateful, you will have ascertained the substantial strength of feeling in the community about the need for a statue of turbaned Sikh soldiers in our capital. More than 80,000 turbaned individuals died for the freedom of this country – our

country. Given that considerable context, Mr Speaker, when giving your advice, perhaps you would be kind enough to impress on the House authorities and the police the need to take this matter very seriously and to bring the assailant to justice.[24]

The Speaker responded thus:

I am grateful to the Hon. Gentleman for his point of order and for his courtesy in offering me advance notice of his intention to raise it. First, let me take this opportunity from the Chair to empathise with the hon. Gentleman and all decent people across the House on this subject. It was a truly appalling incident. I feel a great sense of shame that such an act could have been perpetrated in our country. The hon. Gentleman's friend and visitor to Parliament must have been very shaken by his experience. The act can have been motivated only by hatred, ignorance or – more likely – an extremely regrettable combination of the two. The matter is under active consideration by the police. It would therefore be inappropriate for me to comment in detail upon it. In any case, I would not be able to do myself, although I have received a report of the incident.

He went on:

Let me make it clear that I take the matter extremely seriously, as, I am sure, do the House authorities. It is imperative that visitors to this place are – to the best of our ability and that of the police and security staff here – safe from physical attack and abuse. Moreover, I say to the hon. Gentleman that if, I am provided with an address, I would like to write, on behalf of the House, to the hon. Gentleman's visitor to express our regret about the attack that he experienced. I think that we will have to leave it there for today, but I am grateful to the hon. Gentleman for airing the matter.[25]

The fact the incident was raised in the Commons chamber by a turban-wearing Sikh himself, and that the Speaker made a commitment to write to Ravneet Pal Singh to express his personal sympathy was unprecedented. The attack inadvertently, though briefly, elevated the post-9/11 Sikh problem with British parliamentarians. Many of Tanmanjeet Dhesi's fellow politicians (especially those in the Labour Party) expressed their disgust at the incident on social media. If nothing else, this raised a wider awareness of the Sikh issue (both nationally and internationally), and how Sikh turban-wearing men are subject to hatred directed at them because they are the 'Muslim-looking other'.

Alongside this political outcry, others spoke out. For example, Tina Daheley (@TinaDaheley), a prominent BBC journalist of Sikh heritage, tweeted:

while Gucci sends white models down the catwalk wearing turbans, a Sikh environmentalist has his turban ripped off outside parliament in a hate attack. As someone whose family has been on the receiving end of this sh** for decades, this is utterly depressing.[26]

It was clear that this incident was a case of a religiously motivated hate crime due to 'mistaken identity', because the assailant specifically said, 'Muslim go home', before attempting to remove Ravneet's turban. Unlike traditional racism, the motivation here was an antipathy towards Muslims per se. 'Mistaken identity', as previously discussed, is a controversial term, but this case shows how the visual marker of the Sikh turban has been consistently subjected to vilification, contempt and hatred, with its subliminal association with prominent Muslim extremists like Osama bin Laden and Ayatollah Khomeini. In this context, Sikh turbans are no different to Muslim *hijabs*. The only difference is the gender of the victims. The case also highlighted how anti-immigrant rhetoric has become commonplace since 2016 and is putting communities at risk.

Given the circumstances and the immediate report to the MET, the incident was recorded an 'Islamophobic hate crime'. As discussed previously, this is problematic and gives legitimacy to the claim from Sikh groups that Sikhs have become 'invisible' victims of hatred directed at the 'Muslim-looking other'. Whilst this was a high-profile incident by virtue of its location, it does not change the fortunes of Sikhs or other non-Muslim victims of Islamophobia in the context of parity in public policy.

Government and community action

It cannot be right that in 2018, 17 years on from Al Qaeda's attacks on America, British Sikhs, such as award-winning artist Suman Kaur, are made to feel like marginalized victims because 'the general response from government agencies and media is to increase awareness of support available to Muslims affected by hate. But what about everyone else?' Whilst attacks may not be on the same level as those on Muslims and Jews, it is clear that things do need to change in order to achieve parity for all faiths and assuage these kinds of legitimate concerns.

The attack on Ravneet Singh, whilst bringing the issue of 'mistaken identity' into the public domain, does not mean that all is fine and that the issue has been resolved. Nor does it suggest that the issue is transient; rather, it is clear that hate crime against Sikhs and their religious places of worship are on the rise. Hence, the question that needs to be asked is, how does one counter the problem? Watching from the sidelines, it sometimes feels like that the politicians and the community are pulling in different directions. For example, politicians think money and legal remedies can solve the problem, and it may do so to a certain degree, but it overlooks the underlying issues of difference, community tensions and the lack of religious literacy. It also seems that there is no coordinated or joined up thinking in the community. Within the UK Sikh community, there are several groups pertaining to be representatives of the Sikh community, such as SFUK and NSO, but they do not work together. Instead, they are all addressing it in their own capacity, but it is clear that to make a real difference they need to be working together.

Responses from both community and policymakers need to be workable and grounded ideas that can be employed and utilized by professionals who engage with this issue, not only as the police, the Crown Prosecution Service (hereinafter CPS) and teachers but also community members. Most importantly, there needs to be increased cross-collaboration on policy developments and programmes to curb the problem between government and the various faith communities that are prone to such attacks.

Government policies

Whilst support for the Abrahamic faiths is needed to curb Islamophobia and anti-Semitism, government and professional bodies need to be aware and demonstrate awareness of the wider problem recognizing community needs and vulnerabilities of the *Dharmic* faiths. The 'Action against hate' report (2016), which focused on Muslims and Jews, made no reference to Sikhs or Hindus who had encountered race hate crime; however, the 2018 'Action against hate' 'refresh' has acknowledged this to a limited extent.

Government funding and resources

Subsequent to 'Action against hate' (2016), the former home secretary Amber Rudd announced a renewal of £13.4 million annual funding for Jewish security.[27] This sum is in stark contrast with the funding previously allocated to all other faiths for protection of religious buildings, which as previously discussed was £2.4 million, in the 'places of worship: security-funding scheme' first announced back in July 2016.[28] In percentage terms, if one takes the two figures, it is clear that the government has allocated 80 per cent of funding commitment for the security of religious buildings to British Jews, compared to 20 per cent for other faiths (where funding is available only for churches, mosques, temples and *gurdwara*s).

There should be appropriate reallocation of the £13.4 million funding from the CST to other faiths, and this should only be paid in circumstances where groups can demonstrate a compelling case for extra security, for example after a terror attack such as the case of Finsbury Park mosque. It would be fair and proportionate to reallocate some of the CST funding for additional CCTV, for example, in the absence of funding availability via the Places of Worship Security Funding Scheme. Whilst the allocation of funding has not been something that the *Dharmic* faiths have focused on, there does need to be more awareness of such funding opportunities in the first instance, and government needs to make more funds accessible to these faiths. Given the arson attack on a *gurdwara* and mosque in Leeds on the same night in June 2018,[29] and the firebombing of Edinburgh *gurdwara* and the Methodist church in August 2018,[30] it would make sense for this to be translated into more funding and support for the smaller *dharmic* faiths.

Whilst in the past there was limited meaningful political will to tackle the Sikh issue, it seems that following complaints after the publication of its 2016 'Abrahamic-centric' hate crime action plan, and the recent rise in attacks on Sikhs and their places of worship in 2018 has resulted in more awareness of hate crime affecting Sikhs.

In February 2017, the HO announced that Sikhs and Hindus would receive some support in reporting hate crime via the police sponsored site True Vision. MHCLG also confirmed that all police forces in England and Wales will have to report on religious hate crime according to religion, including the Sikh faith. In 2018, there was the publication of the 'Action against hate' 'refresh' report.[31] Whilst these announcements and publications are welcomed, there has been no progress with the government's commitment to support Hindu and Sikhs to report hate crime via True Vision, despite the project being announced in early 2017. In April 2017, Sikh groups launched Sikh Aware UK,[32] an online hate crime-reporting portal, but not much has been reported, nor are any statistics available from this project.

The 'Action against hate' 'refresh' report (2018)[33] also failed to address the issue in detail despite all the incidents that occurred in the UK throughout 2018. Whilst there is a cursory reference to an attack on a *gurdwara*, what this does is to marginalize the Sikh community, who feel that their concerns are simply not being heard. A major announcement included 'reinforced' support for Muslims and Jews with Ministerial Roundtables on anti-Semitism and Islamophobia to be chaired by the Secretary of State for MHCLG and HO. It is believed that a Roundtable working group will be put in place for the Sikh community in 2019.

Recording and reporting of hate crime

The subjectivism that has been a characteristic of much of the thinking about racial and other prejudices since the Macpherson Report of 1999 has meant that any act that a victim or a witness *perceives* as motivated by racial (or other prejudice) is now regarded as a hate crime incident. For example, the *Evening Standard* ran a story on 26 June 2018, under the headline 'Muslim woman afraid to leave home after car is torched in hate crime attack'.[34] It was reported, 'police have confirmed that they are treating the attack as a hate crime after the victim told them it was religiously motivated because she is the only Muslim living in the street'. Through the authors' research it is clear that the same application applies to the recording of 'Islamophobic hate crime', which has resulted in the marginalization of the 'Muslim-looking other' and has been misleading when it comes to the reporting of hate crime statistics in the press.

As a result, the perception that Sikhs are not being listened to by government and the feeling of being 'invisible' has been compounded by the fact that crimes/ attacks against them (and other non-Muslims) have been incorrectly logged as 'Islamophobic' hate crimes. For example, a victim is recorded as having been targeted for anti-Muslim sentiment based on the 'perception of the victim' or 'any other person' as shown through FOIs, which has demonstrated that many non-Muslims are recorded as victims of 'Islamophobic hate crime' by forces like the MET. In January 2016, it was revealed that 28 per cent of victims of 'Islamophobic hate crime' recorded in 2015 were in fact not crimes against Muslims, but against non-Muslims and those of no recorded faith. The respective figure for 2016 was 25 per cent, and the non-Muslim component comprised of Christians, Sikhs, Hindus, Buddhists, atheists, agnostics and remarkably even Jews. A breakdown of the total numbers by faith was not available.

However, as we have seen, the appropriate recording of hate crime is fraught with difficulty, raising concern about data integrity in the first place. In July 2018 Her Majesty's Inspectorate of Constabulary and Fire & Rescue Services (hereinafter HMICFRS) released a report titled *Understanding the Difference: The Initial Police Response to Hate Crime*.[35] HMICFRS expressed concern about the incorrect flagging of hate crime, which they said had 'serious implications for forces in terms of their ability to understand hate crime and how it affects victims and their communities, and then [to] respond appropriately'.[36] The report found inconsistencies recording hate crime amongst forces, and made a series of recommendations,[37] one of which is to break down statistics for victims into separate sub-categories for a better understanding of what is going on. The authors agree with this approach as there must be greater clarity when the issuing authorities publish hate crime statistics so that people of all faiths and none know the size of the problem for their respective communities. As things stand, they do not, and the status quo is causing disquiet.

Moreover, HMICFRS expressed concern about the implications of using perception-based reporting, suggesting that:

> this can lead to confusion over whose perception is being recorded (that of the victim, or of the police officer dealing with the report, for instance), and to inconsistencies in how different police officers in the same force flag similar incidents.[38]

They say that hate crime flags are not being used when they should be, and they are wrongly used, or used without any justification. This puts into real question the integrity of data given to the HO and fits with the authors' observations about the recording of 'Islamophobic hate crime'.[39] There must be a consistent cross-agency approach, with the NPCC's hate crime lead working with the HO and MHCLG to tackle the important issue of data integrity. The authors believe that the 'perceived' and 'actual' victims should both be recorded as a matter of routine. Moreover, it should be made clear whose initial perception is being recorded – is it the police officer, the victim, a witness or someone else? The authors are under no illusions that this is a simple and straightforward task.

The reality is that transparency has been lacking for some time, and a simple change to the MET's 'Hate crime or special crime dashboard', for example, could make a difference. Navigating the site in its current form is indeed useful. For example, one can look at all of London's 32 boroughs and ascertain the number of 'Islamophobic' hate crimes in each one. For example, one can look at the suburb of Ealing in West London between February 2017 and February 2018.[40] However, when looking at this the authors are unable to see a breakdown of the non-Muslim victims within this category. They had assumed that, as the London Borough of Ealing includes Southall or 'Little Punjab', there would almost certainly have been some Sikhs amongst the 131 victims recorded and displayed on the dashboard during this period. This data however is unavailable. The same approach could well be applied to the 'racist and religious hate crime' category.

British Muslims have effectively lobbied to change public policy on hate crime statistics, the extension of recording 'Islamophobic hate crime' across all British police forces in 2015[41] being a further example. British Sikhs have in contrast been hitherto ineffectual in this regard.

Given the significant numbers of non-Muslim victims of Islamophobic hate crimes revealed through FOIs to the MET, the authors suggest that it would be sensible for police authorities (particularly large ones like the MET) to routinely provide the breakdown of religions. The 2018 'Statistics on hate crimes recorded by the police and information on hate crime from the Crime Survey for England and Wales', which showed that 2 per cent of religious hate crime offences were targeted against Sikhs (117 offences), was very helpful. Indeed, such breakdown, reporting and sharing of data on hate crime will provide reassurance to Sikh organizations that the problem is being taken seriously and that the police are sharing data on hate crime as they do with Tell MAMA and the CST. This would also open a dialogue between the various agencies and providers, and would be a far more inclusive approach.

Government and police activity has evidently heightened a sense of invisibility and disillusionment in the Sikh community, which has been further compounded by its absence from the national intra-faith work that has been done on hate crime, as it is not viewed as a priority group. The authors believe the lack of partnership on an intra-faith level is one of the reasons that the post-9/11 Sikh experience has become a peripheral issue in the eyes of policymakers.

One must be cognisant of the messaging of neo-Nazi groups like NA, which promotes an anti-immigrant narrative as well as the idea that Britain is on the brink of some kind of 'race-war'.[42] These dangerous and incendiary narratives give oxygen to an already polarized society, which is having serious consequences for community cohesion. As we know, this narrative influenced the attack on Sikh dentist Dr Bhambra. All groups who face such hatred (including faith groups like Jews and Muslims) must work together to counter this kind of poisonous worldview with a counter-narrative. One sees this happening briefly after terror attacks, but such often-short-lived solidarity needs to be both continuous and consistent. We must engage and learn from one other, and push back against conspiracies peddled by extremists – be they Islamists or far-right Neo-Nazis.

It would therefore be advantageous to forge meaningful intra-faith partnerships to tackle hate crime moving forward. For example, communities, but also government, should advocate for communities, organizations and APPGs that address the issue to be inclusive of all faiths, if possible. Official campaigns to limit the number of racist and religious hate crimes and encourage reporting need to be inclusive, so the narrative and imagery should include people of all backgrounds who may be affected. Additionally, government initiatives to tackle Islamophobia and anti-Semitism, whether via Cross-Government Working Groups, such as on Anti-Muslim Hatred, or initiatives and funding to curb the problem must demonstrate parity or at least include the voices of other faith representatives where appropriate. This was recently reflected in the appointment of the Chair of CS, Jasvir Singh, to the Cross-Government Working Group on Anti-Muslim Hatred as an Independent Member.

That said, intra-faith partnerships do not go without their own challenges, and one must take a pragmatic approach. Tell MAMA, the Muslim hate crime monitor, organized a 'round-table' meeting to discuss hate crime affecting Sikhs in February 2018.[43] This was a positive attempt to reach out to members of the Sikh community.

However in early 2018, the NSO referred to a 2008 government sponsored Muslim–Sikh project organized by Faith Matters (the group behind Tell MAMA), which was designed to address 'the growing gulf between Sikhs and Muslims in certain localised areas of England'.[44] It was held in Corrymeela, Ballycastle, between 4 and 6 July 2008, a centre famous for conflict resolution at the height of sectarian troubles in Northern Ireland. The project is reported to have cost the taxpayer £33,600. At the end of the residential course, four out of nine of the Sikh participants felt disgruntled and published an 'Alternative Report' (dated 1 October 2008) to express their concerns. They wrote: 'In the view of many Sikh participants, the whole exercise proved faulty and dysfunctional; and failed to enable a wholesome and engaged dialogue on the critical Sikh-Muslims issues.'[45] The founder of Faith Matters, Fiyaz Mughal, discussed the project in an article published by Faith Matters titled 'Cohesive communities: Bridging divides between Muslim and Sikh communities':

> As the name suggests, the Cohesive Communities project was a chance for key issues to be aired and a start to the interaction process between both faiths. It was not meant as a basis to provide legitimisation for either community to use the report or its findings against the other and we firmly adhere to this principal'[46]

The NSO pointed out that despite assurances given by Faith Matters in the article above, in June 2012 tweets published by @FaithMattersUK made derogatory references to Sikh participants in Corrymeela, which were later removed following a complaint. They wrote:

> We believe the 2012 tweets made by @FaithMattersUK, particularly the comparing of Sikhs who entered interfaith dialogue in good faith with Faith Matters to the EDL, and the accompanying hashtag #wolvesinsheeps clothing, are simply not compatible with the aim in creating harmonious

relations between British Sikhs and Muslims, or promoting the concept of 'cohesive communities.'[47]

The CST have also highlighted that whilst they have met with various Sikh organizations and given advice, nothing has come to fruition regarding intra-faith partnerships or long-term exchange of practices with British Sikhs to tackle hate crime. This is a serious failure on the part of the Sikh community, who could have learned a lot from CST.

Print media and online media representation

Media coverage of race hate crime against some communities appears to be increasing in the UK, especially since the 2017 terrorist attacks and the EU referendum in 2016. Much of the current focus is on the Muslim community and Islamophobia, and the rising anti-Semitism problem in the UK. Most recently the media has paid particular attention to the anti-Semitism crisis in the Labour Party, which has resulted in the party being defined by one of its former MPs, Chuka Umunna (the MP for Streatham) as 'institutionally racist' in line with his reading of the Macpherson Report.[48] Against this backdrop, the media focus on anti-Sikh prejudice pales into insignificance despite the fact Sikhs have also been targets of violence since 9/11, and now more so since the EU referendum. In 2018 Sikhs in both the UK and US have encountered a number of attacks.

The media disinterest, like the wider political marginalization (as evidenced by the authors' Hansard audit), was something that respondents referred to repeatedly. What became clear was that this could lead, and has led, to the unintended consequence of Sikhs not reporting incidents because they feel they will not be taken seriously enough. Moreover, when journalists have reported on 'Islamophobic' hate crime statistics, with articles about 'spikes' in incidents in London, they have not always acknowledged non-Muslim victims because they do not have the breakdown of figures, and this makes members of other communities feel that their experiences are not important. Whilst writing this book the authors saw evidence of such reporting in an article published by *The Guardian* on 7 June 2017 headlined 'Anti-Muslim hate crimes increase fivefold since London Bridge attacks', and a similar story in the *Evening Standard* on 17 October 2017, titled 'Shocking figures reveal spike in anti-Islam hate crime in London'.[49] Hardeep Singh, referring to the MET FOI data, argued that the articles were 'inaccurate and misleading' because victims of the 'Islamic hate crime' mentioned in the articles were 'not necessarily Muslim'. A suitable correction was made in the *Evening Standard* on March 2018 when the words 'to make clear that not all victims of Islamophobia crimes were Muslims' were added to the original article.[50] A similar complaint to *The Guardian* was repeatedly ignored.[51] What is clear is that media representatives have a duty of care to report accurately, and journalists should be required to disaggregate information where available, and be religiously competent. Here organizations, such as

IPSO,[52] IMPRESS[53] (an independent press regulator in the UK) and the Religion Media Centre[54] have an important role to play.

Engaging the press and changing the narrative are matters that can be influenced. Take the exemplars of American Sikh writers/activists like Valarie Kaur and Professor Simran Jeet Singh, who have made regular contributions to influential publications like *The New York Times*[55] and *The Washington Post*.[56] In the same way, there is nothing stopping British Sikhs, and Sikh organizations like SikhPA, from contributing to the debate, and the authors acknowledge that some individuals like journalist Sunny Hundal have already begun to do so with opinion-editorials in publications like *The Guardian*.[57]

Social media

Whilst this invisibility of the Sikh experience in the media may be problematic, so in fact is its visibility on social media due to misrepresentation. There have been many examples of Sikhs being misrepresented and misidentified. In 2017 a US airline passenger posted an image of a turbaned Sikh passenger on his flight, alongside the caption 'never mind I might not make it to Indy (Indianapolis)'. He went on to take another picture of the Sikh (this time asleep), writing 'update I'm still alive'. Professor Simran Jeet Singh took to Twitter in response to the posts, saying they demonstrated, 'what it's like for anyone who appears to be Muslim to travel by plane'.[58]

In the UK, there have been two instances that stand out. First, a football match between Manchester United and Bournemouth at Old Trafford on 14 May 2016 was cancelled due to a bomb scare. An Arsenal supporter, 'Arsenal Craig', blamed Sikh football fans for the evacuation, posting an image of Sikh turban-wearing men with a caption that read: 'Bomb threat at Old Trafford, I know where my investigation would start.'[59] Second, after the Manchester terror attack at the Ariana Grande concert on 22 May 2017, *Cosmopolitan* magazine misidentified a turban-wearing Sikh taxi driver offering free rides to those who had been caught up in the attack as a Muslim in a tweet, which was later corrected.[60] These three high-profile tweets demonstrate a lack of religious literacy, but also show that whilst turban-wearing Sikh men have been misidentified as Muslim on social media, it was activism on social media that corrected the misidentification.

Having analysed 500 tweets from 100 Twitter users, Imran Awan states, 'online Islamophobia must be given the same level of attention as street level Islamophobia'.[61] As previously mentioned, the authors are not sure if an equivalence can be made between these environments and the grey area of subjectivity around what constitutes 'offence' and who adjudicates what is a 'phobia' amplifies the difficulty in this regard.

However, with reference to social media the issue is complicated because there has been no agreed international consensus on the definition of Islamophobia since the Runnymede Trust's initial attempt to formulate one in their 1997 report. The APPG on British Muslims conducted an inquiry into what the 'working definition of Islamophobia/Anti-Muslim hatred' should be. In their report *Islamophobia Defined* (published November 2018) they suggested, 'Islamophobia is rooted in racism and is a type of racism that targets expressions of Muslimness or perceived Muslimness'.[62] In contrast to this, Britain was one of the first countries to adopt the IHRA definition of anti-Semitism in 2016.[63]

However, it is important to acknowledge that the APPG definition on Islamophobia faced significant criticism. The National Secular Society (hereinafter NSS) warned MPs that the term Islamophobia 'confuses hatred of, and discrimination against, Muslims with criticism of Islam'.[64] They coordinated a letter titled 'no to definition of Islamophobia' published in *The Sunday Times*.[65] Meanwhile, referring to the original 1997 Runnymede report, Trevor Phillips stated there were reasons the notion that Muslims should be characterized as a racial group was rejected at the time. In a *Times* article he said:

> First, Muslims themselves rejected the idea that they constitute anything like a single separate 'race' in the way that, say, black Africans might. Second, Britain is home to a uniquely wide range of Muslim communities. They differ in origin, with sizeable contingents with roots in the Indian sub-continent, the Middle East, sub-Saharan Africa, central and southeastern Asia, and Europe. And third, the facts of race are not a matter of personal choice; we cannot simply declare ourselves to be white, black or Asian. On the other hand, most of those who follow Islam pride themselves on the fact that they have actively chosen to adhere to a centuries-old belief system.[66]

Trevor Phillips went on to argue that defining Islamophobia as 'anti-Muslim' racism could in fact disadvantage and isolate the Muslim community, and not allow them to have prayer rooms and special holiday arrangements because 'combating racial disadvantage necessitates the opposite, ensuring that people are treated similarly irrespective of their ethnicity'. He continued:

> There's a final, important lesson to be learned from the APPG's report. It speaks of Muslims as if maltreatment by white Britons were their only defining experience. It thus misrepresents the attitudes of most non-Muslims and diminishes Muslim identity to that of the perpetual victim. Before the government or any institution adopts a definition that treats British Muslims in this way, much deeper thought is required.[67]

In an article for *Spiked* Hardeep Singh expressed reservations too, saying: '"Islamophobia" is not always rooted in racism. For a start, racism cannot adequately describe discrimination against either white converts to Islam or European Muslims like Bosniaks, Kosovars and Albanians.'[68] Whilst highlighting how religious symbols like the *dastaar* have been conflated with the 'enemy', he went on:

> Similarly, some orthodox Rastafarian priests were prevented from boarding a US flight after 9/11. More absurd still, Swedish hipsters with beards were

stopped by police who mistook them for members of ISIS. White British hipsters have not been spared this ignominy, either. In these cases, it was clearly their hirsute countenance, rather than their race, that led to them to be mistreated.[69]

Significantly, *The Jewish Chronicle* reported that the leading advocacy group, the Board of Deputies of British Jews (BoD), did not formally support the definition.[70]

The authors believe that the word 'Islamophobia' is vague for the purposes of any definition. It conflates attacks on Muslims with those on non-Muslims, but also with criticism of Islam, and of the bad behaviour of a minority of Muslims. 'Anti-Muslim' hate, like 'anti-Sikh' hate, is far clearer language. In the interests of free speech, the authors also believe consideration must be given to legitimate criticism of negative aspects of religion in the context of any definition moving forward.[71]

It is uncertain whether government will adopt the proposed APPG definition; however policymakers are increasingly considering the echo chambers of social media when it comes to hate crime. A 2016–17 inquiry into hate crime and its violent consequences by the Home Affairs Committee included a wide range of issues including the role of social media. Citing Twitter, Facebook and YouTube the inquiry notes the positive use of these platforms (used by billions) to challenge bigotry (using handles like @EverydaySexism and hashtags such as #aintnomuslimbruv),[72] but also found:

> There is a great deal of evidence that these platforms are being used to spread hate, abuse and extremism. That trend continues to grow at an alarming rate but it remains unchecked and, even where it is illegal, largely unpoliced.[73]

In 2017, former Director of Public Prosecutions Alison Saunders signalled that the CPS would crack down on social media hate crime, suggesting: 'Whether shouted in their face on the street, daubed on their wall or tweeted into their living room, the impact of hateful abuse on a victim can be equally devastating.'[74] The authors are not entirely sure they agree with Saunders' view, given that individuals have the option to mute or block abusers on social media – options they do not have on the street.

Furthermore, we do not believe governments should be policing thought, and laws that criminalize speech are indeed problematic. Bestselling Canadian author and psychology professor from the University of Toronto, Jordan B. Peterson expressed his concerns about this when referring to police adverts in Scotland encouraging people to report 'offensive' behaviour online. He told an audience on BBC *Question Time*:

> one of the things I do see happening in the UK as an outsider, and is quite terrifying to me, is that there are increasing restrictions put on people's

ability to speak forthrightly and the consequence of that restriction and the criminalization of what hypothetically constitutes offensive speech is going to be the cure that is so much worse than the disease, that we can hardly imagine it.[75]

However, the authors acknowledge that in some instances there may be a fine line between freedom of speech and so-called 'hate speech', which continues to be a contentious issue, especially with the views of some tabloid newspaper columnists and, more frequently, 'offensive' posts on social media platforms. That said, the issue of subjectivity remains problematic, raising the questions, who adjudicates what is 'offensive', 'hate' or 'phobia', and how is it defined or proven?

The authors also acknowledge that the online space allows anonymity, which gives rise to a more brazen approach to words published. For example, anonymous Twitter users can be difficult to identify if they hide their Internet Protocol address, giving 'trolls' an added sense of impunity. This makes the likelihood of potential prosecution for criminal offences related to online abuse, harassment and malicious communications far more challenging for prosecuting authorities.[76] Moreover, someone posting comments about faith can have their words read by individuals across the globe, and thus be exposed to increased susceptibility to a hostile reception. It is understood there is little scope in being able to distinguish between online hate originating in the UK and that from overseas. Nevertheless, according to a report in *The Times*, in 2016 the British police arrested nine people a day for posting 'offensive messages online'.[77]

Despite the above caveats, the government can influence companies to implement swift take-down policies. It is imperative that social media providers, such as Facebook, Twitter and YouTube, police and monitor their own content. Social media companies talk about using algorithmic solutions to reduce harmful content, but as noted at Mark Zuckerberg's testimony to Congress (10–11 April 2018), technological solutions are not the only answer. Instead, more investment in employing people to monitor their sites for inappropriate material is needed, including the ability to immediately remove 'offensive' material when detected or reported.

Thus, when material is unequivocally anti-Semitic or Islamophobic, the public needs to see social media providers, but also police and CPS, taking appropriate action. Last year the CPS announced that online hate crimes would be treated just as seriously as offences committed in person, it will be interesting to see if this happens. Nevertheless, hate crime incidents targeting protected characteristics, whether in person or online, must be dealt with robustly, and the victims supported appropriately. However, at the same time, one must be mindful of curbing free speech as Jordan B. Peterson points out, and protecting the liberty to speak openly about matters of public interest, however controversial or distasteful views may be.

Improving religious literacy – government, media and schools

Whilst the UK is a super-diverse country, made up of people from different religions, beliefs and cultures it is evident that there is a lack of knowledge and religious literacy about all these communities. This lack of religious literacy has
fuelled ignorance that might lead to misunderstanding, and even bigotry. Whilst
some of the initiatives mentioned above are a positive step forward, they do not
address the root cause of the problem, which in the context of 'mistaken identity' comes through a lack of understanding. For example, Hopkins et al. in their
research found that people did not know the difference between Hindus, Sikhs
and Muslims.[78] Jasvir Singh, the Chair of CS said: 'Sikhs often find themselves
confused with Muslims, and there is an obvious need to improve faith literacy in
British society generally.'[79]

The authors believe that this need to improve understanding of religion
applies across the board, whether that be amongst the general public, media or
government circles. Admittedly, they are by no means the first to make this suggestion. Peter Hopkins[80] and colleagues advocated 'for better education and
information in schools, colleges, universities and government departments to
increase understanding of ethnic, religious and cultural differences'.[81] It is essential that professionals in the media and government should have a basic understanding of that diversity.

When focusing on religious literacy for the purpose of this analysis, the
authors use the definition of religious literacy as defined by the APPG on Religious Education:

2.3 Religious literacy can be understood as composing four main elements:

- A basic level of knowledge about both the particular beliefs, practices
  and traditions of the main religious traditions in Britain, and of the
  shape of our changing religious landscape today. This must be comple-
  mented by a conceptual understanding of what religious belief systems
  are, and how they may function in the lives of individuals.
- An awareness of how beliefs, inherited traditions and textual interpreta-
  tions might manifest into the actions, practices and daily lives of individuals. Crucial to this is an understanding of the diversity within
  religious traditions, and an awareness of the way in which the same
  text, or religious principle, can be interpreted in different ways by
  different individuals.
- A critical awareness, meaning that an individual has the ability to
  recognize, analyse and critique religious stereotypes, and engage effectively with, and take a nuanced approach towards, the questions raised
  by religion. A sophisticated ability to engage with religious groups in a
  way which promotes respect and plurality, and which enables effective
  communication about religion.[82]

Education

Schools need to teach about different religions and worldviews that make up modern Britain. It is essential that Religious Education (hereinafter RE) taught in schools need to be more robust. However, there has been a historical downgrading of RE. At primary school level the teaching of RE, whilst required, is not always adequate because the focus is mainly on ensuring that the 3Rs (writing, literacy and numeracy) are met. At secondary school level, RE is taught to all children up to Year 9, but again the quality and amount of time spent on the subject is questionable. The lack of teaching prior to Year 10, and the recent changes to the General Certificate in Secondary Education (hereinafter GCSE) curriculum with only two faiths now needing to be studied, is only going to add to the growing religious illiteracy. This will be particularly evident at GCSE level because some of the smaller faiths will be ignored, because it is evident that most schools will focus on the Abrahamic faiths (Christianity/Islam; Islam/ Judaism or Christianity/Judaism).

The government's historical downgrading of RE in schools has been addressed by a number of Commissions and Reports, and in 2013 the APPG on Religious Education published a report suggesting that government policies had undermined the teaching of RE, and from their survey of 430 schools, they found that ten out 130 secondary schools broke the law by not teaching RE to some pupils.[83] In the introduction to a 2016 report 'Improving religious literacy: A contribution to the debate', the Chair of the APPG, Fiona Bruce MP, writes:

> It is clear that the provision of high quality school-based RE, and good teaching and learning about religion beyond the school years in the whole of life context, cannot be allowed to fall off the agenda of the government or Parliament, particularly in these uncertain and changing times.[84]

The Commission on Religious Education,[85] in their report 'A new vision for Religious Education in schools', stated:

> Young people today are growing up in a world where there is increasing awareness of the diversity of religious and non-religious worldviews, and they will need to live and work well with people with very different worldviews from themselves. One need only glance at a newspaper to know that it is impossible fully to understand the world without understanding worldviews – both religious and non-religious.[86]

The report also recommended that the alongside the five religious traditions that are already taught other traditions, including non-religious views like Humanism, Secularism, Atheism and Agnosticism, should be taught and hence the 'subject should be called Religion and Worldviews to reflect the new emphasis'.[87] This, alongside lobbying from groups like the NSS, who amongst other things, are asking around whether RE should be 'absorbed as part of a wider subject'[88] raises concerns, because with an increased pool of subject choices, some of the smaller faith traditions, such as Sikhism, are likely to fall even further behind on the curriculum agenda at all levels including GCSE.

Professional bodies and religious literacy

It is clear that there is a lack of religious literacy in various professional bodies, and that since 9/11 things have not improved. Former Detective Sergeant Gurpal Virdi observed that some MET officers did not know the difference between Sikhs and the Taliban in the aftermath of 9/11.[89] This kind of ignorance must be challenged, especially given that police forces like the MET and West Midlands police serve significant Sikh communities: approximately 127,400 and 130,500 respectively.[90] It also needs to be challenged in other professions.

More recently, the need for this has been highlighted when prominent officials have demonstrated a lack of knowledge of who Sikhs are. For example, in April 2015 the Republican presidential candidate Mitt Romney, whilst paying tribute to Sikhs killed in the Wisconsin *gurdwara* massacre in 2012,[91] confused 'Sikh' with 'Sheikh',[92] and most recently a top British diplomat, Sir Simon Macdonald, referred to Amritsar's Golden Temple (Sikhism's holiest shrine) as the 'Golden Mosque' in April 2018.[93] These two prominent examples point to the need for improving religious literacy to be extended to diversity training for all employees in the public and private sectors. It is essential to educate the majority around different faiths and cultures so that one can break down any unconscious fears, biases and misperceptions so that everyone, irrespective of their race and faith, is respected and appreciated.

Those who work with children also need to be religiously and culturally literate. Under its 'prevention' arm the government's hate crime action plan, 'Action against hate' (2016), states it will tackle bullying in schools with a 'new programme to equip teachers to facilitate conversations about "difficult topics" and carry out a new assessment of the level of anti-Muslim, anti-Semitic, homophobic, racist and other bullying in schools'. This involves collaboration with the Anne Frank Trust and Streetwise, who run educational programmes. However, the government's overall approach to hate crime strategy is not equitable because it ignores the Sikh situation. Sikh boys, especially those wearing *patkas* (small piece of cloth covering long hair), must also be considered in the context of Islamophobia as there is evidence from the US[94] and UK that young Sikh school boys whose long hair is tied up in a bun at the top of the head (*joora*), covered with a *patka* are bullied. These young boys have been attacked for looking different and have been called names such as 'egg head', 'bobble head' or 'topknot'. Tanmanjeet Singh Dhesi, the first turban-wearing Sikh Member of Parliament, highlighted in an interview how 'At school, you get discriminated against. ... One student tried to take off my turban then'.[95]

Stories of bullying in schools do not become public knowledge because they are dealt with by the school in-house. However, many Sikh families have members or know of young Sikhs who have gone through it. One of those rarely reported stories in the media particularly stands out as an example of the tragic consequences of bullying. In 1996, Vijay Singh, a 13-year-old boy from Manchester who attended a predominantly white school, took his own life due to racism and bullying. Racist bullying of young Sikhs continues today, primarily due to their distinct identity, however most cases either are dealt with improperly, or remain unreported.

While some young Sikhs can withstand such bullying and discrimination, and indeed claim to be strengthened by their experience, many will go through an identity crisis and feel the need to eliminate cultural and religious markers that invite prejudice and discrimination. For example, whilst it is common to see young boys at primary school wearing a turban or *patka*, it is less common in secondary schools. By then, the bullying and challenges have made some question their identity and religion and many, in order to fit in with societal norms and to stop being misidentified as Muslims in particular, cut their hair. This was discussed in the recent BBC documentary 'My Turban and Me'.[96] Sanjeev Kohli's mother discussed how she gave her sons the options to cut their hair because she saw boys remove the turban from Sikh boys and kick it like a football. Thus, it is peculiar that the government has not chosen to extend 'prevention' projects to children from all 'visible' faith minorities. The Department for Education and MHCLG need to review their policies to make public policy more inclusive and ensure that teachers receive better training to recognizing bullying and supporting those who may be bullied due to their religious identity.

It is important to note a positive outcome from bullying directed at Sikh boys with *patkas* is the case of Balraj Singh Notay. He had been bullied at two football camps in 2017, but was later an England mascot, after his father, Dr Jasjit Singh, got in touch with the anti-racism football charity Kick It Out. Referring to Notay in an opinion-editorial, Troy Townsend, Kick It Out's education manager writes, 'the fact that it was also his 9th birthday that same day just made the show of diversity that much sweeter'.[97]

The responsibility for improving religious literacy is one that everyone needs to undertake. Government needs to take responsibility with reference to policy and training of government departments and civil servants. It is also imperative that educational provision, particularly RE for young people, needs to be strengthened so that young people can learn about religious diversity.

The media has a responsibility in the way it communicates news. For example, the BBC needs expert editorial teams to encourage public engagement and to commission more documentaries and stories about religious communities that focus on positive as well as negative perspectives. Other media outlets also need to ensure that reporters and editors have some level of religious literacy. The community itself needs to develop partnerships with bodies like IPSO, with the aim of helping to improve the understanding of journalists – and hence that of the wider public – of Sikhism. Some positive steps, for example a 'journalists' guide to Sikhism', is being developed by the NSO. Groups like the SikhPA are also working to address inaccuracies around Sikhism in the print media and have taken up issues with IPSO.

Community activism

Questions need to be asked about how Sikh individuals or community organizations can engage with government to widen the current 'Abrahamic-centric' approach. What, if anything, can be done at a local level? What should the overall strategic objectives be? Moreover, how does all the above fit in with Sikh ethos of *sarbat da bhalla* (the prosperity of all humanity), which recognizes 'equality for all'.

Hate crimes against Muslims, Jews or any other group are deplorable and go against the values and teachings of the Sikh *dharam*. Guru Tegh Bahadur died defending *dharam* and the rights of other religious traditions to practise their faith, and scriptural sayings such as '[the Sikhs] recognize the human race as one'[98] highlight how, whilst the Sikh *dharam* recognizes that religious identity can become a source of social tension due to a lack of religious literacy or blind hatred, all have to work together for the betterment of society.

However, the majority of Sikhs draw on the religious tenet of *sarbat da bhalla* as a guiding principle bringing about positive change for the greater good. Religious leaders and community groups have stepped up as activists and have engaged with government to confront challenges presented by race hate crime. Ordinary citizens and community groups are also playing a powerful role in come out against 'all forms of hate' by educating people about their identity without emphasizing difference, and without creating a narrative of 'them' and 'us' that is prevalent in political discourse.

One famous example of this 'othering' is when Senator McCain, during the 2008 American presidential campaign was told by a woman: 'I can't trust Obama. I have read about him and he's not, he's not uh – he's an Arab.' McCain responded by replying:

> No, ma'am. He's a decent family man [and] citizen that I just happen to have disagreements with on fundamental issues and that's what this campaign's all about. He's not [an Arab].[99]

McCain was criticized for his response because it was seen to be furthering anti-Arab and anti-Muslim sentiments. Sikhs, however, have avoided doing this, as Canadian NDP leader, Jagmmet Singh did when a woman attacked him. When asked in an interview by Hasan Minhaj, 'Why do you not just go "Hey, I'm not Muslim"?', Professor Simran Jeet Singh responded by saying, 'It is just not an option for us to throw another community under the bus. Even if it means things are harder for us.'[100] Valarie Kaur embodies these values through her work in the Revolutionary Love Project – an initiative aiming to fight for universal social justice – and in the UK, Jasvir Singh has expressed the same sentiment in a video.[101]

However, one cannot deny that in the UK, just like in the US, one sees a focus on 'othering', and an emphasis on difference, for example in the NSC campaign 'We Are Sikhs' in the US,[102] and the production of T-shirts after the 7/7 London bombings emblazoned with, 'Don't freak I'm Sikh' in the UK.

Another variation of this was 'Don't panic I'm not Islamic', but it is unclear who was behind this messaging. Adopting this stance does nothing to eradicate the root cause of the problem, instead it contributes to an unhelpful narrative – 'do not be racist to us because we are not one of them'.

Many UK Sikhs have felt some level of discontent with policymakers and have made challenges to institutional arrangements. Some Sikh organizations, such as SN and CS, have collected data on the issue to lobby for the separate recording of anti-Sikh hate crime. Organisations have also worked with community members who have been affected so as to have the incidents recorded correctly.

Victims have also worked with outside agencies to ensure that attacks are recorded correctly as demonstrated in the case of the Sikh Taxi driver in Bristol whose turban was pulled off and burnt in September 2014.[103] In this case, the victim and the Bristol organization Stand against Racism and Inequality fought to ensure that the attack was recorded as a hate crime and that the perpetrator was prosecuted. This case also highlights how statistics compiled by police are incomplete because they may not always record incidences accurately. As a result of incorrect reporting and underreporting the Sikh community have felt that the police and True Vision are not doing enough to support Sikhs, and in April 2017, Sikh groups launched Sikh Aware UK – a reporting portal for individuals to report incidents online. Sikh Council UK launched this initiative after it had consulted CST.

Intra-community working is essential if racial and religiously motivated hate crimes are to be tackled effectively. This is what will have maximum impact on government and policy. UK Sikh organizations, along with leading Sikhs, must have a strategic long-term approach, and there is no room for parochialism. Hate crime affects many communities. It is likely to stay with us over the long term; therefore, getting it right is not merely important: it is critical for future proofing the Sikh presence in Britain. It is important for the community to engage in intra-faith collaboration. One has seen effective collaboration between British Jews and Muslims – most notably with CST and Tell MAMA. The MHCLG report *Integrated Communities Strategy Green Paper* talks of delivering the hate crime action plan by 'strengthening local partnerships to identify innovative practices to address hate crime and promote greater reporting of incidents'.[104]

Whilst communities themselves must engage in genuine intra-faith dialogue, projects and outreach to develop and enhance religious literacy in the community are also critical. Whilst engaging in these activities, participants must not be afraid to have difficult conversations about aspects of some religious traditions that could be viewed as divisive in themselves.

Local activism and developing positive relations with local police authorities

When it comes to local activism, the work of Northampton-based Amarjit Singh Atwal deserves wider recognition. He has taken both practical and proactive steps to collaborate with his local police force in addressing incidents of hate crime in his area, which accommodates approximately 400 Sikh families. It is forming these critical relationships in a meaningful way and taking personal responsibility by stepping up into a leadership role that have resulted in tangible results. For example, individuals who told members of the *gurdwara* 'to go back to Pakistan' in 2015 were brought to justice. When the *gurdwara* (near St George's Street) was on the receiving end of malicious hate mail in 2017, Atwal reported the incidents to the police, telling his local newspaper, *Northampton Chronicle & Echo*, 'The reason I reported this is because I want more people to report hate crimes.'[105] This is local activism at its best, and by stepping up into a leadership role Atwal has made a tangible difference.

Amarjit Atwal sits on the local Hate Crime Security Panel, has organized visits to the *gurdwara* for police recruits, and has forged positive and meaningful relationships at all levels of Northampton Police – from local officers through to the Chief Constable. This in part has been facilitated by an intelligent use of social media, which Atwal effectively employs as a tool to tackle issues as and when they arise. Of course, this kind of work is voluntary and requires a commitment that not everyone has the time, inclination or energy (let alone motivation) to provide. The authors believe that Atwal's model of 'partnership working' with authorities bridges an important gap between the police and the community. His professional approach is amplified by his willingness to give interviews and talk with the local media. The authors take the view that this way of working is an exemplar, and shows how a proactive, dedicated and collaborative approach can pay dividends. It provides communities confidence in local policing. Our recommendation would be that lessons are learned from Amarjit Singh Atwal's model of collaboration, and these should be captured and implemented in other localities where hate crime has been identified as a significant problem. This will require a proactive community approach and the authors believe *gurdwaras* could assign funds to set up a mentoring programme for those willing to volunteer to do this essential community work.

Media and social media activism

Educating non-Sikhs about the Sikh faith and getting them to experience it at first hand has become a theme for many Sikh organizations. In response to Ravneet Singh's case, the Sikh Channel organized a 'turban tying' day in parliament on 28 March 2018. Many non-Sikhs at the Parliament of the World Religions in 2018 walked around the conference with Sikh turbans tied on their heads. This follows on from similar initiatives by American Sikhs to help raise awareness about the Sikh faith and identity amongst Americans by producing documentaries on TV channels. The *United Shades of America* episode 'Sikhs in America' with W. Kamau Bell, screened on the Cable News Network, did exactly this and won an Emmy in 2018.[106] As a public broadcaster, the BBC should consider an hour-long documentary of this kind, given its commitment to religious programming. Having documentaries and programmes about people of other faiths can help correct misconceptions and allow viewers to experience the perspective of the 'other'.

The authors are not aware of any criminal prosecutions for online hate crime against the British Sikh community, but have noted how prominently Sikhs have highlighted incidents through their use of social media. British Sikh humanitarian Ravi Singh from Khalsa Aid is not shy in flagging occasions where he has been mistaken for being a member of the 'Taliban' or 'ISIS'. A more recent example of this is Amandeep Singh Bhogal @Amandeepbhogal, a 'Conservative campaigner' who has 17.3 thousand Twitter followers (at the time of writing). On 5 April 2018, he tweets 'Wow! So I am outside CCHQ and this crazy man with a heavy European accent walks up to me and gets all lippy asking what I was "upto" here in Westminster, that I looked suspiciously like a terrorist.' He went on, 'Asked him to calm down & he spits in my direction what is wrong with some people'. The tweet was shared over 600 times and liked by over 1,500; it elicited more than 600 comments in response.[107]

Although the experience must have been unpleasant, people like Bhogal have the ability to rise above it and possess a platform to raise the Sikh issue to a wide audience, including fellow Conservatives like Home Secretary Sajid Javid and former Foreign Secretary Boris Johnson. This kind of social media activism is critical in highlighting the issue to the wider public, and more importantly policymakers, because Sikhs have historically not been viewed as a priority group by the UK government when it comes to hate crime, probably because there were no specific data to work with. Thus, it is imperative that more data is collected and problems highlighted through grassroots activism. Victims, whether attacked in person or on social media, need to step forward and report incidences to the police and share experiences. For example, if hate is directed at individuals via social media, they should tag Sikh organizations and lodge a complaint about the offending accounts with Twitter or Facebook, as well as flagging with True Vision and the relevant police authority directly, if deemed proportionate given the particular set of circumstances and nature of the offending words. A proactive approach is certainly required, but one in which individuals feel supported and are shown solidarity.

Final remarks

In conclusion, it is vitally important to recognize that religious/racial hate crime occurs outside the much-publicized and very topical Islamophobic and anti-Semitic spheres. Indeed, it is crucial to understand how cases of 'mistaken identity' (for example, Sikhs being mistaken for Muslims) can and do occur, and how irrespective of the victim's background being subject to prejudice and hate has an emotional and physical effect on individuals and the wider community. A poignant example of the long-lasting effects of hate crime is the work of the Sikh Healing Collective in the US, which to this day continues to support victims of the 2012 Wisconsin *gurdwara* massacre, addressing the mental health impact on victims and their families, particularly children who lost parents to hate.

There are some clear challenges ahead in tackling *racialization, Islamophobia and mistaken identity* from a Sikh perspective, and some of the recommendations here will go some way in providing a workable framework moving forward. Semantics will also assist – this applies not only to hate crime recording, but also to media coverage. One must be clear in language: attacks on Sikhs, for example, should be described as 'anti-Sikh', even if the motivation is 'Islamophobic'. As previously suggested, the authors believe that police authorities should record both the 'actual' and the 'perceived' victim of hate crimes. This will assist in identifying motivation, whilst accurately providing the background of the victim.

Although the authors are unsure whether a generic solution is the answer, hate crime is an evolving area and one that requires a multi-faceted, multi-organizational, intra-community and systematic approach, which demonstrates parity in public policy for people of all faiths and none. Implementing examples of best practice, educational projects, realistic intra-faith cooperation, and equitable government initiatives, if consistent and principled in approach, will have a positive impact on all affected by racist or religiously motivated hate crime. There must be accurate recording and reporting, and equitable investment in resources, to tackle what in the case of Sikhs has hitherto been an egregious policy blind spot by successive British governments since 9/11.

Notes

1 C. Wootson Jr (2018). 'An ex-deputy rammed a truck into a store because he thought the owners were Muslim, police say'. *The Washington Post.* [online] Available at: www.washingtonpost.com/news/acts-of-faith/wp/2018/03/07/an-ex-deputy-rammed-a-truck-into-a-store-because-he-thought-the-owners-were-muslim-police-say/?utm_term=.f97d534361e8 [Accessed 26 June 2018].
2 E. Love (2009). 'Confronting Islamophobia in the United States: Framing civil rights activism among Middle Eastern Americans'. *Patterns of Prejudice,* 43(3–4), pp. 401–425.
3 A. Thompson (2017). 'Sikhs in America: A history of hate'. *ProPublica.* [online] Available at: www.propublica.org/article/sikhs-in-america-hate-crime-victims-and-bias [Accessed 5 November 2017]. A notable case of the 'Middle Eastern-looking' other or 'Muslim-looking other' is that of Jean Charles de Menezes. The Brazilian electrician was shot dead by the MET on 22 July 2005 on the tube. He was suspected of being an Islamic extremist in the aftermath of the 7/7 London bombings and the 21/7 attempted attacks.
4 M. Kwan (2008). 'From oral histories to visual narratives: re-presenting the post-September 11 experiences of the Muslim women in the USA'. *Social & Cultural Geography,* 9(6), pp. 653–669; K. Y. Joshi (2006). 'The racialization of Hinduism, Islam, and Sikhism in the United States'. *Equity & Excellence in Education,* 39(3), pp. 211–226.
5 Home Office, *Hate Crime, England and Wales, 2017 to 2018.*
6 Copsey et al., 'Anti-Muslim hate crime and the far right'.
7 ITV News, 'Sikh taxi driver had turban ripped off and burnt'.
8 Tell MAMA (2017). 'Beyond the Incident: Outcomes for victims of Anti-Muslim Prejudice'. Tell MAMA Annual Report 2017. [online] Available at: https://tellmamauk.org/wp-content/uploads/2018/07/Tell-MAMA-Report-2017.pdf [Accessed 7 September 2018].

9 University of Essex. Institute for Social and Economic Research, NatCen Social Research (2016). Understanding Society: Innovation Panel, Waves 1–7, 2008–2014. [data collection]. 6th Edition. UK Data Service. SN: 6849, http://doi.org/10.5255/UKDA-SN-6849-7 [Accessed 12 September 2018].

10 Ibid.

11 Home Office, *Hate Crime, England and Wales, 2017 to 2018.*

12 Notably in Britain, the number of hate crimes recorded by the police in July 2016 was 41 per cent higher in July 2016 than in July 2015, and a sharp increase was observed after the EU referendum.

13 Following the Brexit referendum Dr M. Ali Abbasi tweeted: 'Last night a Sikh radiographer colleague of mine was told by a patient "shouldn't you be on a plane back to Pakistan? We voted you out."'

14 Perraudin, 'Man arrested over fires at mosque and Sikh temple in Leeds'.

15 Watson, 'Man arrested following firebomb attack on Leith Sikh temple'.

16 At this time the news emerged of Gucci's use of turbans as a fashion accessory during Milan Fashion Week. Aljazeera.com, 'Gucci accused of culturally appropriating Sikh turban'. This episode also attracted much outrage on social media. For example, a social media influencer, with over a million followers, Harjinder Singh Kukreja (@SinghLions) tweeted,

> Dear @gucci, the Sikh Turban is not a hot new accessory for white models but an article of faith for practising Sikhs. Your models have used Turbans as 'hats' whereas practising Sikhs tie them neatly fold-by-fold. Using fake Sikhs/Turbans is worse than selling fake Gucci products.

Twitter (2018). Harjinder Singh Kukreja on Twitter. [online] Available at: https://twitter.com/SinghLions/status/966708208667676673/photo/1 [Accessed 6 March 2018].

17 K. Forrester (2018). 'Sikh MP Tan Dhesi "disgusted" after guest has turban ripped off outside Parliament'. *Huffington Post UK*. [online] Available at: www.huffingtonpost.co.uk/entry/sikh-mp-tan-dhesi-disgusted-and-embarrassed-after-guest-has-turban-ripped-off-outside-parliament_uk_5a8eea6ae4b0ae162f21b106 [Accessed 4 March 2018].

18 T. Bachelor (2018). 'Sikh man has turban ripped off in "racist attack" outside Parliament'. *The Independent*. [online] Available at: www.independent.co.uk/news/uk/crime/sikh-man-turban-ripped-off-parliament-hate-crime-police-london-portcullis-house-a8222376.html [Accessed 26 June 2018].

19 Forrester, 'Sikh MP Tan Dhesi "disgusted" after guest has turban ripped off'.

20 M. Coulter (2018). 'Sikh man "has turban ripped off in racist attack outside Parliament"'. *Evening Standard*. [online] Available at: www.standard.co.uk/news/crime/sikh-man-has-turban-ripped-off-in-racist-attack-outside-parliament-while-waiting-to-meet-labour-mp-a3773391.html [Accessed 7 September 2018].

21 D. Goyal (2018). 'Sikh man faces racial attack outside UK Parliament, attacker shouted "Muslim go back"'. *The Indian Express*. [online] Available at: https://indianexpress.com/article/india/racial-attack-on-sikh-man-from-ludhiana-outside-uk-parliament-in-london-attacker-shouted-muslim-go-back-5073567/ [Accessed 26 June 2018].

22 *The Tribune* (2018). 'EcoSikh activist attacked in UK'. [online] Available at: www.tribuneindia.com/news/diaspora/ecosikh-activist-attacked-in-uk/548404.html [Accessed 26 June 2018].

23 According to www.parliament.uk, a point of order is an appeal to the Chair or Speaker for clarification or for a ruling on a matter of procedure in the House of Commons. The MP must explain their reasons for believing the rules of the House have been broken and the Speaker decides whether it is a valid point of order or not.

24 Hansard. HC Deb (26 February 2018). Points of Order vol. 636 col. 565. [online] Available at: https://hansard.parliament.uk/Commons/2018-02-26/debates/C159EB9F-4F36-48C9-906F-AF22A70CE306/PointsOfOrder [Accessed: 4 March 2018].

25 Ibid.

26 Twitter (2018). Tina Daheley on Twitter. [online] Available at: https://twitter.com/TinaDaheley/status/966711681874366466 [Accessed 4 March 2018].

27 *Jewish News* (2018). 'Home Secretary commits to renew £13.4 million in security funding at CST dinner'. *Jewish News*. [online] Available at: http://jewishnews.times-ofisrael.com/home-sec-cst-dinner-2018/ [Accessed 21 March 2018].

28 Home Office, 'Places of worship: Security-funding scheme'.

29 G. Newton (2018). 'Photos show fire damage to Leeds mosque and Sikh temple as police investigate hate crime arson attacks'. *Yorkshire Evening Post*. [online] Available at: www.yorkshireeveningpost.co.uk/news/photos-show-fire-damage-to-leeds-mosque-and-sikh-temple-as-police-investigate-hate-crime-arson-attacks-1-9193972 [Accessed 4 July 2018].

30 D. King (2018). 'Vigil to be held in solidarity with Sikh community in Leith'. *Edinburgh Evening News*. [online] Available at: www.edinburghnews.scotsman.com/our-region/edinburgh/vigil-to-be-held-in-solidarity-with-sikh-community-in-leith-1-4791538 [Accessed 8 September 2018].

31 Home Office and Ministry of Housing, Communities & Local Government (2018). Action against hate: The UK government's plan for tackling hate crime – 'two years on'. https://assets.publishing.service.gov.uk/government/uploads/system/uploads/attachment_data/file/748175/Hate_crime_refresh_2018_FINAL_WEB.PDF [Accessed 5 December 2018].

32 Sikh Aware UK, 'About Us'.

33 Home Office and MHCLG, Action against hate – 'two years on'.

34 Chaplain, 'Thousands of football fans gather for anti-extremism march'.

35 HMICFRS (2018). *Understanding the Difference: The Initial Police Response to Hate Crime*. [online] Available at: www.justiceinspectorates.gov.uk/hmicfrs/publications/understanding-the-difference-the-initial-police-response-to-hate-crime/ [Accessed 12 September 2018].

36 Ibid.

37 Tweet from Richard Norrie (29 November 2018) referring to HMICFRIS report: 'An audit of 700 hate crimes recorded by an unnamed police force, found as many as 1/2 of religious flags were incorrect and should have been flagged as race.' Twitter (2018). Richard Norrie on Twitter. [online] Available at: https://twitter.com/RichardNorrie/status/1068264726705119234 [Accessed 29 November 2018].

38 Ibid.

39 Ibid.

40 Metropolitan Police (2018). 'Hate crime or special crime dashboard'. *Metropolitan Police*. [online] Available at: www.met.police.uk/sd/stats-and-data/met/hate-crime-dashboard/ [Accessed 5 November 2018].

41 BBC News, 'Anti-Muslim crimes get own category'.

42 D. De Simone (2018). 'The new parents and the UK's neo-Nazi terror threat'. BBC News. [online] Available at: www.bbc.co.uk/news/stories-45919730 [Accessed 18 November 2018].

43 Twitter (2018). [online] Available at: https://twitter.com/TellMamaUK/status/963144132842504192 [Accessed 23 December 2018].

44 Network of Sikh Organisations (2018). 'Faith Matters and British Sikhs'. Network of Sikh Organisations. [online] Available at: http://nsouk.co.uk/faith-matters-and-british-sikhs/ [Accessed 23 December 2018].

45 Ibid.

46 Faith Matters (2010). 'Cohesive communities: Bridging divides between Muslim and Sikh communities'. [online] Available at: www.faith-matters.org/2010/02/26/cohesive-communities/ [Accessed 23 December 2018].
47 Network of Sikh Organisations, 'Faith Matters and British Sikhs'.
48 P. Walker (2018). 'Chuka Umunna says Labour is institutionally racist'. *The Guardian*. [online] Available at: www.theguardian.com/politics/2018/sep/09/chuka-umunna-labour-is-institutionally-racist [Accessed 9 September 2018].
49 Chaplain and Bentham, 'Shocking figures reveal spike in anti-Islam hate crime'.
50 A. Kakar (2018). 'Guardian accused of self-regulation failure by Network of Sikh Organisations over hate crime complaint'. *Press Gazette*. [online] Available at: www.pressgazette.co.uk/guardian-accused-of-self-regulation-failure-by-network-of-sikh-organisations-over-hate-crime-complaint/ [Accessed 12 September 2018].
51 Ibid.
52 Independent Press Standards Organisation (2018). [online] Available at: www.ipso.co.uk/.
53 Impress (2018). [online] Available at: www.impress.press/.
54 Religion Media Centre (2018). Religion Media Centre: Home. [online] Available at: https://religionmediacentre.org.uk/.
55 S. Singh (2012). Opinion: 'Hate crime reporting shouldn't ignore American Sikhs'. *The New York Times* [online] Available at: www.nytimes.com/2012/08/24/opinion/do-american-sikhs-count.html [Accessed 18 January 2018]; Sidhu and Gohil, *Civil Rights in Wartime*.
56 V. Kaur (2017). '"Breathe! Push!" Watch this Sikh activist's powerful prayer for America'. *The Washington Post*. [online] Available at: www.washingtonpost.com/news/acts-of-faith/wp/2017/03/06/breathe-push-watch-this-sikh-activists-powerful-prayer-for-america/?utm_term=.8b591a02ac30 [Accessed 17 May 2017].
57 Hundal, 'Wisconsin temple shooting: Sikhs have been silent scapegoats since 9/11'.
58 G. Wilford (2017). 'Racist Snapchat story targeting Sikh man on a plane causes outrage'. *The Independent*. [online] Available at: www.independent.co.uk/news/world/americas/snapchat-racist-twitter-sikh-terrorism-muslim-islamophobia-airplane-passenger-outrage-racism-hate-a7807161.html [Accessed 4 October 2017].
59 P. Mogul (2016). 'Arsenal fan blames Sikh Manchester United supporters for Old Trafford evacuation'. *International Business Times UK*. [online] Available at: www.ibtimes.co.uk/manchester-united-bomb-scare-twitter-fury-arsenal-supporter-blames-sikh-football-fans-1560259 [Accessed 8 September 2018].
60 C. Garcia (2017). 'Cosmopolitan caught misrepresenting Sikh man as a Muslim to push liberal narrative'. *The Blaze*. [online] Available at: www.theblaze.com/news/2017/05/23/cosmopolitan-caught-misrepresenting-sikh-man-as-a-muslim-to-push-liberal-narrative [Accessed 8 September 2018].
61 I. Awan (2014). 'Islamophobia and Twitter: A typology of online hate against Muslims on social media'. *Policy & Internet*, 6(2), pp. 133–150.
62 C. Allen (2018). 'Why UK's working definition of Islamophobia as a "type of racism" is a historic step'.
63 P. Walker (2016). 'UK adopts antisemitism definition to combat hate crime against Jews'. *The Guardian*. [online] Available at: www.theguardian.com/society/2016/dec/12/antisemitism-definition-government-combat-hate-crime-jews-israel [Accessed 9 July 2018].
64 National Secular Society (2018). 'Home Secretary urged not to adopt definition of "Islamophobia"'. [online] Available at: www.secularism.org.uk/news/2018/12/home-secretary-urged-not-to-adopt-definition-of-islamophobia [Accessed 16 December 2018].
65 The letter was worded as follows:

The government must resist growing pressure to adopt a definition of Islamophobia. A recent report from the all-party parliamentary group on British Muslims proposes a definition that conflates hatred of Muslims with criticism of Islam. This is simply wrong. In a liberal secular society, individuals must be protected, but the same cannot be said of ideas, and this proposal would render legitimate comment about Islam beyond the bounds of reasonable public debate. Far from combating prejudice, erroneous claims of Islamophobia have become a cover for it. Lesbian, gay, bisexual and transgender campaigners, as well as feminists, have been called Islamophobes for criticizing the views of Muslim clerics on homosexuality and women's rights. Even liberal and secular Muslims have been branded Islamophobes. A commitment to tackle the real and pressing problem of anti-Muslim bigotry should not, and need not, infringe on the basic right to speak freely. The government must not treat the civil liberties of its citizens as an afterthought.

The signatories were Stephen Evans, Chief Executive, National Secular Society; Mohammed Amin; Amina Lone, co-director, Social Action and Research Foundation; Maajid Nawaz, founder, Quilliam; Yasmin Rehman; Pragna Patel, Southall Black Sisters; Gita Sahgal, Centre for Secular Space. *The Times* (2018). Letters to the Editor. [online] Available at: www.thetimes.co.uk/edition/comment/letters-to-the-editor-take-the-deal-the-alternative-is-chaos-nsxvpt6jw [Accessed 16 December 2018].
66 T. Phillips (2019). 'It's wrong to treat British Muslims as a racial group'. *The Times*. [online] Available at: www.thetimes.co.uk/article/it-s-wrong-to-treat-british-muslims-as-a-racial-group-9xj8bf0vx [Accessed 4 January 2019].
67 Ibid.
68 H. Singh (2019). 'We must be free to criticise Islam'. *Spiked Online*. [online] Available at: www.spiked-online.com/2019/01/04/we-must-be-free-to-criticise-islam/ [Accessed 4 January 2019].
69 Ibid.
70 L. Harpin (2019). 'Board of Deputies nearly backed Islamophobia definition "decisively influenced" by controversial group'. *The Jewish Chronicle.* [online] Available at: https:// www.thejc.com/news/uk-news/board-of-deputies-nearly-backed-islamophobia-definition-decisively-influenced-by-controversial-1.478393.
71 The NSS and others have suggested the term 'Islamophobia' should be used to silence those trying to battle Islamist bigotry. Secular and liberal Muslims (and ex-Muslims) have been labelled 'Islamophobes' for challenging Muslim clerics on issues such as gay and women's rights. Flashpoints have included forced *hijab* wearing and gender segregation in schools.
72 House of Commons Home Affairs Committee (2017). Hate crime: Abuse, hate and extremism online. 14th report of Session 2016–17. [online] Available at: https:// publications.parliament.uk/pa/cm201617/cmselect/cmhaff/609/609.pdf [Accessed 4 July 2018].
73 Ibid.
74 V. Dodd (2017). 'CPS to crack down on social media hate crime, says Alison Saunders'. *The Guardian.* [online] Available at: www.theguardian.com/society/2017/aug/21/cps-to-crack-down-on-social-media-hate-says-alison-saunders [Accessed 5 July 2018].
75 Guido Fawkes (2018). 'Jordan Peterson's warning against criminalising speech'. [online] Available at: https://order-order.com/2018/11/09/jordan-petersons-warning-criminalising-speech/ [Accessed 12 November 2018].
76 There are number of laws that can assist individuals subjected to 'racially motivated' or 'religiously motivated' hate crime online. This includes the Crime and Disorders Act (1998), the Public Order Act (1986), the Malicious Communications Act (1998) and the Communications Act (2003).

77 C. Parker (2017). 'Police arresting nine people a day in fight against web trolls'. *The Times*. [online] Available at: www.thetimes.co.uk/article/police-arresting-nine-people-a-day-in-fight-against-web-trolls-b8nkpgp2d [Accessed 19 September 2018].

78 Newcastle University (2017). 'Mistaken for being Muslim'. [online] Available at: www.ncl.ac.uk/press/news/2017/03/islamophobia-otherethnicgroups/ [Accessed 8 October 2017].

79 C. May (2018). 'UK's top diplomat "sorry" for mosque gaffe'. BBC News. [online] Available at: www.bbc.co.uk/news/uk-43876304 [Accessed 3 July 2018].

80 Hopkins et al., 'Encountering misrecognition'.

81 Newcastle University, 'Mistaken for being Muslim'.

82 APPG on Religious Education (2016). 'Improving religious literacy: A contribution to the debate'. Available at: www.reonline.org.uk/wp-content/uploads/2016/07/APPG-on-RE-Improving-Religious-Literacy-full-report.pdf [Accessed 26 June 2018].

83 E. Malnick (2013). 'MPs attack Government's "downgrading" of religious education'. *The Telegraph*. [online] Available at: www.telegraph.co.uk/education/educationnews/9934940/MPs-attack-Governments-downgrading-of-religious-education.html [Accessed 26 June 2018].

84 APPG on Religious Education, 'Improving religious literacy: A contribution to the debate'.

85 Commission on Religious Education (2018). 'A new vision for Religious Education in schools'. [online] Available at: www.commissiononre.org.uk/ [Accessed 5 November 2018].

86 Commission on Religious Education (2018). 'Religion and worldviews: The way forward. A national plan for RE'. [online] Available at: www.commissiononre.org.uk/final-report-religion-and-worldviews-the-way-forward-a-national-plan-for-re/.

87 J. Burns (2018). 'Teach religion and worldviews instead of RE'. BBC News. [online] Available at: www.bbc.co.uk/news/education-45451489 [Accessed 9 September 2018].

88 National Secular Society (2018). '21st century RE for all'. [online] Available at: www.secularism.org.uk/21st-century-re-for-all/ [Accessed 21 July 2018].

89 This highlights how things have not changed since the Macpherson Inquiry, which noted in section 6.27, para 3.2, that:

> institutional racism … permeates the Metropolitan Police Service. This issue above all others is central to the attitudes, values and beliefs, which lead officers to act, albeit unconsciously and for the most part unintentionally, and treat others differently solely because of their ethnicity or culture.

C. MacPherson (1999). *The Stephen Lawrence Inquiry*. London: TSO.

90 London Datastore, 'Population by Religion, Borough'.

91 After Wisconsin, the authors also witnessed the ignorance of a Fox News host who asked Sikhs: 'Have there been any prior acts of violence against members of the temple? Any anti-Semitic acts?' See YouTube (2012). Fox News Asks If There Were Any Anti-Semitic Acts Against The Wisconsin Sikh Temple. [online] Available at: www.youtube.com/watch?v=URsxydjAtb4 [Accessed 14 December 2017].

92 *The Telegraph*, 'Mitt Romney confuses "Sikh" with "sheikh"'.

93 May, 'UK's top diplomat "sorry" for mosque gaffe'.

94 A prominent US case, in which a boy is filming his classmates on a bus whilst they refer to him as a 'terrorist', shows exactly why. The *patka*-wearing boy is on a bus pointing a camera at his face whilst a female classmate is referring to him as 'terrorist, terrorist'. The 2015 video went viral, but importantly shows how 'visible markers' are all that is required to illicit prejudice in school settings. BBC News, 'Sikh boy labelled a "terrorist"'.

 95 Anoosh Chakelian (2017). '"They tried to take it off at school": Tan Dhesi on being the first Sikh MP with a turban'. *New Statesman*. [online] www.newstatesman.com/politics/uk/2017/08/they-tried-take-it-school-tan-dhesi-being-first-sikh-mp-turban [Accessed 2 January 2019]; Canton, 'First turban-wearing MP in British parliament vows'.

 96 BBC (2018). 'My turban and me'. BBC One. [online] Available at: www.bbc.co.uk/programmes/b09zcvct [Accessed 29 May 2018].

 97 T. Townsend (2018). 'For football to be truly inclusive, we need to see different faces at the top'. *Metro News*. [online] Available at: https://metro.co.uk/2018/09/20/for-football-to-be-truly-inclusive-we-need-to-see-different-faces-at-the-top-7953155/?ito=cbshare [Accessed 25 October 2018].

 98 *Dasam Granth*, Ang 47. [online]. Available at www.searchgurbani.com/dasam-granth/index/chapter/en [Accessed 5 July 2017].

 99 Jonathan Martin and Amie Parnes (2008). 'McCain: Obama not an Arab, crowd boos'. *Politico Magazine* [online] www.politico.com/story/2008/10/mccain-obama-not-an-arab-crowd-boos-014479 [Accessed 15 February 2019].

100 P. Yalamanchili (2016). 'Sikh Americans on the Daily Show explain why throwing Hasan Minhaj under the bus is not an option'. *The Aerogram*. [online] Available at: http://theaerogram.com/sikh-americans-on-daily-show-explain-why-throwing-muslims-under-the-bus-is-not-an-option/ [Accessed 5 July 2017].

101 Twitter (2018). City Sikhs on Twitter. [online] Available at: https://twitter.com/citysikhs/status/1063748105064071168 [Accessed 5 December 2018].

102 We Are Sikhs (2018). We Are Sikhs. [online] Available at: www.wearesikhs.org/ [Accessed 5 January 2018].

103 ITV News, 'Sikh taxi driver had turban ripped off and burnt'.

104 Ministry of Housing, Communities & Local Government (2018). *Integrated Communities Strategy Green Paper*. [online] Available at: https://assets.publishing.service.gov.uk/government/uploads/system/uploads/attachment_data/file/696993/Integrated_Communities_Strategy.pdf [Accessed 23 September 2018].

105 P. Lynch (2017). 'Northampton Sikh leader to racist hate mail writer: "This is unacceptable this day and age"'. *Northampton Chronicle*. [online] Available at: www.northamptonchron.co.uk/news/northampton-sikh-leader-to-racist-hate-mail-writer-this-is-unacceptable-this-day-and-age-1-7893382 [Accessed 6 March 2018].

106 V. Kaur (2018). 'Watch the Emmy-Award winning "Sikhs in America"'. [online] Available at: http://valariekaur.com/2018/09/watch-sikhs-in-america-more-resources/ [Accessed 14 September 2018].

107 Twitter (2018). Amandeep SinghBhogal on Twitter. [online] Available at: https://twitter.com/AmandeepBhogal/status/981589944148877313 [Accessed 9 April 2018].

Glossary

Adi Granth	The name for the original version of the *Guru Granth Sahib*. It was compiled by the fifth Guru, Guru Arjan Dev, and installed at the *Harmandir Sahib* in 1604.
Allah	Arabic word for God
Akal Takht	Building in *Harmandir Sahib*/Golden Temple complex, literally 'Throne of the Timeless'
Amritdhari	Initiated Sikh who wears the Five Ks
Amrit Sanskar/ Amrit Pahul	Initiation ceremony, also referred to as *Khande di Pahul*
Ang	Page
Bhagat	Devotee
Bhakti movement	Twelfth-century devotional movement in India
Burkha	Item of clothing worn by women in the Islamic tradition that covers the whole body and face
Chardi kala	Literally translates as 'high spirits'
Dasam Granth	Book containing the writings of Guru Gobind Singh, compiled by Bhai Mani Singh
Dastaar	Sikh turban, also referred to as *pagri*, or *pagg/pagh*
Dharam	Sikh duties, values, traditions and moral ethos that constitute the Sikh way of life
Dulband	Turban/headwear of Persian origin
Dupatta	Long scarf worn by women, also referred to as *chunni*
Gurdwara	Sikh place of worship, means 'door to Guru'
Gurmukhi	The script in which the primary scripture of Sikhism is written – literally means 'from the mouth of the Guru'
Guru Granth Sahib	The tenth Guru, Guru Gobind Singh, added the verses of Guru Tegh Bahadur (the ninth Guru) to the *Adi Granth* and renamed the revised volume the *Guru Granth Sahib*. It contains the compositions of six Sikh Gurus: Guru Nanak, Guru Angad, Guru Amar Das, Guru Ram Das, Guru Arjan and Guru Teg Bahadur. It also contains teachings of Hindu religious leaders, such as Ramananda and Namdev, and Muslim saints (Kabir and the Sufi Sheikh Farid). It is referred to as the 'Eternal Living Guru for Sikhs'.
Haram	Forbidden or proscribed by Islamic law

Harmandir Sahib	Also known as *Darbar Sahib*, or the Golden Temple, in Amristar, Punjab, India
Hijab	Head covering worn by Muslim women
Hukam	The Will of God
Janam Sakhis	Hagiographical account of the life of Guru Nanak
Joora	Punjabi word that refers to hair in bun or topknot
Jihad	Struggle against enemies of Islam
Jihadi(st)	One who has carried out jihad
Jilab	Full-length outer garment worn by some Muslim women
Kaffir	Derogatory term for non-Muslim
Kaffiyeh	Middle Eastern headdress fashioned from a square scarf
Kara	Steel/iron bangle worn by initiated Sikhs
Karta Purakh	The Creator
Keshdhari	A Sikh who keeps uncut hair
Kesh	Unshorn hair preserved by initiated Sikhs
Khalsa	Initiated Sikhs, means community of the 'pure'
Kippah	Brimless cap usually made of cloth worn by Jews
Kirpan	Sikh ceremonial sword carried by initiated Sikhs
Kshatriya	Hindu warrior caste
Langar	Free vegetarian meal provided for all visitors to a *gurdwara*
Miri–piri	Sikh concept of duality of spiritual and temporal existence
***Mona* Sikh**	A Sikh who cuts his/her hair, also known as a *Sehajdhari* Sikh
Niqab	Veil worn by Muslim women, covering the face bar the eyes
Panj Kakar	Five articles of faith worn by initiated Sikh brotherhood/ community
Panj Pyare	Literally, the 'five beloved ones': the name given to the five men who were prepared to sacrifice their lives. They were the first five members of the khalsa.
Panth	Word referring to the global Sikh brotherhood/community
Parchaar	Educational discourse by Sikhs
Patka	Small piece of cloth covering long hair normally worn by young boys
Quran	Islam's foundational religious text
Rehat Maryada	Code of conduct and conventions for Sikhs
Rehatnama	Code of conduct
Sant	Saint
Sarbat da bhalla	Sikh teachings promoting 'the prosperity of all humanity'
Sati	Practice of self-immolation by widows on their husband's funeral pyres
Shaheed	Martyr
Sharia	Islamic law
Sikh	(Sanskrit: *Shishya*): Literally, 'disciple' or learner
Sikhi	Short for Sikhism
Ummah	Arabic word referring to global community of Muslims

Bibliography

Books

Allen, C. (2016). *Islamophobia*. London: Routledge.

Awan, I. and Zempi, I. (2016). *Islamophobia: Lived Experiences of Online and Offline Victimisation*. Bristol: Policy Press.

Banakar, R. (2016). *Rights in Context*. London: Routledge.

Beetham, D. (1970). *Transport and Turbans: A Comparative Study in Local Politics*. Published for the Institute of Race Relations, London: Oxford University Press.

Bhangu, S. Rattan. *Sri Guru Panth Parkash*. Volumes I and II. English translation by Kulwant Singh. Chandigarh: Institute of Sikh Studies.

Bidwell, S. (1987). *The Turban Victory*. Kent, UK: Sikh Missionary Society.

Dasam Granth. Search Gurbani. [online] Available at www.searchgurbani.com/dasam-granth/index/chapter/en [Accessed 1 May 2019].

Dhanda, P. (2015). *My Political Race: An Outsider's Journey to the Heart of British Politics*. London: Biteback Publishing.

Esteves, Olivier (2018). *The 'Desegregation' of English Schools: Bussing, Race and Urban Space, 1960s–80s*. Manchester: Manchester University Press.

Guru Granth Sahib. Search Gurbani. [online] Available at www.searchgurbani.com/guru-granth-sahib/ang-by-ang [Accessed 1 May 2019].

Hall, N. (2013). *Hate Crime*. London: Routledge.

Jacobsen, K. and Myrvold, K. (2016). *Sikhs in Europe – Migration, Identity and Representations*. London: Routledge.

Jhutti-Johal, J. (2011). *Sikhism Today*. London: Continuum.

McLeod, W. H. (1980). *Early Sikh Tradition: A Study of the Janam-sākhīs*. Oxford: Clarendon Press.

McLeod, W. H. (1984). *Textual Sources for the Study of Sikhism*. Manchester: Manchester University Press.

McLeod, W. H. (2003). *Sikhs of the Khalsa: A History of the Khalsa Rahit*. New Delhi: Oxford University Press.

McGraw, B. A. (2016). *The Wiley-Blackwell Companion to Religion and Politics in the US*. West Sussex: Wiley-Blackwell.

Ondaatje, M. (2009). *The English Patient*: Special Edition. London: A&C Black.

Padam, Piara Singh (1989) *Rehatname*. Amritsar: Singh Brothers.

Poulter, S. (1998). *Ethnicity, Law and Human Rights: The English Experience*. Oxford: Clarendon Press.

Rowe, M. (ed.) (2013). *Policing Beyond Macpherson*. London: Routledge.

Sarna, N. (2010). *The Book of Nanak*. New Delhi: Penguin Books India.

Schofield, C. (2013). *Enoch Powell and the making of postcolonial Britain*. Cambridge: Cambridge University Press.

Shiromani Gurdwara Parbandhak Committee (1945/1950). *The Code of Conduct and Conventions: English Version of the Sikh Rehat Maryada*. [online] Available at: http://sgpc.net/sikh-rehat-maryada-in-english/ [Accessed 30 April 2019].

Sian, K. P. (2013). *Unsettling Sikh and Muslim Conflict: Mistaken Identities, Forced Conversions, and Postcolonial Formations*. Lanham, MD: Lexington Books.

Sidhu, D. S. and Gohil, N. S. (2016). *Civil Rights in Wartime: The Post-9/11 Sikh Experience*. London: Routledge.

Singh, G. (trans.) (1987). *Translation of the Guru Granth Sahib*. 7th Edition. New Delhi: Allied.

Singh, G. (2014). *The Testimonies of Indian Soldiers and the Two World Wars: Between Self and Sepoy*. London: A&C Black.

Singh, G. and Tatla, D. S. (2006). *Sikhs in Britain: The Making of a Community*. London: Zed Books.

Singh, K. (1977). *A History of the Sikhs*, Vol. 1. New Delhi: Oxford University Press.

Singh, P. (1999). *The Sikhs*. London: John Murray Publishers.

Singh, P. and Barrier, N. G. (eds) (2001). *Sikh identity: Continuity and change*. New Delhi: Manohar.

Singh, T. (1977). *The Turban and the Sword of the Sikhs*. Kent, UK: Sikh Missionary Society.

Tatla, D. S. (1998). *The Sikh Diaspora*. London: Taylor & Francis.

Journals

Abel, J. A. (2005). 'Americans under attack: The need for federal hate crime legislation in light of post-September 11 attacks on Arab Americans and Muslims'. *Asian Law Journal*, 12, p. 41.

Ahluwalia, M. and Pellettiere, L. (2010). 'Sikh men post-9/11: Misidentification, discrimination, and coping'. *Asian American Journal of Psychology*, 1(4), pp. 303–314.

Awan, I. (2014). 'Islamophobia and Twitter: A typology of online hate against Muslims on social media'. *Policy & Internet*, 6(2), pp. 133–150.

Bebber, B. (2017). 'Model migrants? Sikh activism and race relations organisations in Britain'. *Contemporary British History*, 31(4), pp. 568–592.

Benier, K. (2017). 'The harms of hate: Comparing the neighbouring practices and interactions of hate crime victims, non-hate crime victims and non-victims'. Available at: *International Review of Victimology*, 23(2), pp. 179–201. https://doi.org/10.1177/0269758017693087 [Accessed 22 December 2018].

Bindman, Geoffrey, QC (2008). 'The right to wear a turban'. *New Law Journal*. [online] Available at: www.newlawjournal.co.uk/content/right-wear-turban [Accessed 15 October 2017].

Blee, K. M. (2005). 'Racial violence in the United States'. *Ethnic and Racial Studies*, 28(4), pp. 599–619.

Chakraborti, N. (2014). 'Re-thinking hate crime: Fresh challenges for policy and practice'. *Journal of Interpersonal Violence*, 30(10), pp. 1738–1754.

Chakraborti, N. and Garland, J. (2012). 'Reconceptualizing hate crime victimization through the lens of vulnerability and "difference"'. *Theoretical Criminology*, 16(4), pp. 499–514.

Chakraborti, N., Garland, J. and Hardy, S. J. (2014). *The Leicester Hate Crime Project: Findings and Conclusions*. Retrieved from www2.le.ac.uk/departments/criminology/hate/documents/fc-full-report [Accessed 23 December 2018].

Frost, D. (2008). 'Islamophobia: examining causal links between the media and "race hate" from "below"'. *International Journal of Sociology and Social Policy*, 28(11/12), pp. 564–578.

Gatrad, R., Jhutti-Johal, J., Gill, P. S. and Sheikh, A. (2005). 'Sikh birth customs'. *Archives of Disease in Childhood*, 90(6), pp. 560–563.

Gohil, N. S. and Sidhu, D. S. (2008). 'The Sikh turban: Post-9/11 challenges to this article of faith'. *Rutgers Journal of Law and Religion*, 9, pp. 10–72.

Grewal, I. (2013). 'Racial sovereignty and "shooter" violence: Oak Creek massacre, normative citizenship and the state'. *Sikh Formations: Religion, Culture and Theory*, 9(2), pp. 187–197.

Hanes, E. and Machin, S. (2014). 'Hate crime in the wake of terror attacks: Evidence from 7/7 and 9/11'. *Journal of Contemporary Criminal Justice*, 30(3), pp. 247–267.

Hopkins, P., Botterill, K., Sanghera, G. and Arshad, R. (2017). 'Encountering misrecognition: Being mistaken for being Muslim'. *Annals of the American Association of Geographers*, 107(4), pp. 934–948.

Jakobsh, D. (2008). '3HO/Sikh Dharma of the Western Hemisphere: The forgotten new religious movement?' *Religion Compass*, 2(3), pp. 385–408.

Joshi, K. (2006). 'The racialization of Hinduism, Islam, and Sikhism in the United States'. *Equity & Excellence in Education*, 39(3), pp. 211–226.

Juss, S. (1995). 'The constitution and Sikhs in Britain'. *Bingham Young University Law Review*. Issue 2, Article 6, pp. 481–533.

Juss, S. (2012). 'Kirpans, law, and religious symbols in schools'. *Journal of Church and State*, 55(4), pp. 758–795.

Kalra, V. (2005). 'Locating the Sikh pagh'. *Sikh Formations: Religion, Culture and Theory*, 1(1), pp. 75–92.

Kurien, P. (2018). 'Shifting US racial and ethnic identities and Sikh American activism'. *The Russell Sage Foundation Journal of the Social Sciences*, 4(5), p. 81.

Kwan, M. (2008). 'From oral histories to visual narratives: re-presenting the post-September 11 experiences of the Muslim women in the USA'. *Social & Cultural Geography*, 9(6), pp. 653–669.

Liebau, Heike (2017). 'Martial races: Theory of'. *International Encyclopedia of the First World War*. [online] Available at: https://encyclopedia.1914-1918-online.net/article/martial_races_theory_of [Accessed 8 October 2017].

Love, E. (2009). 'Confronting Islamophobia in the United States: Framing civil rights activism among Middle Eastern Americans'. *Patterns of Prejudice*, 43(3–4), pp. 401–425.

Mason, G. (2005). 'Hate crime and the image of the stranger'. *British Journal of Criminology*, 45(6), pp. 837–859.

McLeod, W. H. (1999). 'Discord in the Sikh Panth'. *Journal of the American Oriental Society*, 119(3), p. 381.

Neal, S. (2003). 'The Scarman Report, the Macpherson Report and the media: how newspapers respond to race-centred social policy interventions'. *Journal of Social Policy*, 32(1), pp. 55–74.

Puar, J. (2008). '"The turban is not a hat": Queer diaspora and practices of profiling'. *Sikh Formations: Religion, Culture and Theory*, 4(1), pp. 47–91.

Puar, J. and Rai, A. (2002). 'Monster, terrorist, fag: The War on Terrorism and the pro-duction of docile patriots'. *Social Text*, 20(3), pp. 117–148.

Sian, K. (2010). 'Don't Freak I'm a Sikh'. *Thinking through Islamophobia*, pp. 251–254.

Sian, K. (2011). '"Forced" conversions in the British Sikh diaspora'. *South Asian Popular Culture*, 9(2), pp. 115–130.

Sian, K. (2012). 'Gurdwaras, guns and grudges in "post-racial" America'. *Sikh Formations: Religion, Culture and Theory*, 8(3), pp. 293–297.

Sian, K. (2013). 'Losing my religion: Sikhs in the UK'. *Sikh Formations: Religion, Culture and Theory*, 9(1), pp. 39–50.

Singh, G. (2005). 'British multiculturalism and Sikhs'. *Sikh Formations: Religion, Culture Theory*, 1(2), pp. 157–173.

Tatla, D. S. (2003). 'Sikhs in multicultural societies'. *International Journal on Multicultural Societies*, 5(2), pp. 177–192.

Verma, R. (2006). 'Trauma, cultural survival and identity politics in a post-9/11 era: Reflections by Sikh youth'. *Sikh Formations: Religion, Culture and Theory*, 2(1), pp. 89–101.

Younge, G. (1999). 'The Death of Stephen Lawrence: The Macpherson Report'. *Political Quarterly*, 70(3), pp. 329–334.

Yuval-Davis, N. (1999). 'Institutional racism, cultural diversity and citizenship: Some reflections on reading the Stephen Lawrence Inquiry Report'. *Sociological Research Online*, 4(1), pp. 1–9.

Chapters in books

Jhutti-Johal, J. (2017). 'Sikh Dharma', in Veena R. Howard and Rita D. Sherma (eds), *Dharma: The Hindu, Buddhist, Jain and Sikh Traditions of India*. London: I. B. Tauris.

McLeod, W. H. (2001). 'The turban: Symbol of Sikh identity', in P. Singh and N. G. Barrier (eds), *Sikh identity: Continuity and Change*. New Delhi: Manohar.

Nesbitt, E. (2016). 'Sikh diversity in the UK: Contexts and evolution', in K. A. Jacobson and K. Myrvold (eds), *Sikhs in Europe – Migration, Identity and Representations*. London: Routledge.

Reports

Chakrabarti, S. (2016). *The Shami Chakrabarti Inquiry Report*. [online] Available at: https://labour.org.uk/wp-content/uploads/2017/10/Chakrabarti-Inquiry-Report-30June16.pdf [Accessed 15 January 2018].

Commission on Religious Education (2018). 'A new vision for Religious Education in schools'. [online] Available at: www.commissiononre.org.uk/ [Accessed 5 November 2018].

Commission on Religious Education (2018). 'Religion and worldviews: The way forward. A national plan for RE. [online] Available at: www.commissiononre.org.uk/final-report-religion-and-worldviews-the-way-forward-a-national-plan-for-re/ [Accessed 30 April 2019].

Conway, Gordon (1997). *Islamophobia: A Challenge for Us All*. [online] Available at: www.runnymedetrust.org/companies/17/74/Islamophobia-A-Challenge-for-Us-All.html [Accessed 14 December 2017].

Copsey, N., Dack, J., Littler, M., and Feldman, M. (2013). 'Anti-Muslim hate crime and the far right'. Teeside University. [online] Available at http://tellmamauk.org/wp-content/uploads/2013/07/antimuslim2.pdf [Accessed 4 September 2014].

Farah, Elahi and Khan, Omar (2017). *Islamophobia: Still a Challenge for Us All*. [online] Available at: www.runnymedetrust.org/uploads/Islamophobia%20Report%202018.pdf [Accessed 30 November 2017].

Lipka, M. (2017). 'Muslims and Islam: Key findings in the US and around the world'. Pew Research Center. [online] Available at: www.pewresearch.org/fact-tank/2017/08/09/muslims-and-islam-key-findings-in-the-u-s-and-around-the-world/ [Accessed 22 November 2017].

Metropolitan Police (2017). 'Statement on hate crime in London'. [online] Available at: http://news.met.police.uk/news/statement-on-hate-crime-in-london-245032 [Accessed 27 December 2017].

Metropolitan Police (2018). 'Hate crime or special crime dashboard'. *Metropolitan Police*. [online] Available at: www.met.police.uk/sd/stats-and-data/met/hate-crime-dashboard/ [Accessed 5 November 2018].

University of Cambridge (2009). *Contextualising Islam in Britain*. [online] Available at: www.cam.ac.uk/research/news/contextualising-islam-in-britain-report-released [Accessed 28 November 2017].

Government reports and documents

APPG Inquiry into Electoral Conduct (2013). Report of the All-Party Parliamentary Inquiry into Electoral Conduct. [online] Available at: https://files.graph.cool/cj3e6rg8y906h0104uh8bojao/cj4muuuz500250145fwnqvzat [Accessed 23 November 2017].

APPG on Religious Education (2016). 'Improving religious literacy: A contribution to the debate'. [online] Available at: www.reonline.org.uk/wp-content/uploads/2016/07/APPG-on-RE-Improving-Religious-Literacy-full-report.pdf [Accessed 26 June 2018].

Casey, L. (2016). *The Casey Review: A Review into Opportunity and Integration*. GOV. UK [online] Available at: www.gov.uk/government/publications/the-casey-review-a-review-into-opportunity-and-integration [Accessed 22 December 2017].

Department for Work and Pensions (2015). 'Government overturns turban workplace rule'. GOV.UK. [online] Available at: www.gov.uk/government/news/government-overturns-turban-workplace-rule [Accessed 8 October 2017].

Federal Bureau of Investigation (2018). 2017 'Hate crime statistics'. [online] Available at: https://ucr.fbi.gov/hate-crime/2017 [Accessed 14 November 2018].

Hansard. HC Deb (26 February 2018). Points of Order vol. 636 col. 565. [online] Available at: https://hansard.parliament.uk/Commons/2018-02-26/debates/C159EB9F-4F36-48C9-906F-AF22A70CE306/PointsOfOrder [Accessed: 4 March 2018].

Hansard. HC Deb (15 March 2017) Visible Religious Symbols: European Court Ruling vol. 623 col. 419. [online] Available at: https://hansard.parliament.uk/commons/2017-03-15/debates/599884E8-6E05-41C0-8FD3-B6F5A6E1F45F/VisibleReligiousSymbolsEuropeanCourtRuling [Accessed: 26 November 2017].

Hansard. HC Deb (22 June 2017) Terror Attacks vol. 626 col. 211. [online] Available at: https://hansard.parliament.uk/commons/2017-06-22/debates/D00D2537-BD22-4E4D-8E65-FE170E02848A/TerrorAttacks [Accessed: 26 November 2017].

Hansard. HC Deb (18 July 2018). Drugs Policy vol. 627 col. 748. [online] Available at: https://hansard.parliament.uk/commons/2017-07-18/debates/733C6229-49D0-4559-8F59-5F1244C2DE13/DrugsPolicy [Accessed: 5 December 2017].

Hansard. HL Deb (16 October 1989) Employment Bill, series 5, vol. 511 col. 738. [online] Available at: https://api.parliament.uk/historic-hansard/lords/1989/oct/16/employment-bill [Accessed 26 May 2019].

Hansard. HL Deb (25 June 2015) Communities: Young Muslims vol (unknown) col. 1697. [online] Available at: https://publications.parliament.uk/pa/ld201516/ldhansrd/text/150625-0001.htm#15062547000429 [Accessed: 24 November 2017].

Hansard. HL Deb (14 September 2016) Hate Crime vol. 774 col. 1457. [online] Available at: https://hansard.parliament.uk/lords/2016-09-14/debates/AAC3CAC3-78CC-4B7F-B50C-FFB58FBD7244/HateCrime [Accessed: 8 October 2017].

Hansard. HL Deb (20 December 2018). Islamophobia vol. 794 col. 1937. [online] Available at: https://hansard.parliament.uk/Lords/2018-12-20/debates/2F954D45-1962-4256-A492-22EBF6AEF8F0/Islamophobia [Accessed: 31 December 2018].

HMICFRS (2018). *Understanding the Difference: The Initial Police Response to Hate Crime*. [online] Available at: www.justiceinspectorates.gov.uk/hmicfrs/publications/understanding-the-difference-the-initial-police-response-to-hate-crime/ [Accessed 12 September 2018].

Home Office (2016). 'Action against hate: The UK government's plan for tackling hate crime'. GOV.UK. [online] Available at: www.gov.uk/government/uploads/system/uploads/attachment_data/file/543679/Action_Against_Hate_-_UK_Government_s_Plan_to_Tackle_Hate_Crime_2016.pdf [Accessed 30 December 2017].

Home Office (2016). 'Government awards £700k to tackle hate crime'. GOV.UK. [online] Available at: www.gov.uk/government/news/government-awards-700k-to-tackle-hate-crime [Accessed 19 November 2017].

Home Office (2016). 'Home Secretary visits Britain's biggest gurdwara'. GOV.UK. [online] Available at: www.gov.uk/government/news/home-secretary-visits-britains-biggest-gurdwara [Accessed 2 December 2017].

Home Office (2016). 'National Action becomes first extreme right-wing group to be banned in UK'. GOV.UK. [online] Available at: www.gov.uk/government/news/national-action-becomes-first-extreme-right-wing-group-to-be-banned-in-uk [Accessed 8 October 2017].

Home Office (2017). 'Places of worship: security funding scheme'. GOV.UK. [online] Available at: www.gov.uk/guidance/places-of-worship-security-funding-scheme [Accessed 21 March 2018].

Home Office (2018). *Hate Crime, England and Wales, 2017 to 2018*. Assets.publishing.service.gov.uk. [online] Available at: https://assets.publishing.service.gov.uk/government/uploads/system/uploads/attachment_data/file/748598/hate-crime-1718-hosb2018.pdf [Accessed 18 October 2018].

Home Office and Ministry of Community, Housing & Local Government (2018). Action against hate. The UK government's plan for tackling hate crime – 'two years on'. [online] Available at: https://assets.publishing.service.gov.uk/government/uploads/system/uploads/attachment_data/file/748175/Hate_crime_refresh_2018_FINAL_WEB.PDF [Accessed 5 December 2018].

House of Commons (2014). Hansard Written Answers for 30 April 2014 (pt 0001). [online] Available at: https://publications.parliament.uk/pa/cm201314/cmhansrd/cm140430/text/140430w0001.htm [Accessed 17 November 2017].

House of Commons (2015). Register of All-Party Groups as at 30 July 2015: Islamophobia. [online] Available at: https://publications.parliament.uk/pa/cm/cmallparty/register/islamophobia.htm [Accessed 17 November 2017].

House of Commons (2017). Register of All-Party Parliamentary Groups as at 29 March 2017: Religion in the Media. [online] Available at: https://publications.parliament.uk/pa/cm/cmallparty/170329/religion-in-the-media.htm [Accessed 18 December 2017].

House of Commons Home Affairs Committee (2009). *The Macpherson Report: Ten Years On.* [online] Available at https://publications.parliament.uk/pa/cm200809/cmselect/cmhaff/427/427.pdf [Accessed 20 May 2019].

House of Commons Home Affairs Committee (2017). Hate crime: Abuse, hate and extremism online. 14th report of Session 2016–17. [online] Available at: https://publications.parliament.uk/pa/cm201617/cmselect/cmhaff/609/609.pdf [Accessed 4 July 2018].

House of Commons, Select Committee on Home Affairs (2004). Minutes of Evidence. 'Examination of Witnesses (Questions 100–119)'. [online] Available at: https://publications.parliament.uk/pa/cm200405/cmselect/cmhaff/165/4111602.htm [Accessed 8 October 2017].

House of Commons, Select Committee on Home Affairs (2004). Written Evidence. '24. Memorandum submitted by the Metropolitan Police Diversity Directorate'. [online] Available at: https://publications.parliament.uk/pa/cm200405/cmselect/cmhaff/165ii/165we25.htm [Accessed 24 November 2017].

London Datastore (2018). 'Population by Religion, Borough'. Office for National Statistics (ONS). [online] Available at: https://data.london.gov.uk/dataset/percentage-population-religion-borough [Accessed 3 July 2018].

Macpherson, C. (1999). *The Stephen Lawrence Inquiry: Report of an Inquiry.* London: TSO.

Ministry of Defence (2015). 'Armed Forces commemorate the Battle of Saragarhi'. GOV.UK. [online] Available at: www.gov.uk/government/news/armed-forces-commemorate-the-battle-of-saragarhi [Accessed 8 October 2017].

Ministry of Housing, Communities & Local Government (2013). 'Tell MAMA' (Measuring Anti-Muslim Attacks) speech. GOV.UK. [online] Available at: www.gov.uk/government/speeches/tell-mama-measuring-anti-muslim-attacks-speech [Accessed 7 December 2017].

Ministry of Housing, Communities & Local Government (2017). Draft terms of reference for the Anti-Muslim Hatred Working Group. GOV.UK. [online] Available at: www.gov.uk/government/uploads/system/uploads/attachment_data/file/571139/AMHWG_-_terms_of_reference.pdf [Accessed 28 November 2017].

Ministry of Housing Communities & Local Government (2017). 'New hate crime package to target groups at need'. GOV.UK. [online] Available at: www.gov.uk/government/news/new-hate-crime-package-to-target-groups-at-need [Accessed 19 November 2017].

Ministry of Housing, Communities & Local Government (2018). *Integrated Communities Strategy Green Paper.* [online] Available at: https://assets.publishing.service.gov.uk/government/uploads/system/uploads/attachment_data/file/696993/Integrated_Communities_Strategy.pdf [Accessed 23 September 2018].

Ministry of Housing, Communities & Local Government, and Prime Minister's Office (2016). 'Government leads the way in tackling anti-Semitism'. GOV.UK. [online] Available at: www.gov.uk/government/news/government-leads-the-way-in-tackling-anti-semitism [Accessed 20 November 2017].

Ministry of Housing, Communities & Local Government, Home Office and Ministry of Justice (2016). Hate crime action plan 2016 to 2020. GOV.UK. [online] Available at: www.gov.uk/government/publications/hate-crime-action-plan-2016 [Accessed 7 December 2017].

National Archives (2010). Equality Act 2010. [online] Available at: www.legislation.gov.uk/ukpga/2010/15/section/9 [Accessed 8 October 2017].

National Archives (2015). Deregulation Act 2015 – *Explanatory Notes*. [online] Available at: www.legislation.gov.uk/ukpga/2015/20/notes/division/5/6 [Accessed 15 September 2018].

O'Neill, A. (2017). *Hate Crime, England and Wales, 2016/17*. Home Office. [online] Available at: https://assets.publishing.service.gov.uk/government/uploads/system/uploads/attachment_data/file/652136/hate-crime-1617-hosb1717.pdf [Accessed 29 November 2017].

ONS (2011). 'Religion in England and Wales 2011'. [online] Available at: www.ons.gov.uk/peoplepopulationandcommunity/culturalidentity/religion/articles/religioninenglandandwales2011/2012-12-11 [Accessed 2 December 2017].

ONS (2015). 'How religion has changed in England and Wales'. Visual.ONS [online] Available at: https://visual.ons.gov.uk/2011-census-religion/ [Accessed 5 January 2018].

Transport for London (2017). 'TfL and the police join forces to combat hate crime'. [online] Available at: https://tfl.gov.uk/info-for/media/press-releases/2017/october/tfl-and-the-police-join-forces-to-combat-hate-crime [Accessed 24 November 2017].

UK Parliament (2005). Early day motion 645 – London bombings and attacks on Sikhs. [online] Available at: www.parliament.uk/edm/2005-06/645 [Accessed 23 November 2017].

UK Parliament (2017). Written evidence – Network of Sikh Organisations. [online] Available at: http://data.parliament.uk/writtenevidence/committeeevidence.svc/evidencedocument/home-affairs-committee/hate-crime-and-its-violent-consequences/written/45945.html [Accessed 19 November 2017].

Articles and online video content

Abbott, M (2014). 'The Afghan Sikhs fleeing to the UK'. BBC News [online] Available at: www.bbc.co.uk/news/uk-england-29062770 [Accessed 8 October 2017].

Agerholm, H. (2017). 'Women "bearing brunt" of Islamophobic attacks in the UK'. *The Independent*. [online] Available at: www.independent.co.uk/news/uk/home-news/uk-islamophobia-attacks-women-bearing-brunt-hate-crimes-a8036581.html [Accessed 19 December 2017].

Ahmad, A. (2015). 'Captain America dons a turban'. BBC News. [online] Available at: www.bbc.co.uk/news/magazine-30941638 [Accessed 15 September 2018].

Aljazeera (2018). 'Gucci accused of culturally appropriating Sikh turban'. [online] Available at: www.aljazeera.com/news/2018/02/gucci-accused-culturally-appropriating-sikh-turban-180223200944130.html [Accessed 4 March 2018].

Allen, C. (2018). 'Why UK's working definition of Islamophobia as a "type of racism" is a historic step'. *The Conversation*. [online] Available at: https://theconversation.com/why-uks-working-definition-of-islamophobia-as-a-type-of-racism-is-a-historic-step-107657 [Accessed 27 November 2018].

Amin, A. and Jhooti, N. (2019). 'The 4,000-year history of the Sikh turban'. *CNN Style*. [online] Available at: https://edition.cnn.com/style/article/turbans-tales-history/index.html [Accessed 15 February 2019].

Asian Voice (2017). 'Applications open for government-funded security at places of worship'. [online] Available at: www.asian-voice.com/News/UK/Applications-open-for-government-funded-security-at-places-of-worship [Accessed 24 November 2017].

Awan, I. (2017). 'The non-Muslims experiencing Islamophobic attacks'. *News Statesman*. [online] Available at: www.newstatesman.com/politics/staggers/2017/10/non-muslims-experiencing-islamophobic-attacks [Accessed 17 December 2017].

Bachelor, T. (2018). 'Sikh man has turban ripped off in "racist attack" outside Parliament'. *The Independent*. [online] Available at: www.independent.co.uk/news/uk/crime/sikh-man-turban-ripped-off-parliament-hate-crime-police-london-portcullis-house-a8222376.html [Accessed 26 June 2018].

Bassey, A. (2017). 'Sikh TV accused of encouraging vigilantes to target groomers'. *Birmingham Mail* [online]. Available at: www.birminghammail.co.uk/news/midlands-news/birmingham-sikh-tv-channel-accused-13468017 [Accessed 24 December 2017].

Batchelor, T. (2017). 'Islamophobic hate crimes jump fivefold after London Bridge terror attack'. *The Independent*. [online] Available at: www.independent.co.uk/News/uk/crime/london-bridge-attack-latest-rise-islamophobic-hate-crimes-borough-market-stabbing-terror-police-a7777451.html [Accessed 7 December 2017].

Batty, D. (2011). 'Lady Warsi claims Islamophobia is now socially acceptable in Britain'. *The Guardian*. [online] Available at: www.theguardian.com/uk/2011/jan/20/lady-warsi-islamophobia-muslims-prejudice [Accessed 10 October 2018].

BBC News (2001). 'Turbans and beards leave Sikhs vulnerable'. [online] Available at: http://news.bbc.co.uk/1/hi/england/1565146.stm [Accessed 8 October 2017].

BBC News (2005). 'Sikh busmen win turban fight'. [online] Available at: http://news.bbc.co.uk/onthisday/hi/dates/stories/april/9/newsid_2523000/2523691.stm [Accessed 8 October 2017].

BBC News (2005). 'UK Parliament launches Sikh group'. [online] Available at: http://news.bbc.co.uk/1/hi/uk_politics/4675079.stm [Accessed 28 November 2017].

BBC News (2010). 'Troop protest demonstrator denies Luton attack racist'. [online] Available at: http://news.bbc.co.uk/1/hi/england/beds/bucks/herts/8549767.stm [Accessed 8 October 2017].

BBC News (2012). 'Ugandan Asians advert "foolish"'. [online] Available at: www.bbc.co.uk/news/uk-england-leicestershire-19165216 [Accessed 5 January 2018].

BBC News (2013). 'Homeless and hungry Sikh temples'. [online] Available at: www.bbc.co.uk/news/uk-england-21711980 [Accessed 28 November 2017].

BBC News (2013). 'Seven jailed for "revenge attack"'. [online] Available at: www.bbc.co.uk/news/uk-england-leicestershire-22315118 [Accessed 17 January 2018].

BBC News (2013). 'Six jailed over child prostitution'. [online] Available at: www.bbc.co.uk/news/uk-england-23896937 [Accessed 17 January 2018].

BBC News (2015). 'Anti-Islamic graffiti on Sikh temple'. [online] Available at: www.bbc.co.uk/news/uk-scotland-glasgow-west-32284473 [Accessed 12 December 2017].

BBC News (2015). 'Anti-Muslim crimes get own category'. [online] Available at: www.bbc.co.uk/news/uk-34511274 [Accessed 18 November 2017].

BBC News (2015). 'Life term for Rigby revenge attacker'. [online] Available at: www.bbc.co.uk/news/uk-wales-north-east-wales-34218184 [Accessed 8 October 2017].

BBC News (2015). 'The pool of blood that changed my life'. [online] Available at: www.bbc.co.uk/news/magazine-33725217 [Accessed 8 October 2017].

BBC News (2015). 'The Sikh boy labelled a "terrorist" by his classmates'. [online] Available at: www.bbc.co.uk/news/blogs-trending-31695234 [Accessed 30 December 2017].

BBC News (2017). 'Labour nominee dropped "for anti-Semitism"'. [online] Available at: www.bbc.co.uk/news/uk-england-leeds-42009240 [Accessed 18 November 2017].

BBC News (2017). 'The immigrants "bussed" out to school'. [online] Available at: www.bbc.co.uk/news/uk-england-leeds-38689839 [Accessed 5 January 2018].

BBC News (2018). 'Petrol bomb attack on Sikh temple probed'. [online] Available at: www.bbc.co.uk/news/uk-scotland-edinburgh-east-fife-45330820 [Accessed 28 August 2018].

BBC News (2018). 'Police warned to do better on hate crime'. [online] Available at: www.bbc.co.uk/news/uk-44873179 [Accessed 19 July 2018].

BBC News (2018). 'Tommy Robinson banned from Twitter'. [online] Available at: www.bbc.co.uk/news/technology-43572168 [Accessed 14 September 2018].

BBC (2016). 'Sikhs targeted in Islamophobic attacks'. Asian Network Reports – BBC Asian Network. [online] Available at: www.bbc.co.uk/programmes/p03jvnkk [Accessed 10 December 2017].

BBC (2016). 'The selfless Sikh: Faith on the frontline'. BBC One. [online] Available at: www.bbc.co.uk/programmes/b0834s76 [Accessed 19 December 2017].

BBC (2018). 'My turban and me'. BBC One. [online] Available at: www.bbc.co.uk/programmes/b09zcvct [Accessed 29 May 2018].

BBC, Media Centre (2016). 'United States of hate: Muslims under attack'. [online] Available at: www.bbc.co.uk/mediacentre/proginfo/2016/21/united-states-of-hate [Accessed 11 December 2017].

BBC, Press Office (2004). 'Sikhs and the City'. [online] Available at: www.bbc.co.uk/pressoffice/pressreleases/stories/2004/08_august/13/sikhs.shtml [Accessed 8 December 2017].

Beckford, M. (2008). 'Blasphemy laws are lifted'. *The Telegraph*. [online] Available at: www.telegraph.co.uk/news/1942668/Blasphemy-laws-are-lifted.html [Accessed 17 January 2018].

Blackburn, M. (2015). 'Yobs spray "die Muslims die" in graffiti attack – on Sikh temple'. *Gazette Live*. [online] Available at: www.gazettelive.co.uk/news/teesside-news/yobs-spray-die-muslims-die-9985403 [Accessed 14 April 2018].

Boggioni, T. (2018). 'Ex-deputy rams truck into Louisiana store and robs it after mistaking Sikh owners for Muslims'. *Raw Story*. [online] Available at: www.rawstory.com/2018/03/ex-deputy-rams-truck-louisiana-store-robs-mistaking-sikh-owners-muslims/#.WqBnIzOlR9E.twitter [Accessed 8 March 2018].

Booker, C. (2015). 'Enoch Powell and Tony Benn were right on Europe – it was a great deception'. *The Telegraph*. [online] Available at: www.telegraph.co.uk/comment/11673377/Enoch-Powell-and-Tony-Benn-were-right-on-Europe-it-was-a-great-deception.html [Accessed 6 October 2017].

Brandeis University (2016). American Jewish Population Project. [online] Available at: http://ajpp.brandeis.edu/aboutestimates.php [Accessed 13 November 2018].

Brine, Steve (2011). 'Launch of the Sikh Council UK'. [online] Available at: www.steve-brine.com/news/launch-sikh-council-uk [Accessed 1 May 2019].

British Sikh Report (2017). [online] Available at: www.britishsikhreport.org/wp-content/uploads/2017/03/British-Sikh-Report-2017-Online.pdf [Accessed 20 August 2018].

Broadway World (2018). 'RAG HEAD Returns To The Stage'. [online] Available at: www.broadwayworld.com/los-angeles/article/RAG-HEAD-Returns-To-The-Stage-20180822 [Accessed 23 August 2018].

Burns, J. (2018). 'Teach religion and worldviews instead of RE'. BBC News. [online] Available at: www.bbc.co.uk/news/education-45451489 [Accessed 9 September 2018].

Cannold, J. (2013). 'Sikh professor beaten in possible hate crime in New York'. CNN. [online] Available at: http://edition.cnn.com/2013/09/23/justice/new-york-sikh-possible-hate-crime/index.html [Accessed 6 January 2018].

Canton, Naomi (20 June 2017). 'First turban-wearing MP in British parliament vows to be Sikhs' voice worldwide'. *Times of India*. [online] http://timesofindia.indiatimes.com/articleshow/59238710.cms?utm_source=contentofinterest&utm_medium=text&utm_campaign=cppst [Accessed 12 February 2019].

Casciani. D (2014). 'Who are the English Defence League?' BBC News. [online] Available at: http://newsbbc.co.uk/1/hi/8250017.stm [Accessed 8 October 2017].

Centre for the Study of Islam in the UK (2008). 'The role of the media'. [online] Available at: http://sites.cardiff.ac.uk/islamukcentre/rera/online-teaching-resources/muslims-in-britain-online-course/module-4-contemporary-debates/the-role-of-the-media/ [Accessed 17 December 2017].

Chakelian, Anoosh (2017). '"They tried to take it off at school": Tan Dhesi on being the first Sikh MP with a turban'. *New Statesman* [online] www.newstatesman.com/politics/uk/2017/08/they-tried-take-it-school-tan-dhesi-being-first-sikh-mp-turban [Accessed 2 January 2019].

Channel 4 (2016). 'C4 survey and documentary reveals what British Muslims really think'. [online] Available at: www.channel4.com/info/press/news/c4-survey-and-documentary-reveals-what-british-muslims-really-think [Accessed 17 January 2018].

Chaplain, C. (2017). 'Thousands of football fans gather for anti-extremism march'. *Evening Standard.* [online] Available at: www.standard.co.uk/news/london/football-lads-association-march-thousands-gather-in-central-london-in-antiextremism-protest-a3652981.html [Accessed 8 October 2017].

Chaplain, C. and Bentham, M. (2017). 'Shocking figures reveal spike in anti-Islam hate crime in London'. *Evening Standard.* [online] Available at: www.standard.co.uk/news/crime/shocking-figures-reveal-spike-in-antiislam-hate-crime-across-london-with-25-more-offences-reported-a3660501.html [Accessed 7 December 2017].

Chester, N. (2017). 'Why isn't the Government doing more to tackle anti-Sikh discrimination?' *Vice.* [online] Available at: www.vice.com/en_uk/article/ezmyam/why-isnt-the-government-doing-more-to-tackle-anti-sikh-discrimination-89 [Accessed 10 December 2017].

College of Policing (2014). Crime Operational Guidance [online] Available at: www.college.police.uk/What-we-do/Support/Equality/Documents/Hate-Crime-Operational-Guidance.pdf [Accessed 10 December 2017].

Collier, H. (2017). 'Activists clash with police as EDL and anti-fascist groups stage demos'. *Evening Standard.* [online] Available at: www.standard.co.uk/news/london/activists-clash-with-police-as-edl-and-antifascist-groups-stage-rival-protests-a3572441.html [Accessed 8 October 2017].

Community Security Trust (2017). Protecting our Jewish Community: Other Communities. [online] Available at: https://cst.org.uk/about-cst/other-communities [Accessed 18 November 2017].

Coulter, M. (2018). 'Sikh man "has turban ripped off in racist attack outside Parliament"'. *Evening Standard.* [online] Available at: www.standard.co.uk/news/crime/sikh-man-has-turban-ripped-off-in-racist-attack-outside-parliament-while-waiting-to-meet-labour-mp-a3773391.html [Accessed 7 September 2018].

Coventry Telegraph (2004). 'Racist thugs attack dad'. [online] Available at: www.coventrytelegraph.net/news/coventry-news/racist-thugs-attack-dad-3143522 [Accessed 8 October 2017].

Cumming, E. (2018). 'BBC One's "Informer" is as nonsensical as "Bodyguard" – episode one review'. *The Independent.* [online] Available at: www.independent.co.uk/arts-entertainment/tv/reviews/informer-bbc-episode-one-review-plot-cast-paddy-considine-bodyguard-a8586371.html [Accessed 18 October 2018].

Curtis, J. (2016). 'Man jailed for leaving a bacon sandwich outside a mosque is found dead in prison halfway through his 12-month sentence'. *The Daily Mail.* [online] Available at:

www.dailymail.co.uk/news/article-4075328/Man-jailed-leaving-bacon-sandwiched-outside-mosque-dead-prison-half-way-12-month-sentence.html [Accessed 20 November 2017].

Daily Caller, The (2017). 'Cosmopolitan mag confuses a Sikh cab driver for a Muslim'. [online] Available at: http://dailycaller.com/2017/05/23/cosmopolitan-mag-confuses-a-sikh-cab-driver-for-a-muslim/ [Accessed 8 October 2017].

Daisley, S. (2017). 'Britain has an anti-Semitism problem. Here are the numbers that prove it'. *Coffee House*. [online] Available at: https://blogs.spectator.co.uk/2017/09/britain-has-an-anti-semitism-problem-and-now-we-have-the-numbers-to-prove-it/ [Accessed 23 November 2017].

Dakin Andone, C. (2018). 'After brutal attack on a Sikh man, police chief is 'disgusted' to learn his son is one of the suspects'. CNN. [online] Available at: https://edition.cnn.com/2018/08/10/us/sikh-attack-police-chief-son/index.html [Accessed 7 September 2018].

Daniel, B. (2012). 'For Sikhs turban is a proud symbol and a target'. *The Washington Post*. [online] Available at: www.washingtonpost.com/national/on-faith/for-sikhs-turban-is-a-proud-symbol-_-and-a-target/2012/08/06/95d492aa-e012-11e1-8d48-2b1243f34c85_story.html?noredirect=on&utm_term=.365d7dd5eed6 [Accessed 15 October 2017].

Dawood, F. (2016). 'Ugandan Asians dominate economy after exile'. BBC News. [online] Available at: www.bbc.co.uk/news/world-africa-36132151 [Accessed 11 October 2017].

Day, M. (2015). 'Polish police tell British Sikh man "what do you expect after Paris attacks" after nightclub beating'. *The Telegraph*. [online] Available at: www.telegraph.co.uk/news/worldnews/europe/poland/12029627/Polish-police-tell-British-Sikh-man-what-do-you-expect-after-Paris-attacks-after-nightclub-beating.html [Accessed 8 October 2017].

Dean, J. (2015). 'A Sikh man was battered by a racist who called him "bin Laden"'. *The Mirror*. [online] Available at: www.mirror.co.uk/news/world-news/sikh-man-battered-racist-thug-6424786 [Accessed 6 January 2018].

Dearden, L. (2014). 'Israel–Gaza conflict: Anti-Semitic incidents "up 500%" in UK since'. *The Independent*. [online] Available at: www.independent.co.uk/news/uk/home-news/israel-gaza-conflict-anti-semitic-incidents-up-500-in-uk-since-start-of-bombardment-of-gaza-9681324.html [Accessed 28 December 2017].

Dearden, L. (2017). 'Anti-Semitic attacks hit record high in UK'. *The Independent*. [online] Available at: www.independent.co.uk/news/uk/home-news/anti-semitic-hate-crime-attacks-british-jews-assaults-uk-incidents-record-high-cst-research-a7861721.html [Accessed 18 November 2017].

Dearden, L. (2018). 'Britain First leaders jailed for anti-Muslim hate crime'. *The Independent*. [online] Available at: www.independent.co.uk/news/uk/crime/paul-golding-jayda-fransen-britain-first-leaders-guilty-religious-muslim-hate-crime-a8244161.html [Accessed 14 April 2018].

Dearden, L. (2018). 'Huddersfield grooming gang convicted of abusing vulnerable girls'. *The Independent*. [online] Available at: www.independent.co.uk/news/uk/crime/huddersfield-child-abuse-ring-sex-trial-court-grooming-tommy-robinson-reporting-restrictions-a8592176.html [Accessed 20 October 2018].

Dearden, L. (2018). 'Hostility to men could become hate crime under government plans'. *The Independent*. [online] Available at: www.independent.co.uk/news/uk/crime/hate-crime-men-misogyny-misandry-age-women-laws-review-law-commission-action-plan-rise-a8585236.html [Accessed 17 October 2018].

Dearden, L. (2018). 'More than 420 Rotherham grooming gang suspects being investigated in "unprecedented" operation'. *The Independent.* [online] Available at: www.independent.co.uk/news/uk/crime/grooming-gangs-rotherham-suspects-victims-girls-rape-uk-nca-prosecutions-a8609511.html [Accessed 5 December 2018].

Delingpole, J. (2016). 'Trevor Phillips's documentary on Muslims was shocking – but not surprising'. *The Spectator.* [online] Available at: www.spectator.co.uk/2016/04/why-do-we-pretend-that-all-muslims-are-sweet-smiley-and-integrated/ [Accessed 27 November 2017].

De Simone, D. (2018). 'The new parents and the UK's neo-Nazi terror threat'. BBC News. [online] Available at: www.bbc.co.uk/news/stories-45919730 [Accessed 18 November 2018].

Dhanda, P. (2015). *My Political Race.* [online] Available at: www.bitebackpublishing.com/books/my-political-race [Accessed 12 December 2017].

Dizon, J. (2015). 'New H&M ads feature hijab and turban wearing models'. *Tech Times.* [online] Available at: www.techtimes.com/articles/89799/20151001/new-h-m-ads-feature-hijab-and-turban-wearing-models.html [Accessed 19 August 2018].

Dodd, V. (2017). 'CPS to crack down on social media hate crime, says Alison Saunders'. *The Guardian.* [online] Available at: www.theguardian.com/society/2017/aug/21/cps-to-crack-down-on-social-media-hate-says-alison-saunders [Accessed 5 July 2018].

Dodd, V. and Grierson, J. (2017). 'Finsbury Park attack suspect was probably "self-radicalised"'. *The Guardian.* [online] Available at: www.theguardian.com/uk-news/2017/jun/21/finsbury-park-mosque-attack-two-victims-in-critical-care [Accessed 20 November 2017].

Dodd, V. and Marsh, S. (2017). 'Anti-Muslim hate crimes increase fivefold since London Bridge attacks'. *The Guardian* [online] Available at: www.theguardian.com/uk-news/2017/jun/07/anti-muslim-hate-crimes-increase-fivefold-since-london-bridge-attacks [Accessed 7 December 2017].

Economist, The (2018). 'A senior British rabbi takes the fight to Jeremy Corbyn'. [online] Available at: www.economist.com/erasmus/2018/08/29/a-senior-british-rabbi-takes-the-fight-to-jeremy-corbyn [Accessed 16 September 2018].

Empire, Faith & War: The Sikhs and World War One (2016). About. [online] Available at: www.empirefaithwar.com/about#about/intro [Accessed 8 October 2017].

Empire, Faith & War: The Sikhs and World War One (2016). In conversation with the IWM. [online] Available at: www.empirefaithwar.com/blog-entries/harbakhsh-grewal-in-conversation-with-the-imperial-war-museum [Accessed 8 October 2017].

English, R. (2012). 'Sikh soldier makes history as he guards Buckingham Palace wearing turban instead of traditional bearskin'. *Mail Online.* [online] Available at: www.dailymail.co.uk/news/article-2246410/Sikh-soldier-makes-history-guards-Buckingham-Palace-wearing-turban-instead-traditional-bearskin.html [Accessed 8 October 2017].

Faith Matters (2010). 'Cohesive communities: Bridging divides between Muslim and Sikh communities'. [online] Available at: www.faith-matters.org/2010/02/26/cohesive-communities/ [Accessed 23 December 2018].

Farmer, B. (2008). 'BBC favours Muslims, complain Hindus and Sikhs'. *The Telegraph.* [online] Available at: www.telegraph.co.uk/news/religion/2703863/BBC-favours-Muslims-complain-Hindus-and-Sikhs.html [Accessed 8 December 2017].

Financial Times (2004). 'UK hostage Kenneth Bigley beheaded in Iraq'. [online] Available at: www.ft.com/content/aaa83c5a-192c-11d9-80e1-00000e2511c8 [Accessed 8 October 2017].

Forrester, K. (2018). 'Sikh MP Tan Dhesi "disgusted" after guest has turban ripped off outside Parliament'. *Huffington Post UK*. [online] Available at: www.huffingtonpost. co.uk/entry/sikh-mp-tan-dhesi-disgusted-and-embarrassed-after-guest-has-turban-ripped-off-outside-parliament_uk_5a8eea6ae4b0ae162f21b106 [Accessed 4 March 2018].

Fuchs, C. (2018). 'Hate crimes spiked in 2017. Community advocates think there's even more'. NBC News. [online] Available at: www.nbcnews.com/news/amp/ncna938551 [Accessed 24 November 2018].

Fuchs, C. (2018). 'Police investigating alleged assault of California Sikh man as hate crime'. NBC News. [online] Available at: www.nbcnews.com/news/asian-america/police-investigating-alleged-assault-california-sikh-man-hate-crime-n898456 [Accessed 13 September 2018].

Gallup (2016). 'Five key findings on religion in the US'. [online] Available at: https:// news.gallup.com/poll/200186/five-key-findings-religion.aspx [Accessed 13 November 2018].

Garcia, C. (2017). 'Cosmopolitan caught misrepresenting Sikh man as a Muslim to push liberal narrative'. *The Blaze* [online]. Available at: www.theblaze.com/news/2017/ 05/23/cosmopolitan-caught-misrepresenting-sikh-man-as-a-muslim-to-push-liberal-narrative [Accessed 8 September 2018].

Gayle, D. (2017). 'Man who harassed MP Luciana Berger online is jailed for two years'. *The Guardian*. [online] Available at: www.theguardian.com/uk-news/2016/dec/08/ man-joshua-bonehill-paine-harassed-mp-luciana-berger-online-jailed-two-years [Accessed 19 November 2017].

Gillan, A. (2008). '"Proud to be Welsh and a Sikh". Schoolgirl wins court battle to wear religious bangle'. *The Guardian*. [online] Available at: www.theguardian.com/ education/2008/jul/30/schools.religion [Accessed 24 September 2018].

Gilligan, A. (2013). 'Anti-fascists fuel the fire of hate'. *The Telegraph*. [online] Available at: www.telegraph.co.uk/journalists/andrew-gilligan/10122496/Anti-fascists-fuel-the-fire-of-hate.html [Accessed 19 October 2017].

Gilligan, A. (2013). 'Muslim hate monitor to lose backing'. *The Telegraph*. [online] Available at: www.telegraph.co.uk/journalists/andrew-gilligan/10108098/Muslim-hate-monitor-to-lose-backing.html [Accessed 26 November 2017].

Global News (2017). 'House of Commons passes anti-Islamophobia motion M-103'. [online] Available at: https://globalnews.ca/news/3330776/anti-islamophobia-motion-m-103-approved/ [Accessed 31 January 2018].

Goyal, D. (2018). 'Sikh man faces racial attack outside UK Parliament, attacker shouted "Muslim go back"'. *The Indian Express*. [online] Available at: https://indianexpress. com/article/india/racial-attack-on-sikh-man-from-ludhiana-outside-uk-parliament-in-london-attacker-shouted-muslim-go-back-5073567/ [Accessed 26 June 2018].

Goyal, D. (2019). 'Remembering a Sikh postman whose battle benefits the community in UK even today. *The Indian Express*. [online] Available at: https://indianexpress.com/ article/express-sunday-eye/head-heart-5719275/ [Accessed 12 May 2019].

Grewal, H. (2016). 'Interfaith marriage is not the battle young Sikhs should be fighting'. *The Independent*. [online] Available at: www.independent.co.uk/voices/if-young-sikhs-opposing-interfaith-marriage-are-just-asserting-their-religious-identity-here-are-the-a7296631.html [Accessed 8 December 2017].

Guardian, The (2001). G2: 'Leicester's multicultural success: Side by Side' [online] Available at: www.theguardian.com/uk/2001/jan/01/britishidentity.features11 [Accessed 5 January 2018].

Guardian, The (2005). 'Shivani Nagarajah talks to non-Muslim Asians about feeling under siege'. [online] Available at: www.theguardian.com/world/2005/September/05/religion.july7 [Accessed 25 November 2017].

Guido Fawkes (2018). 'Jordan Peterson's warning against criminalising speech'. [online] Available at: https://order-order.com/2018/11/09/jordan-petersons-warning-criminalising-speech/ [Accessed 12 November 2018].

Haag, M. (2018). 'Police chief's son charged in attack on Sikh man in California'. *The New York Times.* [online] Available at: www.nytimes.com/2018/08/09/us/sikh-man-attacked-california.html [Accessed 14 September 2018].

Hafiz, Y. (2013). 'The inspiring way Gap responded to racist graffiti'. *Huffington Post UK.* [online] Available at: www.huffingtonpost.co.uk/entry/gap-ad-sikh-waris-ahluwalia_n_4343586 [Accessed 19 August 2018].

Hamilton, F. (2013). 'EDL chief Tommy Robinson quits after "neo Nazi hijack of group"'. *The Times.* [online] Available at: www.thetimes.co.uk/article/edl-chief-tommy-robinson-quits-after-neo-nazi-hijack-of-group-wgzzxthkxr3 [Accessed 8 October 2017].

Harpin, L. (2019). 'Board of Deputies nearly backed Islamophobia definition "decisively influenced" by controversial group'. *The Jewish Chronicle* [online] Available at: https://www.thejc.com/news/uk-news/board-of-deputies-nearly-backed-islamophobia-definition-decisively-influenced-by-controversial-1.478393 [Accessed 11 January 2019].

Heffer, S. (2015). 'Paris is tragic proof that Enoch Powell was right about threats to our country'. *The Telegraph.* [online] Available at: www.telegraph.co.uk/news/uknews/terrorism-in-the-uk/12009577/Paris-is-tragic-proof-that-Enoch-Powell-was-right-about-threats-to-our-country.html [Accessed 6 October 2017].

Hellen, Nicholas (2017). 'Islamophobia award "puts target on back" of former Equalities Chief Trevor Phillips'. *The Times* [online] Available at: www.thetimes.co.uk/edition/news/islamophobia-award-puts-target-on-back-of-former-equalities-chief-5j3swc7dg [Accessed 30 November 2017].

Hill, E. (2018). 'As a Rotherham grooming gang survivor, I am scared by racism and hate crime in Brexit Britain'. *The Independent.* [online] Available at: www.independent.co.uk/voices/brexit-deal-racism-hate-crime-rotherham-grooming-gang-child-sex-abuse-islamophobia-definition-a8666416.html [Accessed 5 December 2018].

Hindustan Times (2018). '"We Are Sikhs" campaign wins top US public relations award'. [online] Available at: www.hindustantimes.com/world-news/we-are-sikhs-campaign-wins-top-us-public-relations-award/story-gKKdUkb3AtzKct6ffMMs2H.html [Accessed 15 September 2018].

Hope, C. (2016). 'Amber Rudd pledges £13.4million to guard every Jewish school, college, and nursery and synagogue in the UK'. *The Telegraph.* [online] Available at: www.telegraph.co.uk/news/2016/11/30/amber-rudd-pledges-134million-guard-every-jewish-school-college/ [Accessed 17 November 2017].

Howarth, M. (2014). 'A child in Birmingham is now more likely to be a Muslim than Christian'. *Mail Online.* [online] Available at: www.dailymail.co.uk/news/article-2755654/The-changing-face-Britain-A-child-Birmingham-likely-Muslim-Christian.html [Accessed 5 January 2018].

Huffington Post (2014). 'Rapper posts racist message on Instagram'. [online] Available at: www.huffingtonpost.com/2014/03/28/joe-budden-sikh-instagram_n_5051917.html [Accessed 8 October 2017].

Hughes, M. (2012). 'Sikh temple massacre gunman was "white supremacist" Wade Michael Page'. *The Telegraph.* [online] Available at: www.telegraph.co.uk/news/

worldnews/northamerica/usa/9457007/Sikh-temple-massacre-gunman-was-white-supremacist-Wade-Michael-Page.html [Accessed 8 October 2017].

Hundal, S. (2012). 'Wisconsin temple shooting: Sikhs have been silent scapegoats since 9/11'. *The Guardian*. [online] Available at: www.theguardian.com/commentis-free/2012/aug/06/wisconsin-temple-shooting-sikh-scapegoats [Accessed 14 July 2017].

India Today (2017). '32 years of Indira Gandhi assassination, anti-Sikh riots: All you need to know'. [online] Available at: http://indiatoday.intoday.in/story/indira-gandhi-assassination-death-anniversary-things-to-know-operation-blue-star/1/799136.html [Accessed 16 October 2017].

Institute of Race Relations (2005). 'The anti-Muslim backlash begins'. [online] Available at: www.irr.org.uk/nelws/the-anti-muslim-backlash-begins/ [Accessed 13 August 2017].

Irish Examiner (2017). 'Stabbed Sikh is blamed for attacks'. [online] Available at: www.irishexaminer.com/archives/2005/0715/ireland/stabbed-sikh-is-blamed-for-attacksbr-597560583.html [Accessed 10 October 2017].

ITV News (2014). 'Sikh taxi driver had turban ripped off and burnt'. [online] Available at: www.itv.com/news/westcountry/story/2014-12-02/sikh-taxi-driver-had-turban-ripped-off-and-burnt/ [Accessed 4 October 2018].

Iyer, D. (2016). 'In our own words: Reflections on the 15th anniversary of 9/11'. *Color-lines*. [online] Available at: www.colorlines.com/articles/our-own-words-reflections-15th-anniversary-911 [Accessed 15 September 2018].

Jewish News (2018). 'Home Secretary commits to renew £13.4 million in security funding at CST dinner'. *Jewish News*. [online] Available at: http://jewishnews.times-ofisrael.com/home-sec-cst-dinner-2018/ [Accessed 21 March 2018].

Jhutti-Johal, J. (2017). 'Evidence for The Youth Select Committee – racist and religious discrimination from a Sikh perspective'. Byc.org.uk. [online] Available at: www.byc.org.uk/wp-content/uploads/2016/09/050-Jagbir-Jhutti-Johal.pdf [Accessed 12 September 2018].

Jhutti-Johal, J. (2017). 'Research on the Sikh community in the UK is essential to better inform policy, but surveys must be improved'. London School of Economics. [online] Available at: http://blogs.lse.ac.uk/religionglobalsociety/2017/01/research-on-the-sikh-community-in-the-uk-is-essential-to-better-inform-policy-but-surveys-must-be-improved/ [Accessed 30 April 2019].

Jhutti-Johal, J. (2017). 'The problems and challenges going forward'. [online] Available at: https://blog.bham.ac.uk/cpur/2017/06/03/the-problems-and-challenges-going-forward [Accessed 16 October 2017].

Kai-Hwa Wang, F. (2016). '15 years after 9/11 founding, the Sikh Coalition builds a "path forward"'. NBC News. [online] Available at: www.nbcnews.com/news/asian-america/15-years-after-9-11-founding-sikh-coalition-builds-path-n645646 [Accessed 15 September 2018].

Kakar, A. (2018). 'Guardian accused of self-regulation failure by Network of Sikh Organisations over hate crime complaint'. *Press Gazette*. [online] Available at: www.pressgazette.co.uk/guardian-accused-of-self-regulation-failure-by-network-of-sikh-organisations- over-hate-crime-complaint/ [Accessed 12 September 2018].

Kalvapalle, R. (2017). 'Jagmeet Singh speaks out about anti-Islam heckling incident: "Hate doesn't pick and choose"'. *Global News* [online] Available at: https://globalnews.ca/news/3732571/jagmeet-singh-racist-heckler-statement/ [Accessed 16 January 2018].

Kassam, R. (2016). 'UK Equalities Chief who popularised the term "Islamophobia" admits: "I thought Muslims would blend into Britain … I should have known better"'. *Breitbart*. [online] Available at: www.breitbart.com/london/2016/04/10/thought-europes-muslims-gradually-blend-britains-diverse-landscape-known-better/ [Accessed 30 November 2017].

Kaur, V. (2012). 'Two Sikh American activists: Let's retire "mistaken identity"' – OnFaith. [online] Available at: www.onfaith.co/onfaith/2012/08/10/two-sikh-american-activists-lets-retire-mistaken-identity/10590 [Accessed 8 October 2017].

Kaur, V. (2012). 'US military, open your doors to Sikhs'. [online] Available at: http://valariekaur.com/2012/08/the-washington-post-u-s-military-open-your-doors-to-sikhs/ [Accessed 8 October 2017].

Kaur, V. (2017). '"Breathe! Push!" Watch this Sikh activist's powerful prayer for America'. *The Washington Post.* [online] Available at: www.washingtonpost.com/news/acts-of-faith/wp/2017/03/06/breathe-push-watch-this-sikh-activists-powerful-prayer-for-america/?utm_term=.8b591a02ac30 [Accessed 17 May 2017].

Kaur, V. (2018). 'Watch the Emmy-Award winning "Sikhs in America"'. [online] Available at: http://valariekaur.com/2018/09/watch-sikhs-in-america-more-resources/ [Accessed 14 September 2018].

Kern, S. (2015). '"Britain Is the Enemy of Islam": One month of Islam in Britain'. Gatestone Institute. [online] Available at: www.gatestoneinstitute.org/5261/britain-enemy-islam [Accessed 8 October 2017].

Khaleeli, H. (2016). 'The perils of "flying while Muslim"'. *The Guardian.* [online] Available at: www.theguardian.com/world/2016/aug/08/the-perils-of-flying-while-muslim [Accessed 6 December 2017].

Khan, S. (2018). 'We are still ignoring victims of anti-Muslim prejudice'. *Huffington Post UK.* [online] Available at: www.huffingtonpost.co.uk/entry/islamophobia-extremism-hate-crime-racism_uk_5c0566e8e4b066b5cfa475a3 [Accessed 3 December 2018].

@Kharagket (6 March 2019). 'The old Sikh turban style: A tradition lost to the ages'. [online] Available at: https://twitter.com/i/moments/1103380915257032708 [Accessed 7 March 2019].

King, D. (2018). 'Vigil to be held in solidarity with Sikh community in Leith'. *Edinburgh Evening News.* [online] Available at: www.edinburghnews.scotsman.com/our-region/edinburgh/vigil-to-be-held-in-solidarity-with-sikh-community-in-leith-1-4791538 [Accessed 8 September 2018].

Lawler, D., Alexander, H. and Millward, D. (2015). 'San Bernardino shooting: Isil claims attack as reports suggest wife came to US to perpetrate terror'. *The Telegraph.* [online] Available at: www.telegraph.co.uk/news/worldnews/northamerica/usa/12030160/California-shooting-Multiple-victims-reported-in-San-Bernardino-live.html [Accessed 3 July 2018].

Lewis, P. (2010). 'Blair Peach killed by police at 1979 protest, Met report finds'. *The Guardian.* [online] Available at: www.theguardian.com/uk/2010/apr/27/blair-peach-killed-police-met-report [Accessed 8 October 2017].

Lusher, A. (2017). 'Channel 4 mocked for blacking up white woman to disguise her as Muslim'. *The Independent.* [online] Available at: www.independent.co.uk/arts-entertainment/tv/news/my-week-as-a-muslim-channel-4-documentary-black-up-brownface-row-white-woman-islamophobia-racism-a8016911.html [Accessed 11 December 2017].

Lusher, A. (2017). 'Influential Sikh youth group associating with far-right EDL founder Tommy Robinson'. *The Independent.* [online] Available at: www.independent.co.uk/news/uk/home-news/sikh-youth-uk-muslim-film-university-tommy-robinson-edl-sex-groomers-islamophobia-racism-a8002526.html [Accessed 8 December 2017].

Lynch, P. (2017). 'Northampton Sikh leader to racist hate mail writer: "This is unacceptable this day and age"'. *Northampton Chronicle.* [online] Available at: www.northamptonchron.co.uk/news/northampton-sikh-leader-to-racist-hate-mail-writer-this-is-unacceptable-this-day-and-age-1-7893382 [Accessed 6 March 2018].

Malcolm, R. (2018). 'Bridgford man fined for "Muslim peado" comment towards Sikh man'. *Nottingham Post*. [online] Available at: www.nottinghampost.com/news/local-news/west-bridgford-man-fined-muslim-2264283 [Accessed 3 December 2018].

Malnick, E. (2013). 'MPs attack Government's "downgrading" of religious education'. *The Telegraph*. [online] Available at: www.telegraph.co.uk/education/education-news/9934940/MPs-attack-Governments-downgrading-of-religious-education.html [Accessed 26 June 2018].

Mann, T. (2016). 'Christopher Blurton called his Sikh neighbours "ISIS slags" – jailed'. *Metro News*. [online] Available at: http://metro.co.uk/2016/09/18/ex-soldier-jailed-for-racially-abusing-sikh-neighbours-and-calling-them-isis-bitches-6135147/ [Accessed 8 October 2017].

Martin, Jonathan and Parnes, Amie (2008). 'McCain: Obama not an Arab, crowd boos'. *Politico Magazine* [online] www.politico.com/story/2008/10/mccain-obama-not-an-arab-crowd-boos-014479 [Accessed 15 February 2019].

Mason, R. (2015). 'Nigel Farage: British Muslim "fifth column" fuels fear of immigration'. *The Guardian*. [online] Available at: www.theguardian.com/politics/2015/mar/12/nigel-farage-british-muslim-fifth-column-fuels-immigration-fear-ukip [Accessed 8 October 2017].

Mason, V. (2016). 'Hate crime attack at Sikh temple'. *Bradford Telegraph & Argus*. [online] Available at: www.thetelegraphandargus.co.uk/news/14683946.Hate_crime_attack_at_Sikh_temple/ [Accessed 13 March 2018].

May, C. (2018). 'UK's top diplomat "sorry" for mosque gaffe'. BBC News. [online] Available at: www.bbc.co.uk/news/uk-43876304 [Accessed 3 July 2018].

Mejia, P. (2015). 'FBI to track hate crimes against Hindus, Sikhs, Arab Americans'. *Newsweek*. [online] Available at: www.newsweek.com/fbi-track-hate-crimes-against-hindus-sikhs-arab-americans-317563 [Accessed 18 January 2018].

Milmo, C. (2015). 'Rise in abuse on British Muslim schoolchildren following Paris attacks'. *The Independent*. [online] Available at: www.independent.co.uk/news/education/education-news/british-muslim-school-children-suffering-a-backlash-of-abuse-following-paris-attacks-9999393.html [Accessed 2 January 2018].

Mogul, P. (2016). 'Arsenal fan blames Sikh Manchester United supporters for Old Trafford evacuation'. *International Business Times UK*. [online] Available at: www.ibtimes.co.uk/manchester-united-bomb-scare-twitter-fury-arsenal-supporter-blames-sikh-football-fans-1560259 [Accessed 8 September 2018].

Mohamed, B. (2018). 'A new estimate of US Muslim population'. Pew Research Center. [online] Available at: www.pewresearch.org/fact-tank/2018/01/03/new-estimates-show-u-s-muslim-population-continues-to-grow/ [Accessed 13 November 2018].

Molloy, M. (2014). 'Coral Millerchip: Woman jailed for Coventry attack on Joginder Singh'. *Metro News*. [online] Available at: https://metro.co.uk/2014/05/10/w-millerchip-woman-jailed-for-sickening-attack-on-frail-pensioner-in-coventry-4723259/ [Accessed 8 October 2017].

Moore, C. (2016). 'Is it Islamophobic to record "Christianophobic" hate crimes?' *Coffee House*. [online]. Available at: https://blogs.spectator.co.uk/2016/02/is-it-islamophobic-to-record-christianophobic-hate-crimes/ [Accessed 28 November 2017].

Moore, C. (2017). 'The SNP's feat is to make non-Scots equate them with the Scottish people' *The Spectator*. [online] Available at: www.spectator.co.uk/2017/03/the-snps-feat-is-to-make-non-scots-equate-them-with-the-scottish-people/ [Accessed 7 December 2017].

Murphy, Paul P. and Evan Simko-Bednarski, C. (2018). 'Two radio hosts suspended after they refer to America's first Sikh attorney general as "turban man"'. CNN. [online] Available at: https://edition.cnn.com/2018/07/26/us/radio-hosts-nj-sikh-attorney-general-trnd/index.html [Accessed 7 September 2018].

National Police Chiefs' Council (2015). 'Police agree data sharing protocols with the Community Security Trust and Tell MAMA'. National Police Chiefs' Council [online] Available at: https://news.npcc.police.uk/releases/police-agree-data-sharing-protocols-with-the-community-security-trust-and-tell-mama [Accessed 24 December 2017].

National Secular Society (2018). '21st century RE for all'. [online] Available at: www.secularism.org.uk/21st-century-re-for-all/ [Accessed 21 July 2018].

National Secular Society (2018). 'Home Secretary urged not to adopt definition of "Islamophobia"'. [online] Available at: www.secularism.org.uk/news/2018/12/home-secretary-urged-not-to-adopt-definition-of-islamophobia [Accessed 16 December 2018].

National Union of Students (2017). It's Islamophobia Awareness Month @ NUS connect. [online] Available at: www.nusconnect.org.uk/articles/it-s-islamophobia-awareness-month [Accessed 24 November 2017].

National Union of Students (2018). 'The experience of Muslim students in 2017–18'. [online] Available at: www.nusconnect.org.uk/resources/the-experience-of-muslim-students-in-2017-18.

NBC Southern California (2018). 'Man caught on camera beating clerk with bat, bottle'. [online] Available at: www.nbclosangeles.com/news/local/Man-Caught-on-Camera-Beating-Clerk-with-Bat-Bottle_Los-Angeles-475483823.html [Accessed 5 March 2018].

Network of Sikh Organisations (2015). 'Network of Sikh Organisations pushes BBC for on-air correction'. [online] Available at: http://nsouk.co.uk/network-of-sikh-organisations-pushes-bbc-for-on-air-correction/ [Accessed 8 October 2017].

Network of Sikh Organisations (2017). 'Support for Sikh and Hindu hate crime victims'. Network of Sikh Organisations. [online] Available at: http://nsouk.co.uk/support-for-sikh-and-hindu-hate-crime-victims/ [Accessed 18 November 2017].

Network of Sikh Organisations (2018). 'Faith Matters and British Sikhs'. Network of Sikh Organisations. [online] Available at: http://nsouk.co.uk/faith-matters-and-british-sikhs/ [Accessed 23 December 2018].

Newcastle University (2017). 'Mistaken for being Muslim'. [online] Available at: www.ncl.ac.uk/press/news/2017/03/islamophobia-otherethnicgroups/ [Accessed 8 October 2017].

Newton, G. (2018). 'Photos show fire damage to Leeds mosque and Sikh temple as police investigate hate crime arson attacks'. *Yorkshire Evening Post*. [online] Available at: www.yorkshireeveningpost.co.uk/news/photos-show-fire-damage-to-leeds-mosque-and-sikh-temple-as-police-investigate-hate-crime-arson-attacks-1-9193972 [Accessed 4 July 2018].

Parker, C. (2017). 'Police arresting nine people a day in fight against web trolls'. *The Times*. [online] Available at: www.thetimes.co.uk/article/police-arresting-nine-people-a-day-in-fight-against-web-trolls-b8nkpgp2d [Accessed 19 September 2018].

Paterson, S. (2015). '"Dangerous racist" inspired by Jihadi John who tried to behead a Sikh dentist in Tesco in revenge for Lee Rigby's murder is jailed for life'. *The Daily Mail*. [online] Available at: www.dailymail.co.uk/news/article-3230910/Dangerous-racist-inspired-Jihadi-John-tried-behead-Sikh-dentist-Tesco-revenge-Lee-Rigby-s-murder-jailed-life.html [Accessed 8 October 2017].

Paterson, S. (2017). 'One third of British Jews have considered quitting the UK because of anti-Semitic hate crimes reveals shock new survey'. *The Daily Mail*. [online] Available at: www.dailymail.co.uk/news/article-4806578/One-British-Jews-considered-quitting-UK.html [Accessed 18 November 2017].

Pearson, A. (2015). 'The price that Ed Miliband is prepared to pay to win the Muslim vote'. *The Telegraph*. [online] Available at: www.telegraph.co.uk/news/politics/ed-miliband/11570745/The-price-that-Ed-Miliband-is-prepared-to-pay-to-win-the-Muslim-vote.html [Accessed 28 November 2017].

Pells, R. (2016). 'MPs have accused the NUS president of "outright racism"'. *The Independent*. [online] Available at: www.independent.co.uk/news/education/nus-president-malia-bouattia-anti-semitism-parliament-home-affairs-select-committee-israel-a7363591.html [Accessed 16 January 2018].

Perraudin, F. (2018). 'Man arrested over fires at mosque and Sikh temple in Leeds'. *The Guardian*. [online] Available at: www.theguardian.com/uk-news/2018/jun/06/man-arrested-over-fires-at-mosque-and-sikh-temple-in-leeds [Accessed 11 July 2018].

Phillips, Melanie (2017). 'Hate crime through the looking glass'. MelaniePhillips.com. [online] Available at: www.melaniephillips.com/hate-crime-looking-glass/ [Accessed 10 December 2017].

Phillips, T. (2019). 'It's wrong to treat British Muslims as a racial group'. *The Times*. [online] Available at: www.thetimes.co.uk/article/it-s-wrong-to-treat-british-muslims-as-a-racial-group-9xj8bf0vx [Accessed 4 January 2019].

Purewal, B. (no date). 'Indian Workers' Association (Southall): 60 years of struggles and achievements 1956–2016'. [online] www.iwasouthall.org.uk/writing.html [Accessed 20 October 2018].

Purewal, B. (2014). *Young Rebels: The Story of the Southall Youth Movement*. PDF. Booklet accompanying DVD.

Qureshi, Yasmin (2016). 'APPG launch to tackle religion in the media'. [online] Available at: www.yasminqureshi.org.uk/appg_launch_to_tackle_religion_in_the_media [Accessed 8 December 2017].

Rahi, M. (2005). 'Turban and the French law: A question of freedom of conscience'. Globalsikhstudies.net. [online] Available at: www.globalsikhstudies.net/pdf/Turban%20and%20the%20French%20Law-M.S.%20Rahi%20.pdf [Accessed 15 November 2018].

Rebel Media (2017). Tommy Robinson, Shillman Fellow. [online] Available at: www.therebel.media/tommy_robinson [Accessed 8 October 2017].

Richards, V. (2015). '"Insensitive" or "tongue in cheek"? Murdered Charlie Hebdo staff given award – for Islamophobia'. *The Independent*. [online] Available at: www.independent.co.uk/news/world/europe/charlie-hebdo-murdered-staff-given-islamophobe-of-the-year-award-10100317.html [Accessed 30 November 2017].

Roberts, E. (2015). '"An act of terror": Family of dentist attacked by machete-wielding man speak out'. *Wales Online*. [online] Available at: www.walesonline.co.uk/news/wales-news/an-act-terror-sikh-family-9528045 [Accessed 8 October 2017].

Rokos, B. (2017). 'Man who blamed government mind control gets 93 years for San Bernardino slaying'. *San Bernardino Sun*. [online]. Available at: www.sbsun.com/2017/10/13/man-who-blamed-government-mind-control-gets-93-years-for-san-bernardino-murder/ [Accessed 26 June 2018].

Rudgard, O. (2017). 'Muslim population of the UK could triple to 13m following "record" influx'. *The Telegraph*. [online] Available at: www.telegraph.co.uk/news/2017/11/29/muslim-population-uk-could-triple-13m-following-record-influx/ [Accessed 11 July 2018].

Sabin, Lamiat (2017). 'Crimes against Sikhs left out of Tory action plan'. *Morning Star* [online] Available at: www.morningstaronline.co.uk/a-5172-Crimes-against-Sikhs-left-out-of-Tory- action-plan [Accessed 28 November 2017].

Saini, H. (2012). Testimony of Harpreet Singh Saini. Judiciary.senate.gov. [online] Available at: www.judiciary.senate.gov/imo/media/doc/9-19-12SainiTestimony.pdf [Accessed 22 September 2018].

Saini, H. (2015). Opinion: 'There ought to be a law against hate'. *The New York Times*. [online] Available at: www.nytimes.com/2015/07/27/opinion/there-ought-to-be-a-law-against-hate.html [Accessed 23 September 2018].

Saldef.org (2013). 'Turban myths'. [online] Available at: http://saldef.org/policy-research/turban-myths/ [Accessed 8 October 2017].

Sanders, E. (2001). 'Understanding turbans: Don't link them to terrorism'. *The Seattle Times*. Community.seattletimes.nwsource.com. [online] Available at: http://community.seattletimes.nwsource.com/archive/?date=20010927&slug=turban270 [Accessed 8 January 2018].

Saner, E. (2012). 'Why are Sikhs targeted by anti-Muslim extremists?' *The Guardian*. [online] Available at: www.theguardian.com/world/2012/aug/08/sikhs-targeted-anti-muslim-extremists [Accessed 8 October 2017].

Shakeri, S. (2018). 'Defence Minister talks racism, fighting to be seen "as a Canadian"'. *Huffington Post Canada*. [online] Available at: www.huffingtonpost.ca/2018/03/25/defence-minister-harjit-sajjan-racism_a_23394867/?guccounter=1&guce_referrer_us=aHR0cHM6Ly93d3cuZ29vZ2xlLmNvbS8&guce [Accessed 29 January 2018].

Sherwood, H. (2016). 'Sikhs in UK are "invisible to government" despite hate crime increase'. *The Guardian*. [online] Available at: www.theguardian.com/world/2016/nov/25/sikhs-in-uk-are-invisible-to-government-despite-hate-increase [Accessed 28 November 2017].

Siddique, H. (2009) 'Sikh campaigner for BNP set to become party's first non-white member'. *The Guardian*. [online] Available at: www.theguardian.com/politics/2009/nov/20/sikh-man-bnp-member [Accessed 12 January 2018].

Siddique, H. (2010). 'BNP would offer non-white Britons £50,000 to leave UK, says Nick Griffin'. *The Guardian*. [online] Available at: www.theguardian.com/politics/2010/apr/29/bnp-non-white-britons-resettlement-grants [Accessed 8 October 2017].

Sidell, M. (2013). 'GAP slams racist graffiti after ad featuring Sikh jewelry designer Waris Ahluwalia is vandalized with anti-Muslim slurs'. *The Daily Mail*. [online] Available at: www.dailymail.co.uk/femail/article-2513525/Gap-slams-racist-graffiti-ad-featuring-Sikh-Waris-Ahluwalia-vandalized.html [Accessed 5 January 2018].

Sikh Aware UK (2017). About Us. [online] Available at: https://sikhaware.co.uk/about-us/ [Accessed 29 November 2017].

Sikh Coalition (2014). '"Go home, terrorist": A report on the bullying of Sikh American school children.' [online] Available at: www.sikhcoalition.org/resources/go-home-terrorist-a-report-on-the-bullying-of-sikh-american-school-children/ [Accessed 15 September 2018].

Sikh Coalition (2014). National Report on School Bullying Released in Congress. [online] Available at: www.sikhcoalition.org/blog/2014/national-report-on-school-bullying-released-in-congress/ [Accessed 15 September 2018].

Sikh Coalition (2015). 'Veerender Jubbal: Statement in response to fake Paris terrorism photo'. [online] Available at: www.sikhcoalition.org/documents/pdf/2015_Veerender-Jubbal_Statement.pdf [Accessed 4 July 2018].

Sikh Coalition (2016). 'Say no to bullying: What can Sikh youth do?' [online] Available at: www.sikhcoalition.org/resources/say-no-to-bullying-national-pamphlet/ [Accessed 15 September 2018].

Sikh Coalition (2016). The Sikh Project. [online] Available at: www.sikhcoalition.org/our-work/empowering-the-community/the-sikh-project/ [Accessed 15 September 2018].

Sikh Coalition (2018). 'Sikhs implore action & accountability in response to new FBI hate crime stats'. [online] Available at: www.sikhcoalition.org/press-release/sikhs-implore-action-accountability-response-new-fbi-hate-crime-stats/ [Accessed 13 November 2018].

Sikh Coalition (2018). *Successful Sikh Awareness Training with New Jersey Radio Station.* [online] Available at: www.sikhcoalition.org/blog/2018/successful-sikh-awareness-training-new-jersey-radio-station/ [Accessed 8 September 2018].

Sikh Press Association (2016). 'LangarWeek 2016, 3–9 October'. [online] Available at: www.sikhpa.com/campaigns/langarweek/ [Accessed 17 December 2017].

Sikh Press Association (2018). 'Sikh Press Association v. *The Times*'. [online] Available at: www.ipso.co.uk/rulings-and-resolution-statements/ruling/?id=03484-18 [Accessed 23 May 2019].

Sikh Missionary Society (2003). *The Turban Victory – The House of Commons.* [online] Available at: www.gurmat.info/sms/smspublications/theturbanvictory/chapter1.html [Accessed 28 January 2018].

Sikh Network, The (2016). 'UK Sikh Survey 2016'. [online] Available at: www. thesikhnetwork.com/wp-content/uploads/2016/11/UK-Sikh-Survey-2016-Findings-FINAL.pdf.

Sikh Network, The (2017). Cllr Preet Kaur Gill. [online] Available at: www.thesikh network.com/team/cllr-preet-kaur-gill/ [Accessed 28 November 2017].

Sikhsindia.blogspot.co.uk (2009). 'Our shameful treatment of Britain's Sikh saviours'. [online] Available at: http://sikhsindia.blogspot.co.uk/2009/08/our-shameful-treatment-of-britains-sikh.html [Accessed 8 October 2017].

Sikhs in the Army (2016). 'Victoria Cross winners'. [online] Available at: www. sikhsinthearmy.co.uk/vc-winners/4545958279 [Accessed 8 October 2017].

Sikh Spirit (2001). 'Blair condemns attacks on British Sikh community'. [online] Available at: www.sikhspirit.com/khalsa/nso011211.htm [Accessed 22 November 2017].

Singh, H. (2012). 'It's time to stop using the word "Asians"'. *The Telegraph.* [online] Available at: www.telegraph.co.uk/news/religion/9314448/Its-time-to-stop-using-the-word-Asians.html [Accessed 5 December 2017].

Singh, H. (2015). 'Paris attacks: Fake Gamergate image of "Sikh suicide bomber" Veerender Jubbal is no joke'. *International Business Times UK.* [online] Available at: www. ibtimes.co.uk/paris-attacks-fake-gamergate-image-sikh-suicide-bomber-veerender-jubbal-no-joke-1529364 [Accessed 4 July 2018].

Singh, H. (2015). 'Sikh lives matter in Britain too – whether Sikh or Muslim, racists don't discriminate'. *The Telegraph.* [online] Available at: www.telegraph.co.uk/news/religion/11410809/Sikh-lives-matter-in-Britain-too-whether-Sikh-or-Muslim-racists-dont-discriminate.html [Accessed 25 November 2017].

Singh, H. (2015). 'UK Sikhs remain invisible victims of "anti-Muslim" hate crime'. *International Business Times UK.* [online] Available at: www.ibtimes.co.uk/uk-sikhs-remain-invisible-victims-anti-muslim-hate-crime-1510588 [Accessed 25 November 2017].

Singh, H. (2016). 'It's time the Government ended its silence on Sikh hate crime victims'. *Coffee House*. [online] Available at: https://blogs.spectator.co.uk/2016/10/time-government-ended-silence-sikh-hate-crime-victims/ [Accessed 8 Dec. 2017].

Singh, H. (2016). 'The Islamist war against Sikhs is arriving in Europe'. *Coffee House*. [online] Available at: https://blogs.spectator.co.uk/2016/09/islamist-war-sikhs-arriving-europe/ [Accessed 9 October 2017].

Singh, H. (2017). 'Is Britain becoming a Christianophobic country?' *Coffee House*. [online] Available at: https://blogs.spectator.co.uk/2017/11/is-britain-becoming-a-christianophobic-country/ [Accessed 24 December 2017].

Singh, H. (2019). 'We must be free to criticise Islam'. *Spiked Online* [online] Available at: www.spiked-online.com/2019/01/04/we-must-be-free-to-criticise-islam/ [Accessed 4 January 2019].

Singh, Jodh (2019). 'A visual history of the Sikh turban'. Medium. [online] Available at: https://medium.com/@jodhsingh/a-visual-history-of-the-sikh-turban-ca294b58953b [Accessed 7 March 2019].

Singh, R. (2012). 'Satyendra Singh Huja, Mayor of Charlottesville, VA, in his own words'. American Turban. [online] Available at: https://americanturban.com/2012/01/10/satyendra-singh-huja-mayor-of-charlottesville-va-in-his-own-words/ [Accessed 16 August 2018].

Singh, S. (2012). Opinion: 'Hate crime reporting shouldn't ignore American Sikhs'. *The New York Times* [online] Available at: www.nytimes.com/2012/08/24/opinion/do-american-sikhs-count.html [Accessed 18 January 2018].

Singh, S. (2012). 'Revisiting the victim narrative'. [online] Available at: http://archive.jsonline.com/news/opinion/revisiting-the-victim-narrative-dq818fg-184769641.html/ [Accessed 18 January 2018].

Singh, S. and Singh, P. (2012). 'How hate gets counted'. *The New York Times*. [online] Available at: www.nytimes.com/2012/08/24/opinion/do-american-sikhs-count.html [Accessed 3 January 2019].

Sky News (2018). 'UKIP leader Gerard Batten links sexual grooming of girls to Islam'. [online] Available at: https://news.sky.com/story/ukip-leader-gerard-batten-links-sexual-grooming-of-girls-to-islam-11503909 [Accessed 23 September 2018].

Smith, M. (2017). 'Labour MP Fiona Mactaggart quits because she is "bored of political squabbles"'. *The Mirror*. [online] Available at: www.mirror.co.uk/news/politics/labour-mp-fiona-mactaggart-steps-10261079 [Accessed 22 January 2018].

Staufenberg, J. (2015). 'When a bouncer called this Sikh man a terrorist he had an inspiring response'. *The Independent*. [online] Available at: www.independent.co.uk/news/world/europe/british-sikh-punched-and-called-a-terrorist-by-polish-club-bouncer-a6760411.html [Accessed 8 October 2017].

Stewart-Robertson, T. (2015). 'Glasgow Sikh Gurdwara remains defiant after attack with sick Islamophobic graffiti and Nazi swastika'. *Daily Record*. [online] Available at: www.dailyrecord.co.uk/news/local-news/glasgow-sikh-gurdwara-remains-defiant-5512593 [Accessed 7 September 2018].

Sugarman, D. (2018). 'NUS president makes video apology after Judaism left off student survey'. *The Jewish Chronicle* [online] Available at: www.thejc.com/news/uk-news/nus-president-shakira-martin-makes-video-apology-after-judaism-left-off-student-survey-1.451497 [Accessed 15 January 2018].

Sullivan, S. (2018). 'Who is Gurbir Grewal? Jersey's Sikh AG has stared down racial slurs long before radio hosts' insults'. [online] Available at: www.nj.com/politics/

index.ssf/2018/07/gurbir_grewal_jerseys_sikh_ag_stares_down_turban_m.html [Accessed 7 September 2018].

Taher, A. (2016). 'Churches used £2.4m government grant to fend off witches and Satanists'. *Mail Online*. [online] Available at: www.dailymail.co.uk/news/article-3886006/Church-cash-fend-jihadis-witches-Hundreds-government-funding-protect-against-pagans-Halloween.html [Accessed 22 November 2017].

Taylor, M. and Siddique, H. (2012). 'Muslim leaders warn of far right exploitation of Rochdale child sex case'. *The Guardian*. [online] Available at: www.theguardian.com/uk/2012/may/11/far-right-rochdale-sex-case [Accessed 6 November 2017].

Telegraph, The (2007). 'Enoch Powell's "Rivers of Blood" speech'. [online] Available at: www.telegraph.co.uk/comment/3643823/Enoch-Powells-Rivers-of-Blood-speech.html [Accessed 6 October 2017].

Telegraph, The (2012). 'Mitt Romney confuses "Sikh" with "sheikh" while paying tribute to Wisconsin temple shootings'. [online] Available at: www.telegraph.co.uk/news/worldnews/mitt-romney/9461305/Mitt-Romney-confuses-Sikh-with-sheikh-while-paying-tribute-to-Wisconsin-temple-shootings.html [Accessed 27 June 2018].

Tell MAMA (2017). 'Beyond the Incident: Outcomes for victims of Anti-Muslim Prejudice'. Tell MAMA Annual Report 2017. [online] Available at: https://tellmamauk.org/wp-content/uploads/2018/07/Tell-MAMA-Report-2017.pdf [Accessed 7 September 2018].

Tharoor, I. (2015). 'Canada now has the world's most Sikh cabinet'. *The Washington Post*. [online] Available at: www.washingtonpost.com/news/worldviews/wp/2015/11/05/canada-just-appointed-the-worlds-most-sikh-cabinet/?utm_term=.fe231ca3acba [Accessed 27 June 2018].

Thompson, A. (2017). 'Sikhs in America: A history of hate'. *ProPublica*. [online] Available at: www.propublica.org/article/sikhs-in-america-hate-crime-victims-and-bias [Accessed 5 November 2017].

Times, The (2018). Letters to the Editor. [online] Available at: www.thetimes.co.uk/edition/comment/letters-to-the-editor-take-the-deal-the-alternative-is-chaos-nsxvpt6jw [Accessed 16 December 2018].

Townsend, T. (2018). 'For football to be truly inclusive, we need to see different faces at the top'. *Metro News*. [online]. Available at: https://metro.co.uk/2018/09/20/for-football-to-be-truly-inclusive-we-need-to-see-different-faces-at-the-top-7953155/?ito=cbshare [Accessed 25 October 2018].

Travis, A. (2017). 'Anti-Muslim hate crime surges after Manchester and London Bridge attacks'. *The Guardian*. [online] Available at: www.theguardian.com/society/2017/jun/20/anti-muslim-hate-surges-after-manchester-and-london-bridge-attacks [Accessed 7 December 2017].

Tribune, The (2018). 'EcoSikh activist attacked in UK'. [online] Available at: www.tribuneindia.com/news/diaspora/ecosikh-activist-attacked-in-uk/548404.html [Accessed 26 June 2018].

Twitter (2015). The *Sunday Sport* on Twitter. [online] Available at: https://twitter.com/thesundaysport/status/670693059097686017?lang=en [Accessed 24 October 2015].

Twitter (2016). Manpreet Mellhi on Twitter. [online] Available at: https://twitter.com/manpreetmellhi/status/797467133710049280 [Accessed 8 October 2017].

Twitter (2017). LookASingh on Twitter. [online] Available at: https://twitter.com/LookASingh/status/923267900974288896/video/1 [Accessed 4 September 2017].

Twitter (2017). APPG Antisemitism (@APPGAA) on Twitter. [online] Available at: https://twitter.com/APPGAA?ref_src=twsrc%5Egoogle%7Ctwcamp%5Eserp%7Ctwgr%5Eauthor [Accessed 17 November 2017].

Twitter (2017). For Britain (@ForBritainParty) on Twitter. [online] Available at: https://twitter.com/ForBritainParty [Accessed 16 October 2017].

Twitter (2017). Tommy Robinson on Twitter. [online] Available at: https://twitter.com/trobinsonnewera/status/426101533177307137 [Accessed 8 October 2017].

Twitter. (2017). Tommy Robinson on Twitter. [online] Available at: https://twitter.com/trobinsonnewera/status/933349630380859393 [Accessed 27 December 2017].

Twitter (2018). Amandeep SinghBhogal on Twitter. [online] Available at: https://twitter.com/AmandeepBhogal/status/981589944148877313 [Accessed 9 April 2018].

Twitter (2018). City Sikhs on Twitter. [online] Available at: https://twitter.com/citysikhs/status/1063748105064071168 [Accessed 5 December 2018].

Twitter (2018). Harjinder Singh Kukreja on Twitter. [online] Available at: https://twitter.com/SinghLions/status/966708208667676673/photo/1 [Accessed 6 March 2018].

Twitter (2018). Punjab2000.com on Twitter. [online] Available at: https://twitter.com/punjab2000music/status/1012865902549794816 [Accessed 19 August 2018].

Twitter (2018). Tina Daheley on Twitter. [online] Available at: https://twitter.com/TinaDaheley/status/966711681874366466 [Accessed 4 March 2018].

Twitter (2018). Richard Norrie on Twitter. [online] Available at: https://twitter.com/RichardNorrie/status/1068264726705119234 [Accessed 29 November 2018].

UK Parliament (2004). Early day motion 1540 – Mr Nick Griffin and Islamophobia. [online] Available at: www.parliament.uk/edm/2003-04/1540 [Accessed 18 November 2017].

UK Parliament (2017). Race Relations Act 1965. [online] Available at: www.parliament.uk/about/living-heritage/transformingsociety/private-lives/relationships/collections1/race-relations-act-1965/race-relations-act-1965/ [Accessed 8 October 2017].

United Sikhs (2009). Press release: 'UK school bans kirpan forcing Sikh out of school'. [online] Available at: www.unitedsikhs.org/PressReleases/PRSRLS-08-10-2009-00.html [Accessed 26 November 2017].

University of Essex Institute for Social and Economic Research, NatCen Social Research (2016). 'Understanding Society: Innovation Panel, Waves 1–7, 2008–2014 [data collection]'. 6th Edition. UK Data Service. SN: 6849, http://doi.org/10.5255/UKDA-SN-6849-7 [Accessed 12 September 2018].

VICE News (2017). 'Trump's Jerusalem decision is reigniting anti-Semitism in Europe'. [online] Available at: https://news.vice.com/story/trumps-jerusalem-decision-is-reigniting-anti-semitism-in-europe [Accessed 18 December 2017].

Walker, P. (2016). 'UK adopts antisemitism definition to combat hate crime against Jews'. *The Guardian*. [online] Available at: www.theguardian.com/society/2016/dec/12/antisemitism-definition-government-combat-hate-crime-jews-israel [Accessed 9 July 2018].

Walker, P. (2017). 'Theresa May promises to protect mosques after Finsbury Park attack'. *The Guardian*. [online] Available at: www.theguardian.com/uk-news/2017/jun/19/theresa-may-to-chair-cobra-meeting-after-finsbury-park-terror-attack [Accessed 20 November 2017].

Walker, P. (2017). 'Ukip MEP's "death cult" remarks spark new Islamophobia row'. *The Guardian*. [online] Available at: www.theguardian.com/politics/2017/apr/29/ukip-new-islamophobia-row-death-cult-remarks-gerard-batten-paul-nuttall [Accessed 18 November 2017].

Walker, P. (2018). 'Chuka Umunna says Labour is institutionally racist'. *The Guardian*. [online] Available at: www.theguardian.com/politics/2018/September/09/chuka-umunna-labour-is-institutionally-racist [Accessed 9 September 2018].

Walker, P. (2018). 'Gerard Batten drags Ukip further right with harsh anti-Islam agenda'. *The Guardian.* [online] Available at: www.theguardian.com/politics/2018/sep/21/gerard-batten-drags-ukip-further-right-with-harsh-anti-islam-agenda [Accessed 23 September 2018].

Watson, A. (2018). 'Man arrested following firebomb attack on Leith Sikh temple'. *Edinburgh Evening News* [online] Available at: www.edinburghnews.scotsman.com/news/crime/man-arrested-following-firebomb-attack-on-leith-sikh-temple-1-4791315 [Accessed 7 September 2018].

Wightwick, A. (2015). 'Welsh Muslims must be encouraged into public life to tackle extremism'. *Wales Online.* [online] Available at: www.walesonline.co.uk/news/wales-news/poverty-islamophobia-partly-blame-radicalisation-10165980 [Accessed 7 December 2017].

Wigmore, T. (2016). 'What killed the BNP?' *New Statesman* [online] Available at: www.newstatesman.com/politics/staggers/2016/01/what-killed-bnp [Accessed 8 October 2017].

Wilford, G. (2017). 'Racist Snapchat story targeting Sikh man on a plane causes outrage'. *The Independent.* [online] Available at: www.independent.co.uk/news/world/americas/snapchat-racist-twitter-sikh-terrorism-muslim-islamophobia-airplane-passenger-outrage-racism-hate-a7807161.html [Accessed 4 October 2017].

Wootson Jr, C. (2018). 'An ex-deputy rammed a truck into a store because he thought the owners were Muslim, police say'. *The Washington Post.* [online] Available at: www.washingtonpost.com/news/acts-of-faith/wp/2018/03/07/an-ex-deputy-rammed-a-truck-into-a-store-because-he-thought-the-owners-were-muslim-police-say/?utm_term=.f97d534361e8 [Accessed 26 June 2018].

Yalamanchili, P. (2016). 'Sikh Americans on the Daily Show explain why throwing Hasan Minhaj under the bus is not an option'. *The Aerogram.* [online]. Available at: http://theaerogram.com/sikh-americans-on-daily-show-explain-why-throwing-muslims-under-the-bus-is-not-an-option/ [Accessed 5 July 2017].

YouTube (2009). Nick Griffin – Sikhs leave UK & Everybody is Happy. [online] Available at: www.youtube.com/watch?v=9gwFGeYF05E [Accessed 8 October 2017].

YouTube (2011). Guramit Singh of the EDL on BBC Look East discussing the upcoming Luton Demo on Feb 5th 2011. [online] Available at: www.youtube.com/watch?v=oOlzF05BzIQ [Accessed 8 October 2017].

YouTube (2012). Fox News Asks If There Were Any Anti-Semitic Acts Against The Wisconsin Sikh Temple. [online] Available at: www.youtube.com/watch?v=URsxyd-jAtb4 [Accessed 14 December 2017].

YouTube (2013). Tommy Robinson praises Sikhs at Lee Rigby protest at Downing Street. [online] Available at: www.youtube.com/watch?v=Mf_hgM6SXXk [Accessed 7 January 2018].

YouTube (2014). Don't Freak, I'm Sikh. [online] Available at: www.youtube.com/watch?v=Bug3TrH3pWo [Accessed 8 October 2017].

YouTube (2015). 80 year old Sikh man assaulted in Coventry UK by drunk woman DIES. [online] Available at: www.youtube.com/watch?v=v2XrCsoW-UE [Accessed 14 May 2019].

YouTube (2016). Nick Cannon [online] Available at: www.youtube.com/watch?v=cOgeSRP6cAY [Accessed 13 December 2017].

YouTube (2017). Arsenal 2 Man City 2: We Need To Bring David Dein Back! [online] Available at: www.youtube.com/watch?v=Sr0pkjf0arc [Accessed 8 October 2017].

YouTube (2017). Mohan Singh Speaks Truth to!!HUGE!! crowd at the FOOTBALL LADS ALLIANCE. [online] Available at: www.youtube.com/watch?v=GZhyTOtElfg [Accessed 11 January 2018].

YouTube (2017). Tommy Robinson: Sikhs stand with Manchester bombing victims. [online] Available at: www.youtube.com/watch?v=qITyUwl8LxU [Accessed 8 October 2017].

YouTube (2018). Jagmeet Singh 'heckler': Her side of the story. [online] Available at: www.youtube.com/watch?reload=9&v=rfaqa1aCudA [Accessed 31 January 2018].

Zauzmer, J. (2018). 'Uber passenger allegedly pulled a gun on Sikh driver: "I hate turban people"'. *The Washington Post*. [online] Available at: www.washingtonpost.com/news/acts-of-faith/wp/2018/02/15/uber-passenger-allegedly-pulled-a-gun-on-sikh-driver-i-hate-turbanpeople/?utm_term=.1f3dffd13199 [Accessed 5 March 2018].

Films

Beeba Boys (2015). Directed by D. Mehta. Canada: Hamilton Mehta Productions.

Bend it Like Beckham (2002). Directed by G. Chadha. UK: Kintop Pictures.

Darjeeling Limited, The (2007). Directed by W. Anderson. US: Fox Searchlight Pictures, Collage Cinemagraphique, American Empirical Pictures, Dune Entertainment, Cine Mosaic Indian Paintbrush, Scott Rudin Productions.

Grand Budapest Hotel, The (2014). Directed by W. Anderson. US, Germany: American Empirical Pictures, Indian Paintbrush Studio, Babelsberg Scott, Rudin Productions, TSG Entertainment.

Imperium (2016). Directed by D. Ragussis. US: Grindstone Entertainment Group, Sculptor Media, Atomic Features, Tycor International Film Company, Green-Light International.

Inside Man (2006). Directed by S. Lee. US: Universal Pictures, Imagine Entertainment, 40 Acres and a Mule Filmworks.

Learning to Drive (2015). Directed by I. Coixit. US: Lavendar Pictures/Core Pictures.

Life Aquatic with Steve Zissou (2004). Directed by W. Anderson. US: Touchstone Pictures.

Ocean's 8 (2018). Directed by G. Ross. US: Warner Bros. Pictures, Village Roadshow Pictures, Smoke House Pictures, Larger Than Life Productions.

Octopussy (1983). Directed by J. Glen. UK: Eon Productions.

Reluctant Fundamentalist, The (2012). Directed by M. Nair. US, India, Qatar: Mirabai Films, Doha Film Institute, Cine Mosaic.

Singh is Kinng (2008). Directed by A. Bazmee. India: Reliance Entertainment.

Index

Taylor & Francis Group
an **informa** business

Taylor & Francis eBooks

www.taylorfrancis.com

A single destination for eBooks from Taylor & Francis
with increased functionality and an improved user
experience to meet the needs of our customers.

90,000+ eBooks of award-winning academic content in
Humanities, Social Science, Science, Technology, Engineering,
and Medical written by a global network of editors and authors.

TAYLOR & FRANCIS EBOOKS OFFERS:

A streamlined
experience for
our library
customers

A single point
of discovery
for all of our
eBook content

Improved
search and
discovery of
content at both
book and
chapter level

REQUEST A FREE TRIAL
support@taylorfrancis.com

Routledge
Taylor & Francis Group

CRC Press
Taylor & Francis Group